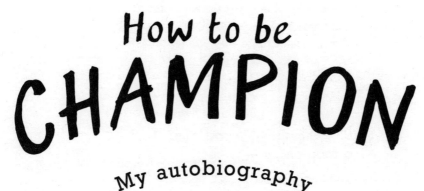

How to be
CHAMPION

My autobiography

SARAH
MILLICAN

TRAPEZE

First published in Great Britain in 2017 by Trapeze,
an imprint of The Orion Publishing Group Ltd
Carmelite House, 50 Victoria Embankment,
London EC4Y 0DZ

An Hachette UK company

1 3 5 7 9 10 8 6 4 2

A CIP catalogue record for this book is
available from the British Library.

ISBN (Hardback): 978 1 4091 7430 1
ISBN (Trade Paperback): 978 1 4091 7431 8
ISBN (eBook): 978 1 4091 7433 2

Typeset by Born Group

Printed in Great Britain by CPI Group (UK) Ltd, Croydon CR0 4YY

www.orionbooks.co.uk

To the loves of my life, Gary and Tuvok

CONTENTS

FOREWORD

Champion *adjective* BRITISH *informal dialect*
1. Excellent. "'Thank ye, lad," the farmer said. "That's champion.'"

WHICH IS A typical dictionary boffin's idea of what a north-
erner sounds like. As soon as I've milked these cows and egged
these chickens, I'll get cracking on my book. I've called it *How
to Be Champion* because that's what I always strive for. Being
champion. And I wanted it, as well as being my autobiography, to be a bit self-helpy. When I described the book to
my best friend, she said, 'Do you mean the sort of book you
wish someone had given you at sixteen?' Exactly that. If I'd
known then that work is better than school, bullies get their
comeuppance by having a boring life, YOU WILL GROW
BOOBS AND THEY WILL BE HUGE, I'd have been much
less anxious and would have started saving for GIANT BRAS.*

---

* Speaking of massive tips, most chapters have How To Be Champion
  tips at the end.

1

I wanted to make it clear that your life doesn't need to be perfect; you don't need to look a certain way to be happy. You don't need to be amazing at everything all of the time. I am, at times, a shoddy daughter, friend, person. Not wife, though. Always brilliant at that. Isn't that right, Gary? He's shouting 'What?' from the other room but I'm choosing to hear 'Yes'. But I try my best and I try to be champion. Champion is Geordie for good or alright. But champion is a better word than alright. Alright can mean great.

'How's the new relationship going?'

'It's alright!'

But it can also mean not quite shit but teetering.

'How's the sex?'

'It's al-right. Sad-face emoticon. Need-to-wank-as-soon-as-he's-left emoticon.'

That's why emoticons exist. Because some words have too many meanings. Take 'better' as another example. It can mean slightly improved.

'How's the sex now you've bought him that manual?'

'It's bet-ter. Zig-zag mouth emoticon.'

Or it can mean totally better. Maximum better.

'How's the genital warts?'

'Better. All cleared up. Gone away. You can't even tell my cock used to look like a witch's chin.'

Champion is a much better word. As a noun, it means the best, victorious, a winner. As in 'We Are the Champions'. It says a lot about you whether the Queen anthem just went through your head or the theme tune to brilliant kids' TV show 'We. Are. The. Champions. De de, de der der.' That's not how I mean it.

I'm all about the adjective. Champion means canny means pretty good means not bad means fair to middling means cracking on with life means nowt's a bother. That's what I want. To always be champion. I think it's important not to give yourself the pressure of having to be amazing all the time. It's also sometimes used as a verb. Because of *Standard Issue*, my no-bullshit women's podcast, I'm often referred to as 'championing' women. Championing. I'm pretty sure that's also French for mushroom.

The title of this book was picked from a list of potentials. I knew I wanted something that was very me. Maybe using a word people associate with me, like nunny or claggy. The obvious title there is perhaps a little graphic though generally true. What about something super-Geordie like 'Gaan Canny', 'I Love Pasties' or 'Hadaway and Shite'? With the latter there was a worry people would think it was an aggressive autobiography from the popular nineties' pop star who asked 'What Is Love?' repeatedly while I danced around De Niro's in South Shields with patent-leather chunky heels and a Mirage and lemonade. I tried to think of what a tabloid newspaper might call my book and came up with 'Cakey Cakey Fat Cunt'.

I asked my husband Gary, who is also a comic and is a genius with words, to help me. I said I liked the word 'champion' and maybe he could come up with some wordplay around that. Now, one thing you need to know about my husband is that he ranks wordplay way above his marriage or indeed anyone's feelings. His suggestion: 'Heavyweight Champion'. He also suggested using the phrase 'older and wider' in the blurb. I have helped him with the title for his next tour: 'Short jokes. Fat man.' And, hilariously, he's actually considering using it.

3

Chapter 1

A Bit About Me

I'M GUESSING YOU'VE bought my book because you know the basics about me (glasses, cake, potty mouth) and would like to know more. Well, before we get into the nitty gritty, here are six stories that sum me up. So if you're cramming for your NVQ in Sarah Millican, inhale these first.

I'm a performer who as a kid was afraid to perform. I was quiet as a mouse at school, but at home I used to make up poems and would read them aloud from behind a curtain. I was about eight and the curtain in the breakfast room only went down to my knees. My mam suggested the curtain thing and, oddly, it gave me confidence. If I did a good job, my mam would give me a banana. When it came to learning about the birds and the bees, my mam said, 'How do you want me to tell you?' and I said 'Can I go behind the curtain?' It was clearly a safe place. Which was fine until I came out and she gave me a banana, like I was supposed to get cracking straight away. She'd also asked which word I wanted her to use for the man's bits and I said 'dick'. I still have sex behind a curtain today.*

I was destined to tell jokes for a living. For Halloween my sister Victoria, being six years older than me, decided she was too old to take this ten-year-old out, so my mam suggested I trick or treated on my own. Great idea, but I was only allowed to trick or treat our house. So I used to go out of the back door and walk around the block, which took less than two minutes, wearing a shawl that was covered in fake blood from Strand, the local card shop. I'd knock on the front door and my mam would leave it a few minutes, to make it exciting. What if she didn't answer? Then she'd open the door and I'd say, 'Trick or treat?' She'd always say 'trick' and I'd tell her a couple of jokes that I'd memorised from Janet and Alan Ahlberg's *The Ha Ha Bonk Book*, which was the first book in my imaginary library (ordered alphabetically, obvs). Then she'd give me a mini Milky Way and I'd go in the house. And that's my job now. But I get cash instead of mini Milky Ways and it's all my own work.

I have a big working-class chip on my shoulder. The first time I bought a first-class train ticket it was by accident, and when the conductor came along to where I was sitting in standard class he said, 'You should be along there,' pointing to the first-class carriage. I said, 'Oh no, I don't think so.' I thought everyone would look like *Downton Abbey* and I was putting my make-up on out of a sandwich bag. He pointed

---

* A curtain of confidence and/or darkness.

to the ticket and said, 'It says first class, look.' I said, 'Oh no, I don't think I'd feel comfortable in first class,' to which he replied, 'Oh no, there's plenty of your sort down there.' Cheeky fucker.

I'm quite dull. I had a hash cake in Amsterdam and fell asleep complaining the cake was rubbish.

I'm rubbish at sticking to things. I tried the clarinet and marriage, didn't put the work in and had them both taken off me. Trying things helps you find out who you are. I am a non-musical married divorcee who takes pictures of puddings and is still partial to Phillip Schofield. Hey, not everyone is an adventurer, right?

I love my animals. One of the best days of my whole life was when a veterinary nurse said I could put clothes on my dog. As per the adoption rules, he'd had his gentleman's surgery (genitalman? Future Marvel character, surely) and we'd been assured he'd bounce back in twenty-four hours or so. It took him a month to recover. A month. He didn't eat or drink for days; we were beside ourselves. Also, he wasn't great with the cones. We tried rigid ones; he refused to move. We tried the floppy ones; he'd just get out of them. We were struggling with how to stop him having access to his stitches when the veterinary nurse said we could put some pants on him. I didn't need asking twice. We stood in Asda kids' section puzzling over which size he'd be. We got age four – as he was age four. I cut a hole out of the bum for his tail and put them on him, taking up the slack with a hairband. He didn't seem to mind them on, but he growled when we tried to take them off or put them back on after a wee, so we went back to trying

the cones. But for two glorious hours I had a medical professional's permission to put pants on my dog. And yes, there's
a photo in the photo section. Go, go. I'll wait.

HOW TO BE CHAMPION

Remember something you were good at as a kid and
bring it back as a hobby now that you're an adult. I
gave gardening a go and also crying whenever I drop
something on the floor and can't find it. Crying always
makes it appear again, oddly.

Chapter 2

What I Was Like at School

GROWING UP IN South Shields, I went to Mortimer Primary and Comprehensive schools. Once, on my way there, I befriended a frog and was genuinely surprised after the bell went at the end of the day that he hadn't waited for me for the seven hours I'd been gone. Or, you know, gone about his day and then come back at 3.50 p.m. to meet me. I was generally good at school: clever, keen and I loved learning. Here's a pretty good summation of what it was like. Feel free to pop on the Sam Cooke classic 'What a Wonderful World' for this bit.

Don't know much about history. We had a mean history teacher who used to initial the centre pages of our exercise books so we couldn't use them for more fun things like drawing and paper cuts. But he wasn't that bright. We used to undo the staples, take the initialled pages out, nab the page underneath for paper aeroplanes and kill lists, and then replace the initialled ones. HA. We won that one. I never did that though. When I say we, I mean 'we' – the kids. We, the kids in the class. We were such a crazy bunch, always up to mischief. All getting along and chatting to each other. When I say we, I really mean 'they'. I was very much looking on in disapproval a lot of the time, siding with the teachers and sometimes grassing people up.

Don't know much biology. We did science double award so I learnt a tiny amount about all three sciences. Also, rumour had it that two of the science teachers were humping so the biology lessons always had an extra frisson. That sort of biology I didn't have to put into practice for a good while yet. Same as sex education. I really should have taken notes to refer back to, though. I remember the period lesson very well. The boys were sent away to watch cartoons while we learnt about 'becoming a woman'. I assume that when I talk about clotting or heavy flow or 'my tits are knacking', my husband's just chuckling to himself about *The Flintstones* and *Scooby-Doo*. Sure that's a great way to prepare men for adulthood. I agree with those who say boys should be in the class too, repeating aloud, 'Sorry your tits are knacking, love. Do you want me to get you some Dairy Milk?' My husband calls Dairy Milk 'lady medicine' because it fixes his lady. During our period lesson, one of the cool girls had something to say. We were all ears. While the nurse was showing us the model of half a woman so we could see where the tampon went, this girl said, 'My friend, right, shoved a tampon so far up that it came out of her bum.' The nurse was momentarily stunned and our shoulders were already starting to go with the beginnings of an eruption of laughter. We just wanted to check it definitely wasn't possible first. To prove it definitely wasn't, the nurse put one finger up the fanny channel and one up the bum and showed us all (a) that they don't meet, and (b) a sexual trick that was not on the curriculum.

Science. See above.

French. I was very good at French but don't remember much now, as was proved on a recent trip to Paris where I panicked and asked for *les nugget de poulet* (oh yes, we eat in classy joints). But at school I was good and I loved it. I did it at A Level too, alongside German, maths and, later on, media studies. I didn't do brilliantly in my A Levels, which will be the first my mam's neighbour hears of it. She thinks I got two As and a B because my mam likes to brag. Presumably she's having a field day now. I was skinny at school and I remember the French teacher once describing me as fat to help everyone learn adjectives. *Merci, chienne.* (That's 'thanks, bitch' in French. Thanks also to Google who provided that, as I can only remember *'ou est la piscine?'* for obvious reasons.)

Geography. We did humanities mostly, which is a combination of geography and history and amounts to colouring in Romans for three years. When we did do geography I enjoyed it. We learnt mostly about New Towns and I remember that farmers leave fields to go to shit every now and again. Fallow, that's it. I got my GCSE results handed to me by my geography teacher, Mr Mizen. They weren't in an envelope, just open for him to see. He read them, winced and handed them to me. Luckily he was joking, as I got two As, three Bs and four Cs. At least I think he was joking – one of the Cs was for geography so who knows.

Trigonometry. I loved maths, though I rarely put my hand up as our brilliant but mad teacher would make the girls do sit-ups if you got it wrong, press-ups if you were a boy. Thank God I didn't know about feminism then. I'd have been shouting my mouth off and then all of the girls would have killed me, and they would have been so much fitter and more able to do so. He thought this would make us all brilliant at maths. For me, it just meant I didn't speak. And it wasn't the sit-ups, it was doing them in front of the whole class. Many years before, when we were learning our times table, we had to stand up and say each one over the course of the term to get them ticked off on the teacher's wall chart. I was so nervous about standing up and talking with everyone looking (and I couldn't see any curtains or mams proffering bananas) that I left it all 'til the last day and got up and did the lot in one go. Odd that this is now my job. I was, and still am in many situations, very shy. I'd still rather stand on stage in front of thousands of people than go to a party where there is anyone I don't know. I only really like my parties.

You can turn the song off now. Or keep it on for the 'la ta ta ta ta ta ta' bit, as that's fun to join in with.

English was the lesson I loved the most. Pretty much as soon as our regular English teacher was off sick with two broken legs, I found our lessons much more engaging. I may have misremembered this and be thinking of Pam Short. As in 'Pam Short's broken both her legs and I wanna dance with you'. If you haven't seen *Strictly Ballroom*, I totally don't mind if you stop reading me to go and watch it.

11

I remember very little about the substitute teacher, just that she made English fun and creative and interesting. She passed the baton on to one of my favourite teachers, Mr O'Shea. I walked into his lesson once wearing my new glasses. They were purple with green speckles and massive. Deirdre Barlow is my closest reference point. I loved them. Because they were so huge, I could see so much of the world at once. On seeing my new specs for the first time, Mr O'Shea said, 'What big glasses you've got,' to which I replied, 'All the better to see you with.' My first zinger – and a literary one too. He must have been so impressed.

We had to write a short story for him once. It could be about anything. I wrote a romance called 'A Chance Encounter'.

Here is an excerpt. In fact, the ending. Well, you're not going to get round to reading the whole thing, are you?

"Lauren, will you marry me?"
Again millions of replies travelled through Lauren's mind, the majority of them being positive. As she observed his muscular, athletic figure and his soft brown eyes her heart melted as she realised just how lucky she was. That was when she made her decision.
"YES...on one condition..."
"Anything...just name it"
"You promise to hold my sickbag on the plane?"
They both chuckled as the final call for the 10:15 flight to the Bahamas was made.

I got a B. I was mostly a B-grade student in English. I was happy with that. A few lessons later, Mr O'Shea taught us about plagiarism and how important it was to be original and only do your own work. He told us a story of a pupil who copied one of Gerald Durrell's stories word for word and handed it in as his own. The teacher hadn't twigged initially and so marked it as normal. Gerald Durrell got a B. This was the first time I considered I could write. And either Gerald Durrell wasn't great or our teachers were HARSH. Either way, I WAS AS GOOD AS GERALD DURRELL. A badge I've worn with pride ever since.

Mr O'Shea was also the first person to stir up any kind of feminism in me. He made us write an essay with the title 'A Woman's Place Is in the Home. Discuss.' I don't remember being very eloquent but I do recall the fury, and even having to mention Margaret Thatcher in a good way. Not sure I'll ever wash that off. Mr O'Shea also taught us how to use a thesaurus. He told us to always look up the synonym you've found in the dictionary to make sure it definitely means what you think it means. The example he gave us that a student had used in previous years was: 'Then the man went into the forest and found haemorrhoids of wood.' Got it.

I loved craft at school. I'm not sure if I was good at it or if it just didn't matter if I was good at it. I keep getting the urge to join the Women's Institute, which in my head is just drinking tea with women in their fifties while fashioning a hanging basket out of an old bra. Sounds like bliss. In my time at school I made a tool rack, a wooden fish, a metal coat-hook and a money box that only held pound coins and therefore always remained empty. Plus a lot of coil pots and ashtrays. My mam once decided to let an ashtray my sister had made her steep in the sink for a while. When she went back, the sink was empty. The ashtray had disintegrated.

I know what became of all the Christmas decorations I made for my parents over the years (including the Santa made from a toilet-roll tube and the sheep made with real sheep wool that we removed from a barbed-wire fence on a school trip). In 2008 my family bought a new Christmas tree, a rather classy affair that had in-built bulbs and needed no decorations. So I got all of the tat I'd made back. I think they were relieved. The best bit about art at school was painting your hands with PVA glue and peeling it off like you were a leper or had eczema. Obviously not that much fun for the kid who did have eczema.

So that was a potted history of my time at school set to the Sam Cooke classic. But it wasn't all colouring-in Romans and being better than, or as good as, Gerald Durrell. Turn to page 27 for the list of things I was bullied for.

HOW TO BE CHAMPION

My dad told me that your school days were the best days of your life. That used to fucking terrify me as my school days were pretty rubbish. If someone says that to you question how popular they were, and if everyone liked them, tell them to fuck off. Work days are better.

Be you in everything you do. Being me at school meant getting verbally bullied and not having many friends. But all of that changed from college onwards. While I was quietly me at school, I was banging the big drum of me at home. As soon as that big wooden front door closed, I was Sarah to the max. And I think young Sarah would have been very happy with what older Sarah does for a living.

Chapter 3

Excellent Things About the Miners' Strike

WHEN I WAS nine there was a miners' strike and, as my dad worked as an electrical engineer down the pit, it affected our family and town. We had £11 a week to do everything with, but I remember it quite positively, probably due to how my parents handled it. I'm sure behind closed doors my mam and dad were having a horrible time, but it brought us closer and taught me the value of money.

So, here is a list of excellent things about the miners' strike. Okay, some of these things aren't great, but I'm determined to take a positive slant. See if you can spot which ones have been shoe-horned into happy times.

I went to school dinners. I had always lived too close to school to go to school dinners. I always went home where my mam had warmed some soup and, when it was really cold, put my slippers on the pipes round the coke boiler. Which is lovely, but school dinners always sounded exciting: special trays with compartments for everything; spongy puddings and custard; scraping your plate into a massive bin with a spatula. I'd heard tell of such a wonderful place but never been. Thanks to the strike, I got free school dinners for a whole year.

I didn't get bullied for having free school dinners. Oddly, I think the bullies drew the line at that. Yeah, her eyesight is bad. Yeah, she's quite clever. Yeah, she's not sucked any cocks yet. That is all on the bullying roster. Her parents have no money? Leave her be, Tracey. But as soon as she's finished her free dinner, she's mine, the glasses-wearing, clever, nine-year-old virgin.

I got seconds at school dinners. (This is a good thing, honest.) Any time sympathy leads to extra food is a good thing. Like when you're ill and people bring Miniature Heroes •sniffs and coughs and shoves another finger of tiny fudge in gob•.

I got sad cuddles off the school dinner ladies. They felt sorry for me and Nicola Symcox (the only other girl in my school year who was affected). Dinner-lady cuddles are some of the best there are. I know this because I now have dinner-lady arms and, boy, am I good at cuddling. (This is not all school-dinner related, by the way, but they were certainly dominant.)

I went on holiday without my sister. The French miners wanted to help the British miners out, so they offered holidays for the kids. My sister was one of three picked from the North East, so she went to some kind of French summer camp. I was too young to be included but got to go on my only ever holiday with just my parents. We went camping in Carlisle and it was one of the best holidays I've ever been on. I got a hula hoop, there was a Care Bear shop, the camp-site had a big tree with a tyre hanging from it and I made a friend, Joanne. Plus I had the sole attention of my parents •does a small dance•. Sole attention is the only attention worth having. I have been known to dance in front of the telly when I'm bored of what my husband is watching. I also clamber on him when he's reading and I'm bored. I am, in short, a needy nightmare.

I got to wear my red wellies for weeks. Read this one really fast please. You know when you first get red wellies and want to wear them all the time even though it might not be raining? Imagine you woke up to find your feet bleeding because your shoes were too small, but you hadn't told your mam and dad because, even though you were only nine, you knew we had no money and that shoes cost money. Then, because it was the summer holidays, you just wore your red wellies the whole time. Sad reason but brilliant outcome.

It was the first hint at what a hero my dad is. He and my uncle Ted used to go down the beach and look for driftwood to burn to keep us warm. Proper hero territory, that.

We got free food. I'm never one to turn down free food. I hate fish and cheese but once ate cheesy fish pie because someone had made it for me. Out of politeness and because it was free, I cut a small slice and covered it in vinaigrette then swallowed it quickly like it was Benylin or cum. Men don't like it if you drizzle Newman's Own Italian dressing on their knobs first, as I've discovered. They're usually fine with Nutella, but check for nut allergies first.

I got to see an avocado for the first time. The local supermarkets would donate end-of-day stuff to the miners and their families – mostly bread and old unlabelled tins. But when Marks & Spencer jumped on the charitable bandwagon they donated thirteen trays of avocados. Bless them. That's like your neighbours making you a pie because you're skint while an old posh aunt sends you a vase. The miners of South Shields had never seen avocados before and had no idea what to do with them. Indeed, I'm not sure I saw another one 'til I went to Australia for the first time in 2009. They put them on everything there: toast, bacon and koalas, obvs.

Christmas was excellent. The French miners donated lots of toys and my dad was one of the co-ordinators. Our garage was full of lovely things for bairns. I picked a cuddly chipmunk as my present and named him Charlie. We also had excellent badges that said 'Santa supports the miners'.

We met a bomb-disposal team. A parcel came through the letterbox right around the time my dad crossed the picket line and went back to work (just before everyone did). My mam rang the police, who sent the bomb squad, an older man and a younger one. Like in *Lethal Weapon*. They opened the parcel, which didn't feel very 'skilled', though they did open it very slowly which must take some training, as I've never been able to do that. As the Mel Gibson one tentatively pulled apart the brown paper, the Danny Glover one shouted 'BANG!' in his ear, and everyone in the room shat his or her pants. Totally the sort of thing they'd do in a film. Turns out it was just my dad's diary/pre-Filofax Filofax. He'd lost it, someone found it and posted it back. Nice people exist. And bomb-disposal-unit guys are proper 'characters'.

I learnt that legs are cheaper than buses. One Saturday during the strike, I went into South Shields town centre with my mam. It was pre-cashpoints, or speed banks as I still call them, and people look at me like I've asked for half a crown of biscuit trimmings. So you had to go into the bank with a cheque to yourself to get money out. The lady on the counter told my mam there wasn't enough in the account to cover that. My mam asked how much there was. She slid it across on a piece of paper. This was back in the day when privacy was a thing. Not like these days when a shop assistant asks for your email address at full volume. I was in Maplin last year buying a voucher for my old tour manager (he loves a cable, does Barry). The bloke on the till said, 'And your email address is . . .' And I said, 'Irrelevant.' You can use that. It's great fun. So my mam asked for the amount that was in the account (not much at all) and we walked home instead of getting the bus. I think this was probably my inspiration when I was at drinking age of spending my last few quid on a McChicken sandwich instead of a taxi. And also why I have okay legs, even if they are still carrying the McChicken-sandwich-filled torso.

HOW TO BE CHAMPION

See bad times in your life as learning experiences.
I know that if I'm ever on the bones of my arse again I
could manage. I've had many times when I've had nowt,
but this was probably the first and the worst. Families
and communities pull together during times like this.
I have almost exclusively excellent memories of the
miners' strike, partly because I was nine, I'm sure, but
also because we all spent a lot time together. And I got
those pity hugs from dinner ladies. I often think it's not
about what happens to you, it's about how you handle it.

Chapter 4

Wearing Glasses

I'VE WORN GLASSES since I was six. That's thirty-five years. There aren't many other things I've done for thirty-five years – probably just breathing and stroking animals a bit too hard. I've only been dancing (in my glasses and without) to Wham! for thirty-two years. And THAT was my main question at the opticians: did I have to wear them for disco dancing?

The only reason I was at the opticians in the first place was because my sister had an appointment so my mam took me along for fun. Don't scoff. This was in the days before PlayStations and the internet. I once had six teeth out on my birthday.

I remember thinking the optician must be rubbish because he wore glasses. You know, like a dentist with black teeth or a bald hairdresser. He had square glasses and a square head and surprisingly nothingy breath. I was up on a high chair doing a quiz; I was having an excellent time. And because at no point did Mr Square McNothing Breath say, 'Wrong!', I assumed I was nailing it. He probably didn't want to embarrass my sister by telling me I'd aced it.

But I didn't ace it. Turned out I needed glasses. That didn't seem fair. It was my sister's fault we were playing this rubbish game, and she was swanning about with her 20/20 vision. Eight years later she joined the four-eyed gang (four eyes are better than two, shut up). So I won that, eh? I did it first. That's what sibling rivalry is about. I did it first so I could show her the ropes – and everything else. Look, you can seeeeee . . .

Four-eyes was just one of the many slurs directed at me during this time. Goggles was another. What does that mean? 'YOU LOOK LIKE A SWIMMER! AAAHAHAHAHAHA!' •goes off and cries in the corner•. Why would they say that? I look like a swimmer? I can't even swim. 'YOU CAN'T EVEN SWIM!! AHAHAHAHA!'

Oh my God, if I was going to list the things I was bullied for at school (and beyond), it would take ages. That's why it's a separate chapter (turn to page 27).

I had an ally, though. One other girl in my whole year wore glasses. You know how you sometimes make friends in the oddest of ways? I thought this could be our moment. We could fight all the bullies. Like in *The Walking Dead** when the goodies have to kill off a queue of zombies and they just take turns and it's awesome – stab, biff, smash, slice! That was

---

* By the way, I did not watch zombie programmes when I was six. I was strictly a Freddy Krueger gal.**

**I didn't watch Freddy Krueger 'til I was ten or so. I'm still scared of knives and burns. My excuse for not cooking.

going to be me and Kayleigh. A line of bullies with perfect vision, all quietly and nervously reciting their insults under their breath, while we stand, wits sharpened, barbs ready, comebacks written down and rehearsed.

'FOUR EYES ARE BETTER THAN TWO.'

'I CAN'T EVEN SWIM.'

'I DON'T LOOK LIKE PEGGY FROM *HI-DE-HI!*' (I totally did. And in some ways I still do.)

But that's not how it worked out, is it? Is it because the bullies and their soldiers refused to queue up, preferring to shout it as they ran past us or to stand on the toilets and yell it over the top while I was dib-dabbing my possum? Nope. It's because Kayleigh, or FUCKING KAYLEIGH as she'd be called now, called me Goggles – while wearing her own actual goggles. It made no sense. My world imploded. She was my one potential ally.

I went home and told my mam. I was always a proper grass/ believed in telling adults when I was being verbally abused by arseholes, and she knew the girl and started to list insults I could aim at her. She was being very protective but, even at six, I knew two wrongs didn't make a right. So I just ignored her. (Don't forget to flip to the Bullied chapter for more on whether ignoring bullies works or is less effective than building your muscles up for years and then going on a Ribena-fuelled rampage.)

My main worry, even at that young age, was how the spectacle-wearing would stunt my sex life. Maybe not in those words exactly, but I was certainly aware of the saying 'boys don't make passes at girls who wear glasses'. I didn't know what passes were. Maybe bits of cardboard with your photo on that get laminated by someone who's allowed? 'Boys don't make passes for girls who wear glasses'. Maybe you needed a pass to dance with a boy. Hence me asking the question of Mr Squarey McNothing Breath: do I have to wear my glasses for disco dancing? He'd listed when I DID need to wear them: reading, writing, watching the telly, looking at the blackboard. I'd like to now add driving and when acting out Wonder Woman/ sexy-secretary scenarios. He said I didn't have to wear them for disco dancing. Phew. Maybe I won't end up a spinster after all, one with zero lanyards.

Clearly I thought my dancing was the way to entice a boy. To be fair, Kimberly House and I did used to make up dances in my backyard (garage if it was raining, but that's where my dad kept his spiders so it had to be properly belting it down). We once made a dance up for the whole year to learn and perform to Five Star's 'Can't Wait Another Minute' (I can still remember bits of it), but one girl couldn't join in as it was against her religion. Nothing more was ever explained to us. It made me shun religion for life. What kind of joyless dicks made up a religion excluding Five Star? Thinking back, it feels like a very smart ruse. Like when I asked if I could wear my pink jogging suit for PE because I once had bronchitis rather than just because it was bloody cold.

So my spectacles-free formation dancing would win a boy's heart, would it? Learn more about how I lost my virginity in the chapter entitled Married!*

---

* This is not a chapter. Just a joke. But you get the message, yes? Good.

HOW TO BE CHAMPION

People who wear glasses are all potential superheroes. Remember that before you take the piss.

Also, if you need to clean your glasses and don't have any fancy sprays or wipes, liquid soap and a run under the tap works brilliantly. If you're not near a sink, spit can cut through smears quite well. Just make sure you haven't just eaten an Aero like I had last week. My husband has just used a KFC hand-wipe and that worked a treat. Lovely lemony glasses.

Chapter 5

Things I've Been Bullied For

1. Wearing glasses

See chapter entitled Wearing Glasses.

2. Not wearing my glasses

Some people clearly think that when you wear glasses they're just glued to your face. You sleep in them (impractical), swim in them (I did once see an old lady swimming with her entire head out of the water, hair dry and glasses on, but she also produced a packet of soft mints from somewhere and I don't think that's the norm), have sex in them (that depends; if I'm acting out a whole sexy-secretary thing then I'll keep them on while I'm doing admin and filing, and hours later, when I've clocked off, I'll take them off and shove my face in a hairy chest). 'Don't you look really weird when you haven't got your glasses on?' is the classic. Not to me. I look like me when I get up, me when I'm having my morning cuppa, me in the bath, me having a poo, me having an orgasm. But you don't see those faces (it would take a real expert to tell the last two apart) so you think I look weird. Like a teacher in jeans. Like Jimmy Carr in jeans. Like a dog in jeans. Actually, that last one is brilliant.

3. Having clip-on sunglasses

I had really bad hay fever one year so my mam got me some sunglasses that clipped on to my normal glasses. They really helped, but I was pointed at and laughed at so much that I stopped wearing them. Yes, I was probably a bit weird at school. Weird in relation to most of the other kids. You know, the ones who were sexually active when it wasn't yet legal, who thought boys were better than pens, who didn't care about exam results, who didn't try. I overheard one girl say to her friend, 'I'd rather be top of B-band than bottom of A-band.' I leaned over and said, 'I'd rather be top of A-band.' I knew what they meant, that given the option they'd rather be king of a crap castle than the lowest of the low the next level up. But I always tried to be the best. I once got 97 per cent in a maths exam and my dad asked me what happened to the other 3. And while that was frustrating at the time, I knew what he was doing. Strive to be the best and you'll probably land nearer than those who didn't bother to bring a pair of shoes to draw to the art lesson so just took their trainers off and drew them. Of course, if they hadn't done that, how would I know that I could probably sketch during chemical warfare?

THINGS I'VE BEEN BULLIED FOR

4. Having a microwave

My mam and dad bought the world's first microwave. Well, they were early adopters at least. It was gigantic and shook the house when it pinged. I think I must have been the first kid in my year at school, maybe even the whole school, to get a microwave. I must have mentioned it one day, while all the other kids were sucking cocks and smoking tabs.

I always felt like a forty-year-old at school. That's one of the reasons I like being in my forties. My age finally caught up with my brain. And my culottes. One day, when I was playing with my friend Kim, we decided to make up names for ourselves. We were saving the world via her bay window, like an early version of *Minority Report*, but instead of Tom Cruise waving his hands about on an invisible screen, it was a bespectacled* eight-year-old in pedal pushers and Jesus sandals. The name I chose was Jackie. *Jackie.* I could have been Anastasia or Sparkle, but no, I chose the persona of a woman in her forties in head-to-toe Marksies. And ta-da! That's what I became.

The microwave slights came to a halt pretty quickly when everyone got one. My dad kept his original one for twenty-five years. Towards the end, the digital light display had died so he bought a kitchen timer and started that at the same time he

---

* Bespectacled is a great word. It always makes me think of eighties pop duo Mel and Kim – 'Bespectacled, Bespectacled. Tay, tay, tay, tay . . .' etc.

29

started the microwave cooking. It did mean that when the time was up it continued cooking, so you had to run to the kitchen and open the door. I still don't trust people who don't have one. My friend Ruth, for example. I stayed with her quite a lot when I started doing stand-up and would always forget and then panic that I had never learnt the old way of cooking. Like when you're not allowed a calculator in an exam and you have to use your brain.

5. Having microwave chips for supper sometimes

Sometimes a friend would come for a sleepover. I preferred that to going to their house; on one occasion I stayed at a friend's house, I forgot clean pants and had to wear some of hers. Another time, when I came home, my dog had been put down and all evidence of it had disappeared, like I'd imagined the dog. To be fair to my parents, we hadn't had him long, he was vicious as hell and turned out to be inbred. But still, I was nervous to stay elsewhere overnight in case my budgies or hamsters vanished. So one time a girl from school stayed and we had Micro Chips for supper. It was a treat. She reported back to the school the next day that I had Micro Chips for supper, then everyone thought I was posh. In the same way I thought the girl whose mam ran a catalogue was rich.

6. Wearing Jesus sandals

Some kids took umbrage. Fuck knows why. Anti-religion? Or maybe my toes were hairy even then. I, personally, liked the way they clacked when I ran along the back lane.

7. Being in a toilet

For some reason when I went to the toilet at school, some girls would stand on the toilets in the cubicles either side of mine and look over the top. I'm not sure what they were looking for, but I've always been a quick wee-er ever since. Maybe they were checking for pubes. Maybe it was just generic bullying. You know the type, not aimed at anything specifically so you can't try to change it and make the bullying stop. I really wish I could meet up again with those girls and force them to watch me shit now. My IBS is regularly awful. Maybe I've had too much pastry, maybe I'm stressed, maybe I forgot and ate a bowlful of sprouts. But farts that make my husband say 'crikey' when he's not actually in *Danger Mouse* must be impressive. Often there's pebble-dashing that sounds like a poorly motor-bike. They could also stay for the inevitable unblocking, tears and sighing.

8. Getting on with the teachers

My sister was in hospital in a big way when I was twelve so my mam kept me off school for five weeks while the NHS saved her life a few times. When I went back to school, I was older and more stupid. Well, I was moved from top class to bottom class for a few subjects because I'd missed five weeks' work. A combination of me turbo catching-up and my mam shouting at the headmaster got me moved back. The older thing didn't go away. When you've seen a close family member nearly die a couple of times, you can't be twelve any more. So I got on really well with the teachers and not the kids. I also, apparently, looked like one of the teachers.

9. Looking like one of the teachers

I had a perm and glasses, and so did Miss Collier the chemistry teacher, so a couple of the smarter bitchy girls shouted her name when I walked by. Or tried to hand their homework in to me. This is the sort of bullying that really hurts: when girls you kind of like are awful to you. Is the sort of thing Susan Collier and I used to chat about while we marked that day's lessons.

10. Walking in front of another girl

A big old bitch a couple of years above me followed me home once. She walked slightly behind me and called me names quietly. I have always believed in grassing people up, or as I call it 'calling people out on bad behaviour'. Only criminals call people grasses, remember that. I told my dad, who went and had a word with her at the bus stop the next day. I wrote in my big navy 1988 desk diary (I was thirteen; why did I need a massive week-to-view diary?) that he put 'the fear of God into her'. I had no idea what that meant at the time. I love a good example of a kid using adult vocab. It's always funny when a six-year-old says 'as fit as a butcher's dog' or describes something as 'better than sex'. Clearly, I don't have kids.

That cow never bothered me again. Not even two years later when we were paired up to go ice-skating on a school trip. Because I was younger and inexperienced, she was told to hold my hand. We skated in silence. I remembered the safety briefing we'd had about pulling your hands into a fist if you fall to save all of your fingers from being sliced off. I tried to fall a couple of times, thinking hospital and no digits would be better than this. But wowsers, she was sturdy. It was the most terrifying hour of my life.

11. Not being able to swim

Someone, somewhere once decided that at school cool people are also athletic, which, as an adult, I can see is utter twaddle. All the cool people I know now are writers, illustrators, comics, doodlers, crafters and creative types. But at school, if you made a brilliant papier-mâché head or a functional tool rack, no one carried you on their shoulders or asked you to the cinema. Cool people at school can swim like fish and suck cocks like champs. I can just about manage both these days, though I haven't quite mastered the breathing technique. I always insist on the little rubber hats. And I hate it when it goes up my nose. And if I'm floundering, Mrs Chidley scoops me out of danger with a big net.

12. Grassing up a girl for making my arms bleed

Never play Chinese burns with someone who hates you. Actually, it wasn't Chinese burns. I split a pack of cards and she dragged half of them down my arm. I've just googled it. It's not a game. So let's recaption this one 'for being a victim of mild torture'.

13. Not having tits

Which is hardly my fault. Sorry boys, I'm not there for you to look at. I'm in school to learn about isosceles triangles and New Towns and to colour in Romans and get out of PE by having a perm. I got boobs and periods in the summer holidays after I left, aged sixteen. I was disappointed, as my mam had promised me I could stay off German when my period started like Dawn Palmer had. She'd also promised that if we ever had a massive garden I could have as many bunnies as Flamingo Land, Yorkshire's ultimate theme-park attraction. I think my mam knows which promises are worth saying yes to.

In PSE (still don't really know what it stands for, but it seemed to be just chatting and playing demeaning games), we used to play a word game. There was a stack of small pieces of paper with different things written on them: 'the person with the nicest eyes'; 'the person I'd like to go on holiday with'. That sort of thing. We'd sit around in a circle and take one and give it to someone appropriate. I'm sure it was aimed at boosting our confidence, and I'm sure Miss Fucking Sparkly Eyes and Mister Fucking Brilliant Holidays went home with a spring in their step. But when your hands are as empty then as when the Christmas cards are handed out, it does a little damage. Also, if someone (Alan Watson) on one occasion passes across a 'nicest eyes' to you, you will fixate on and fantasise about him well into your teens and, at a low moment, your twenties.

14. Not having the right kind of perm

So my mam was a hairdresser, something she'd wanted to do since she was two and only had dolls with painted-on hair – and something she only managed for a few years due to contracting polio in her childhood, which meant she couldn't stand for long periods of time. But it did mean that we got our hair done at home, by a pro. She'd open the larder door, where there was a big mirror, and sit us in front of it. For a treat, the first time I had a perm was at Binns department store. I took a photo of Charlene off *Neighbours*. You now know her as pop goddess Kylie, but she used to be a mechanic with long curly hair. My hair wasn't quite shoulder length but it hadn't occurred to me that a perm would make it shorter. My mam once told me that when her customers came in with an unrealistic picture – her example was 'they had four hairs and a photo of Elizabeth Taylor' – she'd say, 'It's a pair of scissors I've got. Not a wand.'

Now, maybe Binns' hairdressers explained to this eleven-year-old that a perm would take the length up. But I wasn't listening. Maybe I'd have listened if they'd told me I'd look like Kylie's nana and have to take the sneaky stairwell out of the building to go home and wash it immediately. (Cardinal sin of perms: don't wash it straightaway or the curls will drop. GOOD. Maybe then they'll let me pay on buses again and stop giving up their seats on the Metro.)

After that, my mam permed my hair at home. One time, she was supposed to be just perming the roots as I had a lot of growth and she accidentally permed a perm. That's not even a saying, is it? Would you like your perm permed? No one has ever asked that and certainly no one has said yes. Unless they're wanting to convince friends and family they've been electrocuted, while wearing a poodle on their head. She then said she'd trim it 'just to take off the ends'. She didn't open the larder door. I should have known then. She trimmed all the frizz off, and while it did look a lot better, I now had boy-short hair. First thought was always, I'm going to get picked on for this. Anything that made you stand out at school was bad, so with huge trepidation I walked in to school the next day. The day before I'd had shoulder-length curly hair. Today, boy-short hair. Boy short. I'd tried to disguise the shortness by putting a lilac clip in the back, like a fucking idiot. A desperate idiot.

Let's see what the kids think: they didn't even know I was getting my hair done given that (a) I barely spoke to most of them, and telling them something like that would be giving them prep time to write some insults. Never give prep time. And (b) I was supposed to be doing PE but was kept off as I was 'poorly' because my mam didn't think PE was important and perms take ages. I walked into the schoolyard ready. Not to fire back – just with my best ignoring face on. And no one said a word. Not because they thought it looked okay or because they thought it looked bad but didn't want to hurt my feelings. No, they didn't say a word because they didn't notice. It pays to be a wallflower sometimes.* If you'd stopped

---

* Find out about my wallflower years in Chapter 7.

a couple of them throwing some poor kids' school bags on the roof of the sports hall and asked them what was different about me, they'd have asked if I had tits yet or tried to hand their homework in to me. Now I do a telly job and pop my head into the schoolyard of social media to see if the masses approve. Nothing much has changed.

15. For being a lesbian

Which I'm not, though it might have been easier. I bet when it's two girls together there's lots of chat in bed and you don't have to domesticate a man. I came home from school one day and told my mam that the kids at school had called me a lesbian. Looking back, it was probably because I was talking about microwaves while other girls were sucking cocks and smoking tabs. I'd never had a sucker (love bite) and thought all boys smell (still think so, but thanks to Molton Brown's Orange and Bergamot Home Mist you can spray a lot of it away). My mam explained a lesbian as such: 'It means you like girls more than you like boys', which is pretty spot on. And it was true! I did. Girls (the nice ones at least) let me know when someone had stuck a sanitary towel on my school bag and told me about spotty leggings. I went in to school the next day and when someone shouted 'Lesbian!' at me, I said, 'YES! YES I AM!'

16. Being crap at PE

Classic tale of a girl picked last. I was not athletic or popular and it was always the popular girls picking the netball teams.

I only liked being Centre in netball because I knew where I was allowed to go; one time they decided they'd rather be one man down than have me on their team. In rounders I was sent out to the next field, which I'm pretty sure was a park open to the public. My friend Diane and I would just stand and chat and only had to pay attention when Joanne Glenny batted. She'd wallop it and me and Diane would chase after it and then throw it. I always threw high, not far, so it was actually quicker for me to run with the ball. My throw-high-not-far technique nearly killed me once when we got to have a go with a javelin. It went really high but then landed about a foot away from me with a thud and the sort of noise Rolf Harris made before he was accused and convicted of sex offences against bairns.

I recently got back in touch with Joanne Glenny and she remembers a time when she was batting and walloped it. We were on the same team, and as she was speeding past the posts she realised I was ahead of her. She slowed down but was shouted at by the 'bitches' (her word, but I'm very happy with it) for not running me out. Then I shouted at her because I *wanted* to be out. Poor Joanne.

17. For having an I LOVE SCHOOL T-shirt

In the infant school, at about the age of six, my mam put me in a T-shirt that said 'I love school' and underneath in italics *'when it's closed!'* AAAAH – funny joke. And cute, yes. If the internet had existed, I'd have been on her Facebook looking all cute. Cheeky little thing. She loves school but only when she's trapped in it alone with all of the felt-tip pens and blackboards to herself! That's not what it meant. You know what it meant. That's the sort of thing that could have won me friends: 'Look, that girl has a sassy T-shirt, her mam's a funny one, let's be her friend.' But I, ever the cautious one, was so worried I would get expelled from school that I tucked the bottom line into my (Muppets) trousers and wandered around with a T-shirt that just said 'I love school'. I was subsequently bullied for ten years. To be fair, my version of the T-shirt was much more truthful to my character.

18. For wearing a flowery dress that people didn't like. See page 247.

When I started writing this chapter I thought it would be funny to list all of the ridiculous things I was bullied for, but I was horrified by how many there were and that's what instigated the following chapter. So, stop crying, grab a biscuit. The next chapter is more fun.

HOW TO BE CHAMPION

It's hard to give tips for how to handle bullying as it depends what kind it is. It's such a big area. My mam always told me to ignore it, and because mine was wholly verbal that was probably the best idea at the time. But some types of bullying need to be addressed, flagged up to someone else, called out. I would mostly say that you should seek help. Talk it over with someone you trust, an adult if you aren't one yet. And remember that you can be okay. You will be okay. I still have remnants of the shite I went through in me but I am champion due to getting away from the situation, talking to people about it and having some counselling. Also, living well is the best revenge. Have a little watch of my *Outsider* show to see how I did it.

Chapter 6

Good Things that Happened at School

1. A boy bit off his wart to show me he loved me

I didn't have a boyfriend at school. I didn't kiss a boy at school. I didn't dance with a boy at any of the Christmas parties. When I was about twelve I asked my parents how old I had to be before I could have a boyfriend. I wasn't super keen but I like to know the rules so I don't break them. Much like I know not to mix the grape and the grain even though I don't drink booze. Though I do flick the Vs to the rulebook by still eating jam sandwiches. I vaguely remember my mam and dad saying thirteen or fourteen, but truth be told it didn't matter. As long as what they said had a 'teen' on the end, I was well clear.

I didn't ask him to bite his wart off. We'd never spoken. He suffered a huge amount of blood loss but was fine. Warts are living things like hearts. THAT'S WHAT I SHOULD

HAVE SAID TO HIM. He didn't tell me he loved me; another boy did, so it was very possibly a load of shit. Most of the time when I was told a boy liked me, it was a joke, though I think the instance in the swimming pool was genuine, at first. A kid came over and asked me if I'd go out with his friend. Then he spotted the snot in my hair. I had just splashed into the Aqua Blaster's landing pool, the water had gone up my nose and my hair was in my face. And in one fluid (!) movement, I gave myself a proper Pepé Le Pew streak.

2. The one time I was fashionable

We didn't get a school uniform until the senior school, so before that it was very much a free for all of pedal pushers and rara skirts. Think the end party scene in *Footloose*, but through the day, doing maths. I didn't get the rara skirt 'til I proved to my mam that EVERYONE had one. I have no idea how I did that.

We never had much money so my mam had a great idea to make me some skirts. And I loved them. They were pastel colours – pinks, lilacs, turquoises – with elasticated waists and a small split up the back finished with a pretty bow. No matter how much I loved them I was very aware that having home-made clothes was not the done thing – yet another thing to be ready for criticism on. I felt the same way about clothes then as I do now: I want to be covered, clean, warm and look nice. One of the kind girls at school, Louise, didn't ask me where I got my skirt, the question I was dreading. I'm crap at lying and still have price Tourette's today when complimented about anything I'm wearing.

'That's a nice top.'

'Eight quid.'

Louise asked me if my skirt was from Topshop. I still beam at the memory. Topshop, you bugger. TOPSHOP. She said she thought she'd seen it in there, AND her mam ran a catalogue so she knew fashion and always had all the best tops.

3. I was fleetingly the Beyoncé of my school

I hated PE. I could just about get away with rounders and hockey, but I hated netball and always dawdled through a cross-country run, chatting at the back with my friend Diane and then grassing up those who cut through the allotments so that I wasn't technically last.

But they introduced dance and I loved it. I'd always loved dancing. Especially as I didn't even need to wear my glasses for it. If I couldn't be bothered to get my pram out from under all of the camping gear in the cupboard under the stairs, I used to just dance in the hall instead. I joined a dance class for one session; they taught us how to shimmy on the first day and, even at eight, I considered it overly sexual so didn't go back. Instead, my sister and I did what we called 'gymlastics', which mostly involved us wearing leotards and shouting ta-da! with our arms in the air. They're called 'presents', apparently. We called them ta-das. Our name is better.

We were taught dances and we made up dances. I was rarely happier than when in a Lycra catsuit and making fresh bruises by chucking myself about. How things change. I stood up from the sofa the other day to make a cup of tea and my knees said, 'Are you sure?'

4. I discovered I could write

We had a writing competition at junior school judged by the headmaster, Mr Hoban, who was mostly known for chewing something on his way to the stage in assembly. He clearly never got stage fright; when I first started doing stand-up I would get so nervous that I couldn't eat for five hours before my gig. Now, even though I still get nervous, I'm much better at the eating. I can be picking chicken out of my teeth as they're announcing my name. Sometimes, on the last tour we ate Nando's so close to show time that I'd do small, sneaky burps during my first five minutes on stage. We called them 'thoughtful moments'. Look thoughtful, sneak a small, meaty burp out. If you've ever been on the front row and got a whiff of PERi-PERi then that was my belch. Or, in the second half, a chickeny fart.

When writing stories in class I often ran out of time; the teacher would say 'pens down' when I was only three-quarters done. On those occasions, I'd quickly add the line 'So they all went home and had their tea', which seems to end all stories really well. Think about it. Why wouldn't fairies, rabbits, dancers, Care Bears or pterodactyls go home for their tea? See! No reason. The story I wrote for this particular competition came first and was only half done. Another indicator that I could write. And also that Mr Hoban thought going home for your tea was important and final too.

5. I discovered I'm not a daredevil

I've always done as I'm told, and when we went to Lightwater Valley, Yorkshire's ultimate theme-park attraction, with the school, I was no different. I wasn't going to be Estee Caruthers, who was left behind because she didn't get back to the bus for the time we were supposed to. For all I know, she's still there and lives under the log flume with a massive beard and hobbit feet. My friend Kimberly and I broke away from the group (of other kids who didn't like us) and went off on our own. Kimberly was allowed to do anything she liked. She could play in the park across the road from us, whereas I had to make do with the church green that wasn't across a busy road we could get killed on. My mam had told me the things I wasn't allowed on at Lightwater Valley – basically the big rides. I was allowed on the dodgems because I'd been trained well on those. As a kid, I was always the passenger as my dad had a driving licence and I did not. He looped the seat belt over my head so it chafed my armpit and then proceeded to avoid all the other cars. It takes real skill but it's also very boring. It was very similar to just being in my dad's car on any journey.

So we blitzed the dodgems but I started to worry that we were going on too much and someone might stop us (I AM SO MUCH FUN), so we started to swap coats and bags, which made it even more fun. Being rammed by boys you don't know in someone else's coat is the height of entertainment, I can tell you. We didn't just go on the dodgems – we also went on the little train.

I've always liked little trains since we started going on the one at the Marine Park, South Shields' ultimate park-based attraction, every Easter, even the time when some skinheads started a mass brawl and, to keep us safe, my dad pushed my mam, sister and me into a coconut shy while he helped pick up an old policeman who had been knocked to the ground. We still didn't win anything, which is proof that they are fixed. We went on the little train that year as a comedown. That little train is also where I first heard the word 'cheapies', when my mam said she liked the train because it rumbled as it went through the harebells and gave her cheapies. Even if that's not the word you'd use for it, I'm sure you can imagine what I mean and my mam's face as she said it. The little train at Lightwater Valley was great fun. It was only a year ago that, when talking about this to a friend, I realised the little train at Lightwater Valley connects the big rides. You know, the big rides I wasn't allowed on. So it was basically transportation.

6. I was better at maths than my sister

My mam and dad always went to parents' evenings and I always went with them. I wasn't going to miss out on any well dones or hear them second hand when my parents might not remember the compliments word for word. One year, my dad was at work down the pit and unable to come so my sister, Victoria, went in place of him. My mam and sister split up to cover the maximum amount of teachers. I went with Victoria. Because she is six years older than me and had most of the same teachers, a lot of them were commenting that she was too young to be a parent or saying how brilliant she was in their lessons (she was in the netball and rounders teams AND played the flute – fuck's sake). I rolled my eyes so much it hurt then did a little cough so they'd remember they were supposed to be talking about me. Finally, we got to the maths teacher. I'd been waiting for this one. The first thing he said was, 'Well, she's much better at maths than you were,' and I bounced all the way home.

7. I learnt how to say no (to clarinets)

Because my sister played the flute, my parents wondered what my musical instrument might be. I was self-taught on the recorder from an early age. I also taught myself to read music and I got sheet music out of the library to play. My favourite was all of the songs from *The Sound of Music*, which I could play ably on the recorder. That's like being able to paint like an impressionist but shunning oils and watercolours for dog shit. My mam asked which instrument I'd like to try and I said, 'Piano.' My parents couldn't afford a piano so they got me a guitar. I joined Mrs Chilly's lunchtime guitar club but my heart wasn't in it. I learnt 'Little Donkey' and left.

Next I gave the clarinet a go, borrowing one from the school. My mam's rule was always to borrow first to see if I'd stick to it. She was right to do so otherwise we'd have a twice-used Brownies uniform. Plus, divorce is basically handing someone back in, isn't it? Mr Coates was my clarinet teacher; he'd taught my sister the flute and was also one of my mam's teachers from years gone by. They all loved him and he loved our family. Until me. Three hours' practice a day was what he suggested for the summer holidays. He clearly had no idea about the heavy schedule of perfume making, sticker re-ordering, birds' nest spotting, book alphabetising and budgie drawing I had planned. I took the clarinet box in on the first day back at school. I also took my sister to sugar the pill as he loved her. I blew the dust off before opening the box lid. He took the hint. 'You haven't practised, have you?' Nope. 'You don't want to do it any more, do you?' Nope. I've taken the same approach to blow jobs. Totally works. Though my sister finds it awkward.

8. I learnt that touching friends is nice

Whether I was sitting on a wall listening to Kylie's first tape *Kylie* on my Walkman, practising my plan of attack to ask my mam for another budgie or working out how to play multiple person games on my own (hopscotch totally works), I was never surrounded by kids. Aside from that one time, at the age of nine, when I warned some very cynical kids that if they didn't believe in Santa they'd get sticks and ashes for Christmas. Oh, they gathered round to listen to me then, didn't they? And in the senior school, during the winter months, two friends and I asked to clean the science labs to get out of the cold. I might not be that popular but I can swill out a conical flask with the best of them.

One of the best things ever to happen in a schoolyard happened to me a handful of times. When two friends, usually girls, skip around the playground, arms entwined behind each other's backs, it's as close to a platonic PDA as you can get. It's sort of a precursor to sex, in that you have to convince another person to play ONLY with you. And other people will see. If you can get someone to do interlocking skipping then you should lock them into a best-friend contract as soon as poss. That mostly involves calling each other best friend in earshot of others, but you can firm it up by telling each other a secret. That's a good long-term plan, but make sure theirs is true or else everyone will find out about the boil on your bum.

9. I had a rabbit on my knee

When I got to be in the school assembly about pets. Not much more to this story than that, really. My excellent first-year junior teacher Mrs Chilly brought in all of her pets and some she'd borrowed. We didn't ask where from – there were guinea pigs in the room. I got to sit in an assembly with a rabbit on my knee for twenty minutes. I couldn't have been happier; I wouldn't have minded if it had weed on me from stage fright. Much like I once encouraged a poo out of our cat Chief Brody's bum by wiping it continually with a wet cotton pad (to imitate his mother licking his bum. So glad I googled it twice).

10. I learnt that ring binders can lead to happiness

In the fourth year of junior school we did an assembly about talent. The middle-class girl played 'The Entertainer' on Mrs Hopper's piano. Another girl did remedial ballet. Holly Burns sat this one out as she didn't have a talent yet. My friend

Diane's talent was looking after children. She was eleven but she's always been forty really. I did 'looking after animals'. I held up a poster from Athena of a grey, lop-eared rabbit with the words 'You're no bunny 'til some bunny loves you'. I thought, at the time, that it was just about loving your rabbit, which I've always done whether it's in a hutch or up my fanny. Later, I realised it was a Dean Martin song. And given that I've never really listened to the lyrics, I just sang it, along with 'Hazard' and 'It's a Man's World'. I've only in the last five years started actually listening to lyrics and I can't believe that Richard Marx was singing about a murderer, James Brown sang a big old sexist song and Dean Martin's songwriters thought single people were worthless.

In the assembly I showed everyone my ring binder full of rabbit facts. My friend Rachael and I used to get the bus to South Shields Central Library and spend hours in the reference section, copying out of bunny books. We'd grab two of those study booths and snaffle Iced Gems. Eating wasn't allowed in the reference library and Iced Gems violated two rules because of all the loud crunching. To this day it's the most obvious flouting of the rules I've ever been involved in, and the most alive I've ever felt. The head of the first and second year seniors, Mrs Tilbrook, came to watch this assembly. We hadn't been told she was coming so it all felt a bit 'mystery shopper'. Luckily, she was impressed by my ring binder and talent for research, and I got in the senior school (so did everyone else, even the one with no talent). I've always warmed to those who are impressed by stationery.

11. I was great at following instructions*

I was always crap at cooking. I'm better now as it turns out it's just following instructions, doing as you're told.** At school, in home economics, we were never taught how to cook, just asked to bring in a recipe and do it. My sister, years before, had been taught three ways to make a cake, and if that isn't a recipe to happiness I don't know what is.

One time we were asked to bring in ingredients to make a breakfast. There were the show-offs who, having been taught by their parents, made fried eggs and sausages. My parents weren't able to teach me to cook; my dad worked every hour and my mam wasn't great in the kitchen. Actually, that's not true, she couldn't do a flan but could do a dinner, which is a much more useful skill. I'm not even sure I know what a flan is. While other kids were scrambling eggs and making French toast, I poured milk over a bowl of Frosties and sat smugly waiting for the others to finish. These days it would be even quicker. It takes seconds to open a Chunky Kit Kat.

When we made desserts, I did fruit salad. Yes, I can cut up fruit and put it in a bowl. I added the extra flourish of orange juice to stop the apple going brown, but the base of my sister's

---

* I would have made an incredible Nazi.

**I even have a favourite recipe now and it's for the best cake ever. Turn to page 287.

wicker cookery basket wasn't flat and the lid of my casserole dish didn't match. I left a trail of orange juice the entire route home that led a witch to us who pointed and laughed at my dry brown fruit and then left. But. BUT. While I was bad, BAD at home economics (I couldn't open a tin because it was a manual opener and I was used to electric – I'm the same with masturbation), when it came to exams I was brilliant. The test they set us was to answer a list of questions about nutrition and we had the run of all the books in the room. I came top of the class and second top in the year, despite not being able to cook. See, research is my skill.

12. The day Alan Watson gave me 'the person with the nicest eyes' in PSE

13. I got a bodyguard

My friend Joanne Glenny was a down-to-earth, funny, sweet tomboy who broke bones almost weekly. She wasn't brittle-boned, just super rough-and-tumble. On one occasion, when she broke her right arm, thus preventing her from writing, I got some carbon paper and put it under every sheet I wrote on during every class we did together. That way she got all the notes. To say thanks when her cast was taken off, she bought me an A4 pad of lined paper to replace what I'd used and offered to be my bodyguard for a year. She was tough and got on with everyone. I don't remember her ever having to act on her title but I was much more relaxed and confident that year knowing I had back up. We decided that Paul Simon's 'You

Can Call Me Al' was her theme tune, and whenever I hear it now, I always think of her.

14. I was crap at heads

In Mrs Chilly's class, in the first year at junior school, everything was taught through the medium of art. She was nice and creative and a little bit weird. She came in one day wearing sunglasses because she'd tried to bleach her eyelashes and it had gone a bit wrong. She once set us the task of making puppets for a puppet show. The short kids were to be the puppeteers, but everyone got a chance to make a papier-mâché puppet that might be chosen to be in *The Frog Prince*. All the boys set about making the prince; all the girls, me included, the princess. Mrs Chilly explained that heads aren't spherical, that the back juts out a little and to bear that in mind. I did. I always did as I was told. She came across to see how I was doing, saw my papier-mâché princess head, complete with jutting-out back bit, and declared, 'Ah, you're doing the frog!' So I painted my princess green with a heavy heart. But I was the only one who did a frog so I totally got in the show!

15. I got to pick a team

In PE I was always the last to be picked. The PE teacher felt sorry for me so she let me be the referee and gave me her whistle. But as I didn't know the rules of the game, I just stood on the sideline and blew the whistle whenever Mrs Chidley shouted, 'NOOOOOOWWWWWW!'

There was one time when the teacher realised that some kids were always picked last and she said, 'You [me] can pick a team.' Now, I could have picked all the sporty kids and had an amazing team (plus me) that won. But no, I picked all the ones like me. All the glasses, wonky eyes and club feet; it was like the cantina scene in *Star Wars* and I was head alien. If this had been a Hollywood film, there'd have been a montage where the underdogs very quickly learnt how to play netball and hammered it. But no, we got slaughtered. But we had such a brilliant time. For some of those kids, me included, it was the first time they'd held the netball when they weren't putting it in a cupboard. To be honest, I think that's why we lost, because every time they had the ball they kept taking it to the cupboard. If the cupboard had been the goal we would have won eight–nil.

16. I saw a girl squirt cheese in her mouth

Once, on a school trip, we were told to take sandwiches. Whether my friend Gabrielle's parents were busy or lazy I have no idea, but we were all jealous when she unpacked her lunch to reveal two slices of white bread and a full tube of Primula cheese (I don't even like cheese), which she proceeded to squirt directly into her mouth. I remember thinking, I bet this is what being an adult is like.

17. I was popular for the duration of a Kylie Minogue song

Another school trip was to Otterburn Hall, Northumberland's ultimate country-house attraction, which was an odd choice for a school trip. We were there four or five days. I had packed two spare outfits in case I fell in the 'man-made lake'. I didn't see it once, let alone fall in twice. These days, kids would probably go to Disneyland Paris, Paris's ultimate theme-park attraction, but we got Otterburn Hall, the sort of place I'd look at now in case they did big Sunday dinners but wouldn't give a general shit about the antiques and history: 'Ooh, it looks like they'd do big Yorkshires.'

Forgive me in this bit as I often get this school trip and the one to Calais mixed up. Calais was barely French and a spider ran up a girl's leg. Otterburn was rope bridges and a disco. The disco was on the first night and we were urged to bring any mixtapes* we had so Mrs Chidley could play them for everyone to dance to. Well, this was very exciting. I wondered if my mixtape would be a way to get more friends. The disco was well underway when a song came on that I knew was on my tape, Kylie's 'Got to Be Certain'. Everyone was dancing. It's a cracking tune and I could see people chatting to each other about what a great song it was. Maybe even things like 'we should find out whose tape this is and show her how to get her perm as crunchy as ours'. That was something I hadn't figured out yet. Mine was all soft and natural like a nana's; theirs was rock hard and never moved.

Kylie's song ended abruptly and all at once my future popularity was hanging in the balance. Also my future as a DJ was down the shitter. In that moment Mrs Chidley pulled a face, a

---

* If you don't know what a mixtape is I have no time for you.

sort of 'what happened there?' face, but the wondering didn't last long as the loud Metro Radio jingle that denoted how I'd acquired said Stock Aitken and Waterman CLASSIC rang out across the neo-Elizabethan listed building. God knows what the people making the giant Yorkshire puddings must have thought. But while it was loud, it was also a short jingle, and everyone's shoulders came back down hopeful of another banging tune.

This is where I realised my fatal flaw. Surely when Mrs Chidley asked us to hand in any mixtapes for the disco, what she really meant was 'have a think about what's on that personal mixtape you've made just for yourself that no one else has ever listened to, and if you think it will help you get friends who can crisp up your curls, hand it in'. Straight after the success of Kylie and the wobble of the radio jingle came Al Jarreau's theme from *Moonlighting*. Please stop reading to google this. It's best described as a ballad for mams. I loved the programme and loved the theme music; why wouldn't I have it on my private mixtape? I had to spend another four days there talking about 'that loser with the crappy love song on her mixtape'. Luckily, Mrs Chidley kept my secret safe.

18. I discovered I like wearing helmets

We once went to Beamish, the North East's ultimate open-air museum attraction. I would highly recommend it for a glimpse into the past, though to be fair I haven't been in over thirty years so maybe they've updated it and 'the past' is now landlines, Ceefax and Goblin puddings. My mam came as an extra helper and I was thrilled as it meant there was definitely someone who would talk to me. We went down the pretend coal mine and it was great to see the kind of place my dad worked. We went all round the pit cottages and in the shops – it was incredible. By mid-afternoon, one of the kids pointed out that I still had my pit helmet on, a whole forty-five minutes after leaving the mine. I'd been in the tea room, round the shops and in the cottages, and no one had noticed that I still had my helmet on. NOT EVEN MY MAM. I felt silly, but when I got home and told my dad he beamed with pride and said, 'You must have found it comfortable.'

19. An excellent teacher made a difference

My very favourite teacher taught me in the fourth year at junior school: Mr Thomas. I'm pretty sure he was every kid's favourite teacher; he was funny and kind. He noticed that I was shy and every time he saw me, he'd say, 'Head up!' I'd lift my head 'til I got round the corner. Then I'd see him in the playground: 'Head up!' In the corridor: 'Head up!' In the school hall: 'Head up!' He once commented that I must never stand in dog dirt as I was always looking at the floor. Amazingly, that was not true. I stood in it all the time. I used to get narked about being told to put my head up so I thought I'd do something about it. I held my head up all the time so he couldn't shout at me. That showed him. And when I left, he signed my autograph book along with all the other teachers, but above his name he wrote 'Always hold your head high'.

I mentioned him in an article I wrote for a newspaper last year and his daughter got in touch with me. He had sadly passed away several years ago. I was so surprised and touched to hear that he'd been proud of what I'd achieved.

During my wobbles of self-confidence, I try to hold my head high. It always makes me think of him.

HOW TO BE CHAMPION

Yes, some of my best memories of school are animal- and Kylie-based, but school is also where I realised I could write quite well, that I love ballads for mams and where I got annoyed about the patriarchy for the first time. Like a tiny version of me now. Have a think about what your tiny version of you was like. And always hold your head high.

Chapter 7

Being a Wallflower

CHRISTMAS PARTIES ALWAYS spelt hope for me, especially at school. Sure, no boys had shown interest in me all year round, but there was a reason for that. Boys don't like clever girls, girls who are polite, girls who've never touched a cock but could draw you a really good budgie. Boys, weirdly, like girls who suck their hair, have suckers (love bites) on their necks and are repeatedly average in exams. But I wasn't at school to impress boys. I was at school to learn, to find out what I was good at, what I enjoyed and to get ready to shine like billy-o.

But I always thought I had the potential to turn heads. If someone wears make-up and short skirts all the time, what are they going to pull out of the bag at the Christmas party? I was pulling things out of bags like a magician. I liked make-up and jewellery but never wore them at school. I liked dangly earrings and a lipstick by Avon called Café au Lait. And so to the transformation. What would the boy who sneezed on my desk and rubbed it in (but who I was reliably informed loved me) think when I walked into the Christmas party all glammed up? Or the boy who bit off his wart for me? I envisioned them both, their eyes wide open, jaws dropping – running, sneezing and bleeding to ask me to dance, and maybe kiss me in a couple of years.

In the lead up to the party, I'd buy as many women's magazines as my pocket money and the extra few quid I earned from cleaning the house could stretch to (do you need any more *Cinderella* references?), remembering that the festive issues always came out in November. They were my bible. Without them, how would I know that licking my lips and touching his arm would lead to having someone to go to the cinema with on a Saturday afternoon? In reality, it meant I ended up with chapped lips, and have you ever tried to touch a boy's arm while he's jigging about to Madness?

I think I just wanted to be noticed, asked to dance. And on the day, in my Avon lipstick, River Island earrings, White Musk playfully squirted behind my ears because I'd seen someone do it on the telly, in an off-the-shoulder black velvet cocktail dress that I'd feather-dusted many a skirting board for, I moused into the party. And I did dance, but just with girls, and with teachers too, in an innocent, waltzing kind of way. And I had a lovely time. I was just a Plain Jane Super Brain who never got her 'wow' moment.

And I think I know why. I think it's a confidence thing. It didn't matter what I was wearing because I was quiet and invisible. You can't get confidence from a magazine. Maybe it's leaving school and getting out of those gangs you've been in for too long that allows you to blossom and become a proper person. There's no social mobility at school; if you're a dowdy nerd, you're a dowdy nerd for five years. But the minute you leave, you can be a funny girl with nine GCSEs and the whole world ahead of her. Head up, smile, eye contact: that's what makes people look at you.

That's why it pisses me off when people comment on what I wear. It doesn't matter. Fuck what I've got on. If I'm wearing it then I've picked it because I feel good in it. Is my head up? Am I smiling? Then I am currently winning the low self-esteem battle.

Also, there are men who love a smart woman – who find wit sexy. They're just not thirteen.

HOW TO BE CHAMPION

Be yourself or else you'll have to keep up the pretence for ever. Unless you're an actor, then do the opposite.

If you didn't get any attention from people you fancied at school, it doesn't matter. That's not what you're there for. That's why there's no GCSE in fingering. You're there to learn. Being sad about not having a relationship at school is like complaining to a butcher when he won't take your library books off you. Get yourself to the library – there's loads of cocks and fannies there. Hold on, this has gone wrong.

Chapter 8

I've Had Proper Jobs

I'VE ALWAYS ENJOYED working. I am a workaholic these days, which isn't ideal but I'm aware of it so I keep an eye and pull back when needs be. I've always loved spending money I've earned. My parents never gave us money; we got pocket money, yes, but if we wanted some more money, we had to do more chores. The money was oh-so-much sweeter that way. The one thing my dad doesn't like in people is laziness, and I've got that from him. Work hard, do your best. Why wouldn't you? Then you can moan if things don't go your way, sure. But not for long, because there's always more work to be done. We can all improve; I want every tour I do to be better than the last. I'm only thirteen years into this job, and there's a lot still to learn.

We learnt the value of money early when our parents told us that they sent the money to Santa for our Christmas presents. So, every year, we'd be told an amount and we'd pick presents up to that amount. Then my mam and dad would send the money to Santa who was basically just shopping for us. We'd thank him, yes, but we'd thank our parents more.

I've had a fair few jobs in my time. My first official job was when I was sixteen and worked part-time at WHSmith in South Shields. Well, not just when I was sixteen: I was there for four years. Always the bridesmaid, never the full-time worker or off-to-university adventurer. University wasn't really an option for me as there wasn't much spare cash and my dad was already working seven days a week, fifty weeks a year, and, to be honest, I think that's enough. I was the only kid in my year not to fill out the UCCA/PCAS form. Even those falling way below every pass mark were encouraged to fill in the 'form of hope' with fingers, toes and everything else crossed that their next three years were full of boozing, cooking badly and trying to be cool. (I was already pretty good at the first two and the third had been a pipe dream since my flip-up prescription sunglasses at the age of twelve.)

Until a few years ago I had this feeling that I'd missed out and that people looking at me could tell that my education was limited. Like when you think people can tell you're a virgin, which of course they can because you blush every time they mention sex and just say, 'Yeah, me too,' after any stories about conquests and one-night stands. And your 'what are men like?' conversation input is limited to your dad and he's pretty awesome.

I continued my education after getting average A-level grades at South Tyneside College by doing an HND in film and production that was doomed when the European Social Fund withdrew their funding. (Cheers, now we'll never know how that terrible split-screen romantic short film will end.)

At WHSmith, whenever I trained new Saturday staff, I always quietly showed them an extra thing that wasn't on my list. How to open the till if someone threatens you to do so. I'm pretty sure any shop's policy would be to lie over the till and protect the takings. I told them which button opens the till drawer and said 'Give them it. You are more important than cash.' During my four years I saw countless Saturday staff come and go, and only nearly had sex with one. But by the time he fancied me, I'd gone off him.

I owe a lot to that job. I loved my time there. My first job, first colleagues, first work nights out, first wage I earned, first bosses, first staff discount, dealt with my first customer complaints, met my first pervert too (a man who asked for books with pictures of naked pregnant ladies), first uniform and name badge I wore (of many), first overtime, first Christmas bonus. My mam told me later that she'd suggested I get a Saturday job to help bring me out of my shell. And it worked; I'm still in touch with a few of the people I worked with there twenty years ago. Turns out people at work are a vast improvement on kids at school. It was a brilliant time in my life with many memories, some funny, some happy, such as:

- When a man asked when *Elvis* monthly came out, I opened up the massive ring binder from under the counter and went through it. When I shut it, he'd gone. Odd. Ah no, he's on the floor having an epileptic fit. I rang my bell a million times. The rules were once for a member of staff, twice for a supervisor, three times for an emergency and a million times for a giant Elvis fan convulsing on the floor. The staff ran to the man's aid, called 999 and loosened his collar. He was a big bloke and blocked my exit from behind the counter so I panicked. It turns out I am good in an emergency until someone else takes over. Then I fall apart. I felt woozy and, just in time, Kelvin (one of the best people I've ever met) tapped on the counter for me to climb onto it. I did, he swung my legs around, lifted me off and handed me to Gillian, who took me upstairs for sugary tea. That was where my love affair with sugary tea began. The bloke was fine by the way. I realise I've made this all about me. Maybe that's where that started too.

• When *For Women*, the porn mag for the ladies, came out in the early nineties I led a small campaign to get WHSmith to stock it. I had no interest in it but had to tidy titty mags every day, and it felt only fair to have to tidy some cocks too. I never bought that magazine, but someone once bought a copy for me. It was my eighteenth birthday – you know, the porn birthday – and my sister's friend bought me it for a laugh. We sat in Oscars (wine bar, opposite the town hall and at that time the start of any decent pub crawl; it was downhill all the way, in more ways than one) and flicked through it, with lots of shrieking and laughing. You're not allowed to show erect penises so, rather than arousing, it was hilarious. A man standing with one leg up on a hay bale with his dangly cock just hanging there apologetically. Another man leaning against a truck with his willy lying on his leg, like it was tired. Flicking through, it must be similar to what it's like working in a hospital. Constantly confronted with sad knobs and sleepy winkies. The girl that gave me it thought it would be a laugh and it was. Until we moved from that bar to the next. I had the tiniest of handbags with me. Tiny. Only big enough for your purse, keys, a claggy lip gloss and your Suzy Lamplugh rape alarm. Back in the day, rape alarms weren't just a tiny discreet button, they were a fucking aerosol, like a fat Elnett. When you depressed it a huge siren blared out. Great for when you're in danger; not so great when your mam makes you test it every morning before you go to college. I'm sure the neighbours thought we had daily rounds of early-morning *It's a Knockout*. Also, imagine if I'd ever needed it and it was empty because of too much testing. Just SSSSSed in the air like the last day of a deodorant. You know it won't work but at least your pits smell momentarily clean. Still, an aerosol is better than when you used to just have to bash a pan and spoon together. Imagine the size of your handbag then.

- Still the only skirt I've ever had with a dedicated pen slot. I'm surprised they aren't more common.

- We always worked on Christmas Eve and it was great. The day flew by and everyone was in a good mood – we knew time off and food saturation were only a day away. We'd usually dress up in fancy dress. I was Goldilocks one year, complete with bonnet that had long hair attached, pencilled-on freckles and a shiny-yellow fire-hazard of a dress. Not everyone got who I was: men would shout, 'Where are your sheep?' as they went past. Also, when you've had your head down on a till for seven hours, not looking up because there is no end to your queue, you sort of forget you're in fancy dress, and when people laugh at your face you get defensive. Then you accidentally get your plaits caught in the till drawer and remember what you look like. One year, no one could be arsed to get dressed up but me and my friend Lynne. So with the manager's permission, we did it anyway. We decided to do bad taste. We put on too much eighties' blue eyeliner, a lot of red lipstick, dug some clothes out of Lynne's mam's past (sorry, Lynne's mam) and strutted into work looking absolutely terrible. Did everyone laugh and think we looked absolutely terrible? No. Not a single person noticed. No reaction. I think someone even said I looked nicer. Not nice. NICER.

- There was a boy who came in that I slightly knew and low-level loved but thought I was hiding it super well. Until I noticed that every time I spoke to him, my friend on the music department played Andy Williams's 'Can't Take My Eyes Off You'. Loudly.

- The branch in South Shields was very small and on one floor. I worked initially on the till and magazine section then moved to stationery, which only made my addiction to pens and pads worse. On a quiet afternoon you could sometimes find me writhing around among the wire-bound wide-lined jotters. Like in *American Beauty* but fatter and with more paper cuts. Whoever was on the music section would pick the tunes that played out in the shop. Obviously, you had to be careful it wasn't something that might offend the public. Like when a customer complained about a Christmas album because of Gary Glitter. Alison, the Saturday part-timer, would regularly pop on Alanis Morissette's *Jagged Little Pill* at 9 a.m. and we would fill up the shelves while listening to her angsty brilliance (I still love that album to this day). Nothing to worry about here. Until the second song, when twenty-four seconds in the line, 'Would she go down on you in a theatre?' makes a couple of customers look up from the fineliners and Catherine Cookson classics. Look up, slightly puzzled, shake it off, and go back to their hard-backed double-entry accounts books and *Cross Stitcher* monthly. Also, I'm pretty sure that theatre in America means cinema. I'm sure she doesn't mean, 'Would she suck you off during a live performance of *Hamlet*?' 'Is this a dagger I see before me?' •snuffling sucky noises•. Over a minute goes by and everyone relaxes. Must have misheard that previous bit – probably about going down to the theatre. Maybe it's about being in the stalls. Would she sit in the stalls with you? Then, at one-minute forty-five, two teen-agers would run, RUN across the shop to the CD player. Me and Alison. Running like I never had in PE. Thunderous comfortable black shoes stampeding across the shop floor so that hopefully the line 'And are you thinking of me when you fuck her?' would end rather more romantically and abruptly with 'And are you thinking of me?' then some very quick Sting.

- All Saturday staff lie about when things are coming in. We just used to say Wednesday as we didn't work on a Wednesday. Sorry, everyone.

- We did annual audits where the manager needed the part-time staff in for as many hours as you could do. I loved it. LOVED IT. I used to go in for a few hours after college, count shit on a big calculator thing and earn money. It was double-time too, and all in your normal clothes. I think that's when I learnt about working hard and a lot.

Next, I worked in the Virgin cinema in Boldon Colliery. It was my first full-time job; I was twenty-two. I've always loved films, and as a teen I went to the cinema as often as I could. I remember telling my friend Helen that I had a date for the new Keanu Reeves film *Speed* and she got all excited until I said 'September thirtieth!' I used to sneak into films I wasn't old enough to see, but with my dad. When we saw the classic *Tango & Cash* I linked arms with him to make me less likely to have my age checked. Years later, I realised what that looked like. We essentially pretended my dad was a paedophile to get into *Tango & Cash*.

I wondered what it took to be a film critic so when I was seventeen I wrote a couple of reviews and sent them in to *Film Review* magazine for their opinion. They printed my letter and one from some young lad. I can't remember exactly what they said, but they liked him more than me. I was informative and he was sassy. They did say that I might have a chance of writing reviews for a local newspaper so I wrote to them all and the Star series – a group of six free newspapers – said yes. They could only do expenses but I was happy. A column reviewing films in the free paper at the age of seventeen? I was beaming. I wrote for them for four years, and never met any of the newspaper staff. I did it all via the fax machine in my local newsagents. The fax machine was often temperamental and the man who ran the shop would let me go to work and just keep trying 'til it went through. What a hero.

I suspected that a lot of people put the free paper straight in the bin or the litter tray for their cat to wee on, and that those who did read it possibly did so because they couldn't afford to buy a paper. With that in mind, I wrote the weekly column so that it was entertaining without the reader needing to have seen the film. If you can't afford a paper, you probably can't afford the cinema. I once mentioned Richard Gere's leather trousers three times in a review and someone came up to me in the shop the next day to tell me I'd mentioned them three times. Customers would tell me what page I was on when the paper came out. Adorable.

Because the space for actual writing was at the mercy of advertisers, the paper regularly chopped the last paragraph off my column and called it editing. Brutal.

It was a review of *The Preacher's Wife*, starring Denzel Washington and Whitney Houston, that got me fired. FIRED! I wrote quite a scathing review of Ms Houston, confident that she wouldn't be passing through Jarrow any time soon to see it. The film was awful, she was awful; I was funny about it but I was also awful. The editor, who I'd never met, wrote me a damning letter. He said my 'vitriolic diatribe' against the lead actor meant that I would not 'attract a fee' for this review. Neither would he be printing it. Firstly, I looked up both 'vitriolic' and 'diatribe' in my dictionary. Then I replied that none of my reviews attracted a fee and that he should know that. I suggested he try 'editing, for that is your job' and told him that, as I would not change my opinion, he was free to take it or leave it. He left it. And asked for my press pass to be sent back to him immediately. I cut it up into tiny bits and posted it back so he'd have to piece it together to see what it was. He was clearly a MASSIVE Whitney fan. Me too – just not in that piece of shit.

My favourite programme at the time was *Film 93,* so I wrote to the producer and asked if I could have Barry Norman's job, please. I think I used the words 'new blood'. He replied that he had no immediate plans to replace Barry Norman, which I did not take as a definite 'no'.

I tried to get freelance work writing for a magazine. I remember being on the phone to someone at a women's magazine listing the subjects I could write about. After every one she told me they had someone on staff who could write that. It was harsh. But I did manage to sell a piece I'd written as an example of my work to the short-lived *Minx* magazine. It was about being invited to a wedding when you're single. It was two hours' work – one to write it, one to edit to the word count they wanted – and I made £200. They never printed the article but I didn't care. I sold some writing. I was a paid writer. I framed the cheque. Then realised I was being a twat, so I photocopied the cheque, cashed it and framed the photocopy.

Back to working at the cinema. Seventy staff started on the same day, and for the first two weeks we were setting the place up. It was a brand-new, purpose-built cinema; the excitement in the air was palpable. As a big film fan, I was convinced the cinema would be full of my type. It wasn't. Unlike my HND course, where we could regularly nerd-out over films. The course was very cock heavy, with about forty blokes and only six women. One day I heard some of the lads on the course chatting about *Star Wars* – this was back when there were just the three films, Episodes IV, V and VI. I thought, Here's my chance to ingratiate myself, make the fellas aware that I know my films. They were placing the films in order of quality, favourite to least favourite. I joined in with, 'Well, obviously *Empire* is the best . . .'

All men call it *Empire*, not *Star Wars: The Empire Strikes Back*. Just *Empire*. And they all think it's the best one because it's the darkest when actually it's just a bridging film; it doesn't really stand alone. I could see the interest in their faces. A girl who knows about sci-fi? Who knows who directed what? Who knows *Empire* is the best? I continued, 'So, yes, *Empire* first then probably *Star Wars* . . .'

They leaned in.

'Oh, hold on, which is the one with the teddies in it again?'

They stopped leaning in and walked away. And I laughed my arse off.

On opening night at the cinema they played my *Disco Mix 96* double CD. Thankfully there was no Al Jarreau on that one. I was quickly promoted to supervisor as I was good at dealing with problems and was very proactive. A manager once told me I'd never make a good manager because I didn't think I was better than everyone else. I said, 'If that's what it takes then, yep, I'd be crap at it.'

Another time, a manager, different one to the one above but of similar ilk, locked himself in the cash office (we could see him on the CCTV) when we had a power cut and had to empty eleven screens of people, a café-bar, a shop and a kids area in an ordered and non-panicky way. He was the only manager on duty. So six of us went screen to screen, holding a torch up at our faces while we explained what had happened and encouraged customers to leave via the fire exits, handing out raffle tickets to exchange for a free ticket on their next visit.

Then all the staff went home early. Aside from my department, who had to spend two hours chipping cheese off the walls and washing floors. The manager said nothing.

One Boxing Day, I had a taxi booked to take me in to work as there was no public transport. The taxi didn't show up. I rang to complain and thanks to some mix-up they said it was cancelled. The driver came out to get me in the end and, instead of accepting that shit happens and there'd been some miscommunication, he berated me for lying, accusing me of cancelling the taxi so I could throw a sickie then feeling guilty and lying about what I'd done. He was so awful that I shouted something that I think only normally happens in films. I leaned forward and said, 'Stop the fucking car!' He did and I got out, walked back home and called a different taxi firm. I think this was the start of me not taking any shit. I'm pleased to say this is a skill I have nurtured. I'm really good at it now. In my handbag I always carry a small crocheted turd so that I never have to take any shit, because I've already got one.

We had one of those big signs on the side of the cinema to advertise the films we had on that week. You know, like one of those aspirational lightboxes you can buy now, but ours said 'Titanic', not 'Do something for yourself today' or 'More wine please'. I fucking hate aspirational and inspirational signs. They make my stomach muscles tense. Literally the only exercise I get is cringing; I can wander around John Lewis and have a pretty good workout. 'You don't have to brush all of your teeth. Just the ones you want to keep.' CRINGE. 'If at first you don't succeed, try doing it the way your wife told you.' SEXIST CRINGE. There's a kitchen rules one that is so passive-aggressive it practically says 'Eat this or fuck off', but in curly writing. Our massive cinema lightbox would regularly be spelt wrong, but it was such a fanny to go back up that we'd just leave it. Some classics included *Sphere* spelt Spear and the Nick Leeson story *Rouge Trader*. The bad spelling was everywhere. We'd leave work messages for each other on the white board behind the popcorn stand, where I worked. My favourite was: 'Deepest appollogies. There's a projeter falt in sceen 8.'

The first time I ever had a milkshake was at this cinema. There was a milk bar where the kids got hammered (on sugar) and threw balls at the heads of some unfortunate members of staff in Velcro hats. I finished my shift and sat and talked to the nice girl who worked there, while downing five milk-shakes. When I stood up I felt like a cow. I must have looked like a proper lush: me, telling all my woes; her, cleaning the nozzle of the milkshake machine with a tea towel. And in the background, sugared-up kids going hell for leather on a minimum-wage-paid member of staff who is simultaneously thinking about updating her CV and sealing her vagina shut once and for all.

The cinema was opposite a McDonald's and round the corner from a big Asda, so lunchtimes were a doddle. A few of us once went to McDonald's on our lunch break during a crazy-busy time for them. The queues inside were really bad but the drive-thru was empty. None of us could drive so instead we stood in the formation of a car, two in front and two behind, and walked through the drive-thru. Kudos to the 'driver', who even steered a 'wheel' and wound a 'window' down. I think the staff admired our chutzpah and so served us.*

Because I wanted a bit more stability and a bit more money, I next went to work for the Jobcentre. My sister worked for them so, just like musical instruments and the Brownies before it, I copied her. Can I just remind you that I handed in a dusty clarinet case after only a couple of months? Picture the scene with a soundtrack by my sister as James Galway, fluting away a tune called 'I got to Grade 5'. I only joined the Brownies for two weeks. My mam didn't even buy me the uniform; she borrowed one as she didn't think I'd stick at it. There's nothing worse than an accurate insult. At Brownies I didn't like joining in. I only liked the tuck shop. Turns out there are sweets everywhere. Picture the scene: me eating sweets questioning pointless games while my sister dances around us in her GUIDES uniform throwing badges she's earned by cooking and sewing into the air like a rubbish graduation. So, hey, I'm sure this Jobcentre thing is going to go great.

Truth is, it wasn't so bad. Apart from the time a man once weed on his seat while signing on. Still no clue if it was a dirty protest or my job search was hilarious. The first two weeks were just computer-based training in a room with three men with grey hair and glasses. I had my cinema leaving do my first week on the job and came in to work on the Friday via a

---

* It was in this job that I met my first husband. We had a lovely time for about seven years. To see how this turned out, skip to the chapter entitled 'Divorce'.

terrifying journey on the Metro. I was incredibly hungover and swallowed down so much sick I felt full. Only a little squirted its way forcefully out of a tiny gap between my lips, which I seemingly had no control over. That was while I was taking most of my clothes off due to the sweats. The three men with grey hair and glasses turned out to be lovely men who didn't tell anyone how many times I legged it to the loo and came back white as a sheet, smelling of whisky and regurgitated McChicken sandwiches.

During the second week of training, my friend John from the cinema had a house party and I came in to work that Friday in much the same state as the week before. I was never a good drinker so it was rare for me to be hungover at work. In fact, they were probably the only two occasions that year that I was hungover. The following week, when I was fine on the Friday, all three men came up to me surprised. They thought the last two weeks were just Sarah on a Friday. They clearly hadn't met the real me yet. They had no idea of my work-hard, play-hardly-at-all general attitude to life.

One of the men with grey hair and glasses became a good pal and I always sat in the smoking room with him on breaks. I've never smoked; I've never fancied it. My parents both smoked for a long time and my first husband did too. If you need a mint before someone can kiss you, maybe it's not a great thing you're doing there. BUT, the smoking room was always full of more interesting people. See! I risked cancer for good chat. I am an idiot. Sniff my clothes – that's the smell of banter, that.

I worked on what's called 'frontline', which is where people come in to sign on. One day, when I said, 'Next, please,' to the person at the front of the queue, he sat down and said, 'You're new.' I told him I'd been there six months and asked him what made him think I was new. He said, 'You're smiling.'

Part of the job you don't get trained for is counselling. Sometimes broken men and women sit in front of you, and I'd always tried to boost their confidence, give them some pointers that might help and be sympathetic and always positive. An old man cried at my desk once. He was probably only in his sixties but recent events had knocked the life out of him and made him look old-old. His wife had died suddenly and he'd been fired from work for taking time off to grieve. I hope I helped him. I tried. I tried to comfort him as he cried silently at my desk. I tried to boost his confidence about getting him back into work. Warehousing is hard to get a bloke in his sixties back into when twenty-five-year-olds are going for the same jobs. I put him on my caseload, which meant that when it was quiet, I'd do job searches for him and ring him about jobs that had come in. He was always very receptive to help and seemed like such a nice man. I told him to keep his ear to the ground in case a job popped up that didn't get advertised with us. You have to be looking everywhere. Teach a man to fish and all that. I wanted to give him hope. There's always hope.

I found this job hard, in an emotional sense. I would regularly go home and have a little cry about some of the things I'd dealt with. But also, it was probably the job that was furthest from what I really wanted to do, which was write. In WHSmith I was surrounded by books and pens, and even though in the cinema my main job was warming cheese, it was still a place that celebrated art. Working at the Jobcentre made me feel sad and untapped. I was still writing short films and plays in my spare time, but it was a hard job. I used to try to get knocked over on the way in to work. Not to die, just to break a leg or a few ribs and get some time off. Proper time off. It was a busy road but bloody hell, they were careful drivers.

Looking back, I think this was depression, but I didn't use the word at the time. With the disappearance of telephone boxes, I sometimes wonder where people who hate their jobs go to cry. There was one opposite the Jobcentre where I'd either be ringing the bank to consolidate all of my loans into one fucking huge unmanageable one,* as more was going out than coming in, or crying. Crying is good for you; it's like releasing a valve. I don't really know what valves are but I know that opening one up a little stops it blowing later down the line. I think I might have learnt that from *The Simpsons*. While it sounds sad, those cries were very good for me and helped me get back behind my desk to work.

I was worried that staying too long on frontline would desensitise me to emotions, so I was very glad to be headhunted to be part of a new team that would be working out the back of

---

* By this time I was married and living in a rented flat which turned out to be incredibly damp. We thought it was weird that posters peeled off the walls every time we put them up. Turns out the walls were wet and our books were ruined. And our health hitty missy. I once had a cold for a few weeks and couldn't seem to shake it. I was pulled in by my manager and asked to sign a statement: 'Sarah endeavours to eat more oranges.'

Felling Jobcentre, six Metro stops away. It was a call centre where the only thing I'd be doing was job searches. I was one of a team of about ten. We all worked in the same room, which had a small kitchenette off it where one of the girls pinned passive-aggressive poems about cleaning the microwave, and the tea club biscuit-tin lid was never on. Because we were in such a small room with our own loos and everything, we didn't have to go far to get anything. A few of us learnt that you could even wheel your chair to the kitchenette and the printer, meaning there was hardly any need at all to get out of your chair. I put two stone on in four months.

This was one of my favourite jobs. It was such a fun team of positive people determined to help folk find work. One of the women read ten Mills & Boons a week and did poos that sometimes needed breaking up with a stick. One of the men used to take toilet breaks as well as tea breaks. But we still liked him. He had funny names for his friends and they for him. He was once on a break and our boss, a lovely middle-class woman we never saw use the toilet but who definitely knew how to tie a chiffon scarf, answered his phone and delivered a message when he returned. She was quite posh, remember. 'Er, Gavin,' she said. 'There's been a Captain BlackBush on the phone for you.' His funny name was Captain CactusPants, or so I thought. Turns out it was actually Captain Cacked His Pants, as on one occasion he had done just that.

When the phones were quiet, we again had our own case-loads to look after. Mine was clerical and retail but my friend Angela's was warehouse and forklift, so I mentioned my old warehouse man and she said she'd see what she could do. It was on that computer system that I spotted my next job: sound engineer. When I went for the interview and they told me it was for audiobooks, I was thrilled because I was going to be surrounded by books again. They'd had only male interviewees so far who'd thought it was a music role. I got the job, and on the day I left the call centre my friend Angela got a call from my warehouse man. She had put him in for a fair few jobs over the months, and he'd rung to pass a message on to me that he'd got himself one, which was the best leaving present I could have asked for.

Producing audiobooks was like being a kid, but instead of your parent reading to you it's a professional actor who can do all the voices. I was only there eighteen months but I enjoyed it very much. There was a downstairs toilet that became ladies only after someone did a massive turd in it that we could smell in the corridor. Quite old-fashioned, that. And a bit sexist to assume women can't do big stinky poos. The woman who raised the issue did not see the perpetrator but confidently declared it 'a man's smell'. I've spent my life since proving that theory wrong.

We recorded many Mills & Boon books. My favourite title was *Once Upon a Mattress*. There were a couple of authors who came up time and again, including one who in real life was a nurse who moved to Holland and married a doctor. All of her stories were about nurses who moved to Holland and married doctors. Hers usually ended with a chaste kiss, but, as we know, there are different levels of filth: throbbing members, a lot of men in white shirts, erect nipples taking people's eyes out left, right and centre. You can make your own Mills &

Boon title (or indeed any existing ones) by using my Mills & Boon title generator below.

Pick one from each category

Prince	Mistress	Rock Hard	Roulette
Doctor	Daughter	Wet	Christmas
Sheikh	Twins	Throbbing	Passion
Tycoon	Wife	Massive	Magic
Desert King	Virgin	Intense	Betrayal
Billionaire	Bride	Moist	Blackmail
Duke	Virgin Bride	Rounded	Baby
Italian	Virgin Twins	Soft	Secret
Husband	Virgin Daughter	Manly	Secret Baby
		Solid	Secret Baby Blackmail
		Painful	Secret Christmas Baby Blackmail
		Sore	Crouching Tiger Hidden Dragon Hard-on

Some examples:

The Desert King's Mistress's Moist Blackmail

The Sheikh, the Virgin Bride and Their Throbbing Christmas

But you can also have:

The Doctor's Daughter's Massive Baby

Because we recorded the books unabridged, we sold a lot to libraries and often the staff of those libraries wanted to come for a visit. I remember a 10 a.m. visit when a softly spoken woman and gentleman sat behind me while an actress in her sixties MMMed and YESed her way through a nine-page sex scene. Their eyes widened and we all had an exhausted custard cream straight afterwards. I heard tell of a care worker in an old people's home putting on an audiobook for the old ladies in the day room. It got a bit hot and heavy so she stopped the tape, only for every single one of those women to come up to her individually and ask for a borrow.

Through all of the seafaring yarns, potboilers, crime and romance, my favourite book by a country mile was *The Weeping Tree* by Audrey Reimann. It's a romance set during the Second World War and the reader, Lesley Mackie, and I cried so much at the end that we had to stop recording and gather ourselves together. I mentioned the book on a TV show I did with Anne Robinson and Audrey got in touch with me and came to see one of my shows. It was the only book I asked to take home after recording.

My favourite line from any book, however, was this from a Mills & Boon: 'He positioned himself for entry.' Sounds like a fat man trying to get through a doorway.

HOW TO BE CHAMPION

I once did a talk for fourteen- and fifteen-year-old girls at the school where my old college friend Helen is a teacher. One of the things I told them was that university wasn't essential. I remember the teachers all started looking at each other and panicking. I didn't want the kids who couldn't afford to go to think that this would in any way stop them from having a great life. Sure, if you want to be a doctor or lawyer, there's no way around it. But there are plenty of jobs where work experience and being keen and willing to learn can get you a foot in the door.

A quote that always gives me fire in my belly is by Johann Wolfgang von Goethe: 'Whatever you can do or dream you can, begin it. Boldness has genius, power and magic in it.'

Chapter 9

The Big Breakfast

MY FRIEND CATHY and I wanted to get into telly. We'd met on the film and TV production HND course and became good friends, and when I spotted an ad by a production company in the back of the Newcastle *Journal* asking for participants in some kind of youth TV show, we were in. In pairs, all the contributors had to make up a story and get it into the press. Cathy, who lived near Middlesbrough, stayed at mine and we came up with an idea. As Cathy was much more confident and outgoing than me, she'd be in front of the camera and I'd be the one making the video. Our story was that Cathy had been at a hen party where there was a hypnotist who'd made her sing like Madonna. Problem was, he hadn't brought her completely back out of it, so she'd be standing in the queue at the bank and would suddenly burst into song. That was our story. Daft and pretty unbelievable, but given that hypnotism is witchcraft of a sort, we thought someone might go for it.

We rang the *Shields Gazette* and Cathy got chatting to a journalist but then got cut off. We rang the Newcastle *Journal* who didn't believe us for a second. We were working out who to ring next when the doorbell went. We looked out of my mam and dad's bedroom bay window and it was a journalist. SHIT, SHIT. We hadn't even said where I lived (I never discovered how they found us). SHIT. We ran downstairs and Cathy ran in the wrong direction for the door. That's because she'd been drinking white wine from the bottle. It was about 1 p.m. We answered the door and took the journalist – from the *Gazette*, as it happened – to the nearby pub. Cathy told the story and explained that her friend was doing a TV course and wanted to film us for a little project. They didn't bat an eyelid. After a few photos of Cathy vogueing at a bus stop, off they went.

We were then contacted by a local news agency, which is not a shop that sells chocolate and tabs as I had previously thought. They took the story, and again I filmed it and also filmed a bit to camera in secret. Camcorders in those days didn't have a fancy screen, just an eyepiece you looked down. So I had no idea 'til later that the secret piece to camera was just a shot of my massive nose talking.

Cathy and I had a laugh that night in my tiny bedroom, thinking we'd done a good job but we'd have to see what got printed. Then I got a phone call from my sister the next day to say we were front page of the *Gazette*. The woman in the paper shop (ah, that's what they're called) even recognised the back of my head. I'd been an extra in the vogueing shot. Front page. Shit.

Over the course of the next four days, the following things happened.

- The national press picked it up. It was in all of the tabloids and a few of the broadsheets. As Cathy accidentally gave away the name of an actual friend, we're pretty sure that if any of the newspapers had tried to verify the story, they would have failed.
- One of the tabloids superimposed Cathy's face on Madonna during her cone period.
- The *Daily Star* put out an APB on the hypnotist to try to track him down. An APB. Like for a murderer. His name was Rupert Danns because it was nearly an anagram of 'underpants'.
- A journalist from the *Daily Mirror* sat outside my parents' house for five hours, ringing the landline every twenty minutes or so and ringing the doorbell the rest of the time.
- We became slightly paranoid and assumed a man walking his dog in the park was also a journalist.
- *This Morning* offered to fly us to Liverpool and bring a hypnotist in to try to turn Cathy back.
- We were linked to a tragic story in which a girl died due to a mishap with a hypnotist.

Shit.

So it got out of hand, which is an understatement. The TV company we were working for were thrilled with the take-up of the story. Before us, the best they had done was an inch-square story in Scottish newspaper the *Daily Record*. We were fucking everywhere. They knew this would be great on their show.

But it was getting scary. We were in deep and the press attention wasn't letting up. We told the TV company that we wanted to come clean and tell everyone it was a hoax. They refused to help. So, as it was my camcorder we were using because they didn't have enough to go round, I withheld the tape. They went a bit mad. I withheld the tape. Then I gave them a list of all the journalists who were hounding us – names and numbers. I told the TV people to ring them all and tell them it was a hoax, that they'd been had. They did. I gave them the tape, specifically asking them to use the massive-nose piece for audio only.

The journalist from the *Daily Mirror*, upon hearing that it was a hoax, said he was going to 'turn us over'. Cathy was twenty and I was twenty-one, and before this we had done nothing wrong. Good luck, mate.

Then *The Big Breakfast* popped up. More interested in the story now than before, they invited us on the show. We went down to London the night before and stayed in a hotel with a man at a piano in the bar. This was during Zoë Ball's stint so, according to Wikipedia, it was 1996. My first time on telly. My first time having make-up done. Cathy was great at make-up; my only experience was wearing a lot of concealer during a tough week in senior school when a boil took over from my nose. Cathy got in the make-up chair. Obviously we were just the public so we didn't get the kind of overhaul I would now. They put a little powder over the top of her gloriously made-up face. The make-up artist came to me, took one look and shouted over her shoulder, 'I'm gonna need another 20 minutes.' I think it's possible we were shunted down the running order as my face wasn't ready for telly. Or telly wasn't ready for my face.

You know when you don't really like how you look and struggle with it, and then you remember small moments like this that must have contributed. Like when the first boy I kissed laughed. Or a week of having a boil for a nose. Yep, makes total sense. They painted so much make-up on I couldn't properly smile.

We were interviewed by Zoë Ball, who had very claggy legs due to the previous segment where they'd tried to wax them with homemade sugar syrup. She was lovely. Is lovely. When I met her again on *It Takes Two*, *Strictly*'s sister show, she pretended to remember me. That's how lovely she is. We came clean about hoodwinking the press (their word; good word though, yes?) and with the nerves of a twenty-one-year-old bairn on live telly for the first time, I sneaked out a small fart on *The Big Breakfast* couch. My first, and some would say best, claim to fame.

It all died down, we won our episode, they showed my massive nose ('course they did – they're telly people) and our prize was a camcorder. So Cathy's dad bought it off us and we split the money. When the TV show aired, the guest judges pulled us apart because the other videos we were required to do were rushed and so weren't great – forgetting the fact that we'd done the best of any contestants in the history of the show. They needed an 'all about us' video, and as we'd been hounded by the press the whole time we hadn't got round to it. They filmed us at the fair on dodgems, eating candyfloss and saying words they suggested like 'suave' and 'debonair'. Fuck knows why. The guest judges, when describing us, just said, 'fat girls eat sugar'. THAT'S what they focused on. I've never liked Chumbawamba much anyway (at least one of them was a guest judge). Oh, and my favourite bit is that the *Daily Mirror* reporter used to play cricket with my dad. When he told us he was going to turn us over, my dad took great pleasure in telling him where to go because he 'was always shite at cricket anyway'.

HOW TO BE CHAMPION

Hotels with men playing the piano are definitely posh.

Don't give people a picture of your big nose if you don't want them to use it.

Brush the back of your hair in case you end up on the front page of a newspaper.

Chapter 10

Dates I Have Had

The One Who Gave Me My First Sexual Experience

My first sexual experience was when I was seven and Mark Robson shoved grass cuttings down the front of my homemade terry-towelling boob tube. It stayed up with elastic because actual boobs didn't arrive for another nine years.

The One Who Went Off in a Huff

When I was nineteen my friend came back from uni for her birthday party and brought some friends with her. One of them was very flirty and nice and funny; I responded accordingly. He suggested we go for a walk. We did, along the beach. It was lovely and I had flutterings in my chest. He stopped; we were at his B&B. I didn't want to have sex with him right then. He went off in a huff and just went into his accommodation I had to walk back in the dark on my own. An early lesson: not all men are gentlemen. And always wear shoes you can run in.

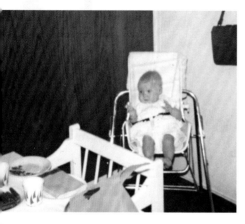

That's me in the corner. That's me in the high chair, being ignored at my sister's party.

Strong men tear up phonebooks in one go. Idiots. One page at a time while sitting on your nana's floor is the best way.

Possibly the first instance of side boob on South Shields beach. My very first wardrobe malfunction.

Shouting in a park. Not my last time doing that. The next time will involve hi-vis jackets and remote-controlled aeroplanes.

That is Bovril on my nose, I promise. How adorable is my older sister? I've never been great at buttoning up. See here, and on the cover of this book.

I came third in a bonny-baby contest. Not bad for a basin cut, slacks and puzzled expression. Look at my dad suggesting I smile at the camera. I was clearly annoyed at being judged on my appearance even then.

Remember when you could get a photo instantly? And it would naturally airbrush you over time? My sis and I doing 'gymlastics' in the hall, which consisted of wearing leotards and saying 'ta-da!' a lot.

Pre-glasses so I must have been four or five. And what an excellent jumper.

The only school photo of my sister and me due to the age gap. We'd had a fight just before this was taken and we weren't speaking. Still turned on the smiley faces, though.

I remember this jumper really well as it came with a matching skirt that was brilliant for twirling in.

My first perm. And some more studious specs.

Above The last year of junior school and the best teacher there ever was, Mr Thomas. You should be able to spot me quite easily. I'm still in regular touch with two kids in this class from over thirty years ago.

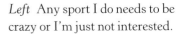

Left Any sport I do needs to be crazy or I'm just not interested.

Above Ah, my lovely granda.
It's either Christmas or it was my
coronation. This is the photo I put
up when he died so I could
remember him as he was.

Right Fake books behind me
and accidentally flicking
the Vs at the photographer.

Above The photo that best captures my youth. I Hoovered and dusted for Athena money, and look at all of the Schofield posters. Schofe with gopher and without. Smiling and serious (which I don't think I knew at the time meant sexy). This is the photo I sent him. He sent it back signed to 'a true fan!' Nice, but I had assumed he would keep it.

Left Me and my excellent friends Kym and Diane, who cleaned science labs with me during break time so we didn't have to stand in the cold. Check out the variety of perms too. And the biggest glasses I've ever had.

Dressed as Goldilocks and ready to work Christmas Eve at WHSmith. Note the *Cheers* pic during my obsession with Kirstie Alley, and the Sylvia Kristel *Emmanuelle* chair in the background that had to be moved every time I wanted to get into the wardrobe.

Late teens, I think, maybe early pub days. And I wasn't comparing myself to the *Mona Lisa*, I promise.

Above left I won a Moose! One of four new-act competitions I entered and the only one I won. (*Amused Moose Comedy Archive*)

Above right Forever a fan of the wraparound dress, this is during my set at the Funny Women final (I came second). We (me, Gary, my bezzie Lizzy and Kate Fox, the wonderful woman who encouraged me to start stand-up) all went to Patisserie Valerie beforehand and I learnt that milkshakes aren't good for nerves. (*Funny Women*)

An early backstage pic of Gary and me. I'm not sure if we were just flirting or dating openly or dating secretly, but this photo still gives me flutters.

The One with the Wonky Eye

I once went on a date with a man to an aquarium. I think if you asked him now he wouldn't think it was a date but I was sure it was. We saw sharks' cocks; what's more sexy than that? Nothing happened after that. Or before. Or during. He was very pretty, way out of my league, but had a slightly wonky eye so I thought that levelled us off.

The One Who Had a Car

I went on a few dates with a nice fella. He had a car and we'd go to cinemas I couldn't get to by bus. He took me to the tree at Hadrian's Wall, as featured in *Robin Hood: Prince of Thieves*, which hadn't long been out at the cinema. It was brilliant and a surprise, but by the time we got there I was bursting for a wee so it was a very quick visit. He cooked for me once and we ate a whole birthday cake, even though it was no one's birthday. He mentioned his friend Jo a lot. Neither of us fancied each other so I finished with him by letter. He is now married to Jo.

The One Who Failed Three Tests

I fancied a bloke for a year and a half before he asked me out. I said yes. He couldn't possibly live up to what I'd built him up to be in eighteen months. I made a cup of coffee for him before we went on our first date. He took a sip and said I'd passed the test. *Really?* I thought. *That's it?* He'd failed two since he came in the door. I did kiss him though (my first kiss), and he laughed at me. Three tests.

The One Who Bet on Dead People

I went out with a man who had a dead pool at the old people's home where he worked. I didn't see him again, though I did write a letter to *Empire* magazine about him (he'd bragged about having every issue). He was dull and HAD A DEAD POOL AT THE OLD PEOPLE'S HOME HE WORKED AT! I asked *Empire* if all male readers were like him. They answered 'God, no . . .'

He got annoyed I'd written in (they printed it) and threatened me via a mutual friend.

The One Who Read My Texts

I went out with a bloke for a few weeks who would drink a pitcher of cocktail while I drank a Coke, and he insisted on buying in rounds. He shouted at me for something I'd texted my friend. I apologised profusely until my friend asked why he was reading my texts. I dumped him by phone then met up with him at a bowling alley so he could give back the money he'd borrowed from me.

The One with No Opinions

I got in touch with an actor I had seen at a local theatre and fancied. I possibly just fancied the character he played in that one play. He picked up on the fact that I was a writer and I said I'd send him a couple of short scripts I'd written for him to read. He said that, as he didn't have any opinions, he would give them to his mam to read. He didn't have any opinions. Parked him there and then.

Now can you see why I marry the good ones?

The First One I Married

I met a man who cracked a joke about *Jaws* that no one got but me. We sparred and very quickly fell in love. He proposed in a café six or seven weeks after we started going out, maybe ten weeks after we met. I said yes. There was literally no reason not to.

HOW TO BE CHAMPION

Be careful and be safe when on dates, but also put your-self out there. I had a friend who dismissed a bloke I pointed out to her because he 'wasn't her type'. She'd been single for years so I suggested that maybe she wasn't doing so well with her type anyway.

Go with your gut instinct. Most of the dates I've listed above were first and last. I don't hang around if it doesn't feel right.

Have some gaps. Being on your own is brilliant and good for you. Let the dust settle after a relationship has ended. Allow yourself to blossom.

Chapter 11

A Love Letter to My Knockers

I LOVE YOU.

You didn't turn up until I left school so no boys ever got to snap my bra strap. It's very hard to twang a vest.

You catch cake crumbs, like nature's bib. I keep my pencils under you; I did that test you're supposed to do and I passed! I can keep a remote control under there. The Sky one.

You stopped men calling me 'mate' on the bus. (I used to get called 'son' a lot as a kid, but that might have been the hair.)

You helped me learn the alphabet. I know up to H.

You make a good, warm pillow for kittens and husbands.

I once cheered up a sad friend by flashing you both and she laughed (from the surprise, I like to think).

You are the bridge between 'just kissing' and 'thank God I've shaved me legs cos we're doing it'.

You save me from suffocation (I sleep on my stomach and you stop me lying too flat).

A LOVE LETTER TO MY KNOCKERS

You're like a built-in bumper. It would be hard to crack a rib with these babies on duty.

You are the reason I don't really want to lose weight (I'll be left with just a gut rather than curves). The right dress just hangs off you like an awning. I used to avoid tops with buttons down the front as they always puckered, but now I'm forty-two I just accept that at some point that day I'll be giving anyone who wants one an eyeful.

In a good bra, you make me feel like a 1950s Hollywood starlet. In a certain nightie, I look like Bubbles DeVere. But, wowsers, is that nightie comfy.

In bed, you keep under my arms warm.

You help me give excellent cushiony hugs. Imagine falling slow-motion into a giant marshmallow that smells of Marksies. And because I give good hugs, I get lots of hugs.

Your release is the best part of my day. Whether I'm at home, on a train, in a cinema or driving (always pull in to release the beasts: safety first; comfy second), taking my bra off is a joy. There are few thrills more intense than driving with no bra on. What if I get pulled over?

'Ma'am, you have your headlights on.'

'They're not my headlights, Officer.' (I clearly think all police are American. And in porn films.)

You are good at motorboating, where someone you know (preferably) puts their face betwixt you and makes the noise of a small engine. This can also be used as self-defence (depending on the size of the boobs and assailant).

You can accidentally click a link on my laptop.

Your size means I can't see my belly. Therefore it mustn't exist.

Underneath you is the first place I get sweaty. A sign to turn the heating down – like a woozy canary in a mine.

I balanced a kitten on one of you once and we watched *Bake Off* together. Now, that's basically how I want to die.

I think sometimes I forget the size of you. Like last week when I trapped a nipple in a Tupperware box. I didn't know it was there until I couldn't shut the fourth side and, remembering how tricky they are to close, I pressed with all of my might . . .

It was your fault; you shouldn't have been resting on the bench.

HOW TO BE CHAMPION

Check your knockers regularly. There's a clip on YouTube of me and buff Dr Christian showing you how to do it. I've just checked and if you put 'sarah millican dr christian tits' into Google it comes up.

Chapter 12

Divorce

DIVORCED AT TWENTY-NINE. Wow, that came as a surprise. I say that like he jumped out of a cake. We weren't sitting having our dinner only for him to pop to the loo and then a few minutes later a five-foot cake wheels itself in. He bursts out. I scramble for the date. Is it my birthday? We're already married so this can't be an elaborate proposal. Is it national knob-in-a-cake day? That's not fair – I was fond of him then. Also, every day is national knob-in-a-cake day, am I right, guys? Ew. I can't think of any good reason for him bursting out of a massive cake so I shout, 'I give up!' And he says, 'Me too – on our marriage!' And I start to think of conniving ways I can keep our Quentin Tarantino DVDs.

No, that's not what happened. I wish it had been; at least then there would have been cake. Once, when I was working in Australia, a friend of a friend I'd met once but really liked came to support me at an awards ceremony, where I'd been nominated. She brought me an all-singing, all-dancing Krispy Kreme doughnut. You know the ones, covered in Jelly Tots, marshmallows, bits of chocolate, like they've been dropped in a child's pocket. She brought it in case I won – CELEBRATION. And also, in case I didn't win – AT LEAST I HAVE A DOUGHNUT. I didn't win but I think a nomination and a fancy doughnut might be better than a win. You'd need to ask the Pajama Men (who beat me). Ditto the time I lost out twice at the British Comedy Awards and came back to our room at the Premier Inn only for my now husband to go foraging for McDonald's and come back with an unasked-for McFlurry. I think two nominations and an unasked-for McFlurry might be better than a win. You'd need to ask either Jo Brand or Samantha Spiro. What I'm saying is, if you're planning to end a relationship, consider having something sweet to hand. Maybe get a Viennetta out of the freezer half an hour before. Just a thought. You'd prepare for a proposal (buy a ring, think of somewhere up high with limited oxygen, wash), so why not for the opposite?

It was around the time of our divorce that I also found out he liked broccoli. Eight years together, you'd think it would have come up before then. We had one appointment with a counsellor in an attempt to save our marriage. They told us there was nothing they could do for us, saying, 'We help people work out what's wrong with their relationship. You already know.' And I suppose we did. He'd been in a crabby mood the weekend before and I asked what was wrong. He clammed up. So I started to list things. Is it work? No. Is it the tabs? (He'd recently given up smoking. I liked to think he was forward planning. When we split, he wouldn't be able to afford to smoke so let's get started on that now. I may be being cynical.

I may also be fucking right.) Is it the tabs? No. A few down the list, I slotted myself in. I've always needed reassurance on everything. God knows I love a 'well done', be it for a school project, a DVD or a big shop where I go through everything I bought with my now husband so he can do complimentary noises and well dones. Indeed, even as I write this book I keep stopping to read bits aloud to him. Well dones are my fuel. And biscuits. Also, is it weird that I'm calling Gary my now husband? Like, *Now That's What I Call Husbands 2*. If you're a bairn, just picture a pig in sunglasses. That's very unfair. He's quite the dish.

So I slotted myself in: Is it me? This was the first one that wasn't quickly answered. Just quiet, awkward: the sound of my world falling apart. I'm fine now, spoiler alert. More than fine. Divorce was the making of me, but more on that later. Let's wallow for a bit. It's good for us. We cried together – it was very sad. I needed comfort and at that time it usually came from him. So it came from him again. It was odd, but he was crying too. I assumed for the same reason, but maybe he'd just stubbed a well-timed toe or perhaps they were tears of relief like when you finally do that big poo you've been brewing all day. Or maybe it was purely that the eight-year broccoli drought was nearly over.

So the counsellor said they couldn't help us and still took our £60, which given that we were splitting up and one of us needed to buy another of everything we shared – bed, washing machine, potato masher, hoover, *Pulp Fiction* – was taking the piss. They sent us packing. In an attempt to chat over what had been discussed at the counselling appointment, I booked us a table somewhere neutral: Frankie & Benny's. It turns out the two-minute walk from the appointment to the restaurant was all we needed. I said, 'Is that it, then?' And he said, 'Yes.'

We walked into Frankie & Benny's exhausted and technically single. Thankfully the balloon man wasn't in that day. On a bank holiday they sometimes employ a balloon man to squeakily twist air-filled bags of rubber into chubby animals for kids who don't look up from their iPhones. You've got to feel bad for balloon men. And that bloke who used to sell jumping beans on King Street in South Shields. Rolling the magical little things on the sort of tray I now eat my dinner off in front of the telly, those small capsules with either a ball bearing or maggot inside, depending on who you speak to. Best not to speak to my now husband (*Now . . . 2*) then. On this matter, he is still six and convinced they were maggots. I could never resist them. Or bouncy balls. Or toffee cakes. Simpler, more innocent times.

While an earthquake in Frankie & Benny's was bringing everything to the ground in my heart and head – think ANY disaster film but with no visible hero – my then husband's belly was empty and ready for scran. We ordered starters and main courses. Even now, ordering a starter seems like decadence but, hell, when chicken wings are on the menu who cares if emotionally you feel like you're falling down a well? Chicken wings are chicken wings. When our starters came, my stomach flipped and I stopped crying for long enough to vomit in the ladies' loos. I came back to see my then husband licking his fingers like he was in an advert. From the outside it must have looked like I was pregnant: me crying and throwing up; him thrilled with himself and eating for two. I pushed my starter towards him. His day was just getting better. I cancelled my main course in between sessions of puke. His arrived and he ate broccoli. And with a background noise of someone nailing a coffin shut, I said, 'You don't like broccoli.'

He said, 'I do. You just never got any in.' Like I had the magic fucking keys to Asda.

I got off the Metro early, went to my parents' house and asked them if I could move back in for a short while/two-and-a-half years. I don't hold any of this against broccoli. I like it now too. Maybe if I'd liked it then, that conversation would have gone very differently.

'Ooh can I have some of your broccoli?'

'Maybe I've been hasty. Nope, still don't love you.' •shoves all broccoli in his gob•

I also don't blame Frankie & Benny's. Their toilets were so clean. I got a good look at the black-and-white chequered floor tiles while I sat on them. I still sometimes get a bad tummy in there, but that's because I eat triple carbs (pizza, chips AND dough balls) and my IBS-stamped belly starts crying shit.

He wasn't the only one discovering new food. Little did I know the joy that lay ahead of me when I walked into work the next day. I'd been there less than half an hour when one of the girls had some spare buttery toast from the canteen. I grabbed it even though I'd never liked butter and had lived twenty-nine years without it. And thus began a new love affair. Butter and I have been together for thirteen years now and we're very happy. No more dry toast, sad potatoes or expensive lube for me. I didn't eat much during that first week, mostly just the odd banana, and I told the doctor that when I went to see her. She was a locum, and when I told her I wasn't eating much but drinking LOADS she was horrified.

'NO! Pop, tea, juice.'

I meant, 'Don't worry, you can survive three weeks on water alone.' She thought I was reassuring her about my alcoholism. 'Don't worry, Doctor, I am SHITFACED all of the time. It's going really well.'

I pride myself on the fact that I only missed half a day at work the whole time, but I know in my heart that I cried at my desk A LOT so I'm not sure how much actual work got done. At this point I was back working for the civil service. I'd left audiobooks because of the antisocial hours and this job, working in the call centre, was more money. I sat opposite an adorable bloke called Paul, and one day he asked how he could help me while I was snuffling behind my monitor. I told him I liked pictures of animals in clothes, so every time I was upset my email would ping and there would be a Yorkshire terrier in a ball gown. Instant wet-faced smile.

Paul was very sweet. We once got in the lift on the ground floor together and he decided to use the time between there and the sixth floor, where we worked, to strip to the waist to show me his new tattoo. While my face reddened, my eyes searched everywhere, taking everything in. You know like when a baby with terrible sight gets glasses put on her and her eyes widen like saucers and take in the world? Like that, but in a trouser suit and apologising. I was excited in case the lift doors opened on our floor while he was still undressed and it looked like we'd ramped up our relationship to different animals in clothes.

What would everyone think? They'd think I was some kind of vixen or cougar or other sexy animal, a bear. Yes, a sexy bear in Marksies workwear. The doors opened while he was still buttoning up his shirt but no one was there. Bugger. I nearly had a rumour about me that wasn't just about eating stuff out of bins.

I told my supervisor at work, a lovely girl going through the same shit, and she told me that there was a third one of us too. In an open-plan office it's tricky to cry in groups, so we commandeered the photocopy room, much to the annoyance of the bloke whose sole job it was to photocopy. In most offices, if the photocopy room door is shut it probably means someone has slapped his wang under the lid for japes. Glance through the glass panel in the door in our office and you'd see one or two women crying. Never three; women are emotional but also very practical. If we're all crying, who's rubbing the backs and telling Tony we don't give a shit if he has priority, he needs to fuck off?

I felt like I needed to fill all of my time. Any moment I wasn't busy, my brain raged with thoughts about an empty future and WHAT HAD I DONE WRONG? I remember going through old diaries looking for any sign of something I'd done that had stopped his love. Of course, I keep a diary not a bloody journal so 'cut and colour 11 a.m.', 'dentist 4 p.m.' and 'Karen's birthday bash, start at Trader Jack's' threw up no solutions whatsoever. I wish someone had snuck my diary away and written 'got married too young', 'grew apart', 'you can do better' or even 'he tells you to stop every time you sing even though your dad says he likes it because it means you're happy' in a variety of coloured glittery gel pens. Good stationery can cushion any blow.

Anne and Jane (names changed to protect those who cried in a photocopy room) and I started to meet for Sunday lunch each week. Long, protracted dinners with much chat and support. I thought we should have a name so I called us the Divorce Club. The other girls (possibly thinking of the potential of future cock) wanted something less obvious. We settled on the Lovely Ladies Club, shortened to LLC, then lengthened to the Elsies.

To kill time on Saturdays and because I needed more money if I was ever going to move out of my parents' house, I got a part-time job in Waterstones in Newcastle. After seven years as a Saturday kid at WHSmith, I was surely a shoo-in. They put me in charge of the maps. Clearly I looked like someone who'd lost her way. I'm not sure alphabetising Ordnance Survey maps helped me find it, but in my break time I'd stand in front of the self-help section. Just stand there, wide eyes scanning, looking for any sign of a way out. The disaster film needed a hero and I knew it was me. I had no idea what I was looking for or if it was even there. Are there books called 'Fuck, What Do I Do Now?' or 'Having Sex with a New Man: The Bits People Shave These Days'. After a few weeks one book jumped out. It was less namby-pamby than some – almost aggressive. It was called *It's Your Life. What Are You Going to Do with It?* (I got to page eighteen and started stand-up.) That's what I wanted. A slap across the face, someone beside me going, COME ON! DO SOMETHING! Like a personal trainer for your heart. Someone in intimidating gym gear timing your gaps between crying with a stopwatch. Someone jogging on the spot in Greggs while you take ages choosing a pastie because you can't make decisions about anything any more. Also, WHICH PASTIE WOULD MAKE HIM LOVE ME AGAIN? AND HOW COULD I NOTIFY HIM I WAS EATING IT?

Then husband and I had stayed in the flat for a further three months after Broccoli Day. We needed to sell the flat, and I suspected that if I moved out and he was in charge of readying and cleaning it for viewings, we'd never sell. Not a slant on him, more blokes in general. Blokes don't hoover unless they've spilt something, and it has to be a large amount of the thing or you can just spread it out and it'll vanish. My now husband won't mop up water spills as 'they'll evaporate'.

When we were selling the flat we booked a time for the estate-agent photographer to come round. I got up, got ready, made myself presentable and answered the door when he came. When I opened the door the bloke looked at my face and said, 'Oh, I've had a rough night an' all!' Cheeky little fucker.

Then husband was also my best friend. I've never done that since. Same as I won't get a car with a built-in sat nav – things should have one purpose. I've had a separate best friend ever since (more on her later). I had stopped any contact with him that wasn't about legal stuff; I didn't think it was healthy. So when something happened and I wanted to tell someone, *Now . . . 1* was understandably the person to tell. He had been for eight years. But I couldn't tell him; I needed to detach. Also, if it was a good thing, he didn't deserve that any more. So I made a rule. I was allowed to write the text and save it in drafts.

'I LIKE BROCCOLI NOW . . .'

'I HAD A CORNED-BEEF PASTIE TODAY . . .'
'WAS IT THE DENTIST APPOINTMENT . . .?'

If, in an hour, I still thought it was a good idea to send it, I was allowed to. I never once sent the text. Turns out an hour is the distance between heart and head, though it's much shorter when I'm wandering around Paperchase or Ryman picking up notebooks I NEED but really don't need. I think the head kicks in at a certain price and, man, stationery is a cheap addiction. I don't know anything about drugs but I'm sure I could get a lot of fancy-shaped Post-it notes for the price of a quarter of cocaine. It's measured like sweets, yes? And the lady pours it from big jars into a paper cone with a twist at the end. The man in our sweet shop taught me how to whistle. See, they're not all paedophiles.

I also changed his name in my phone to 'The Arse'. I cannot recommend this enough. Every time I got a text – 'Text from The Arse' – or he rang – 'The Arse is calling' – it temporarily made me giggle before I dealt with whatever shit was on offer.

I decided to divorce him. That was probably the most pro-active thing I did. I was sick of reacting to things – someone else's feelings, someone else's wishes, someone else's decisions. So I divorced him. When you divorce someone via the unreasonable-behaviour method you need to list things they've done and date-and-time stamp them. I sat with one of the Elsies one Friday night puzzling over what I could say. After half an hour, I was cherry-picking the best ones.

Sunday nights were empty and I needed them filling. My oldest friend Diane said I could join her and her fella at a pub quiz. They'd buy sweets and crisps from the shop nearby and sit with a Coke all night. It was cheap fun. She said sometimes her fella brought his friend from work, 'Tony with the big knob'. He may have been well-endowed but he was a bairn of about twenty. A nice lad but massive cock or normal-sized cock, I was too fragile for anything more than picture rounds and tiebreakers. Tony seemed to think that Diane and her fella were setting us up and would flirt, bless him. One Sunday, it was my turn to buy the snacks, and just as we were doing a word round I asked my pal if I should 'get them out', gesturing to the Asda bag full of Quavers and Creme Eggs. Tony giggled and said, 'YES PLEASE,' brilliantly making a joke about my tits. Just at that precise moment, Diane and I realised the answer to the clue – 'Unlikely – NAHIH' – and both beamed as we shouted, 'NOT A HOPE IN HELL.'

People deal with break-ups in a variety of different ways. Well, just three: cocks, fannies and booze. Often all together. I chose to stand on a stage in front of strangers and try to make them laugh. By Christmas I was doing well; I'd done a few gigs and living at home was bearable. I was worried about Christmas, though: that it would be exactly the same, minus one important person. So my friend Jane, of one of the Elsies, and I went to New York for actual Christmas. She was in the same boat as me and we just wanted to be somewhere entirely different. We booked a hotel on Times Square and drank Manhattans in Manhattan. We even went on an open-top bus on Christmas Eve in the snow like idiots/tourists.

On Christmas Day we had a huge, crazily decadent buffet-style lunch at the Plaza – the most expensive gastroenteritis I've ever had. No matter how fancy, no matter how posh the plates are, a buffet is a buffet and I got the shits all the next day. And for the rest of the week. It was all go at both ends. We got an emergency doctor out and he told me I had the blood pressure of a twenty-year-old. Because I was newly divorced and slightly delirious with a fever, I thought he was flirting with me. He gave me an injection in my bum. HELLO. Bet that wasn't necessary. I bet that was one of the ones he could've chosen an arm or arse for, and because my blood pressure was sexy he wanted a look at my arse. Definitely that and not just a professional man trying to make an incomprehensible British woman stop smelling of sick. He suggested I drink Gatorade to rehydrate me and I still can't drink it to this day. There were too many times it came back up, hot.

My friend Jane refused to leave me, so we watched episodes of *Everybody Loves Raymond* and she read all of the books while I used the toilet. Really used it. On our last day I was feeling a little better and felt so bad about spoiling the holiday that I said we could do whatever Jane wanted. She wanted to eat in Greenwich Village so I sat outside a café until she was finished. I saw Jake Gyllenhaal in the street, and if I hadn't been retching bright-orange Gatorade over a hedge and spitting on a hanky to clean my own face I would probably be married to him now. Especially if I'd told him how young my blood pressure was.

But I can honestly say it was a very different Christmas. So, as far as that goal went, big tick.

How do you know when your divorce ends? When you're not divorced any more? Or are you always divorced, like alcoholics? I don't mean they're always divorced – you know what I mean. When are you not divorced any more? And just single? I read somewhere during this period that hate is not the opposite of love; indifference is the opposite of them both. And this is correct. So I put it to you that you're not divorced any more when you're standing on a Metro platform and a Metro you can't get on slows down, stops, then moves away again and as it gathers speed you see a man you recognise but can't place. You know him from somewhere but can't think where. Did you used to work with him? Oh, no, you were married to him once.

Or when you try to picture him in your mind's eye and you can't quite get the whole face, just the eyebrows and the hair. Like trying to visualise a grandparent who's been dead for more than five years. Just teeth and hands. The rest is very swimmy. That's when you know you're not divorced any more.

Chapter 13

Thirteen Excellent Break-up Tips

REMEMBER, I'M NOT a counsellor, but I have been spectacularly dumped and in time was alright, then bloody champion.

1. Change his name to a swear word in your phone. I used 'The Arse' but 'Dead to Me' or 'Cuntchops' also work.
2. Consider counselling. It has helped me get through a fair few tricky patches.
3. Get a new 'I love you' person. I appointed a good friend to be the person I said 'I love you' to and got 'I love you' from. A small, short-term fix that isn't needed for long but helps.
4. Be kind to yourself. Whether that's treating yourself to a present every now and again or just allowing yourself to wallow when needs be. Also, biscuits. I lost weight, gained weight, lost weight, gained weight. None of it fucking matters.

5. Cry a lot. Crying is so good for you. It's a release – it makes you feel tons better. I'm not saying I enjoy the process but I often feel lighter and less stressed after a good bout. I cried so much at Jojo Moyes's book *Me Before You* I had a headache afterwards from the dehydration. But I read it in the bath so it was kinda helpful. Saved me topping it up.

6. Rediscover you. I went out and bought new music. There were bands 'we' didn't like that I discovered I actually did. I also played them loud in the kitchen when we'd broken up but were still living together.

7. Buy some new knickers. Perhaps don't do what I did and just bin all of your knickers on a whim and have to go commando 'til you have time for a trip to Marksies. I wanted a fresh start, and new knickers are always a good idea. Sometimes I change mine in the middle of the day because it's a very easy way to feel nice.

8. Accept the decision: the single best thing I did at the end of that relationship. Stop asking why. Why? Why? I emailed him a few months after we'd moved out of our flat, when the divorce was going through, and asked why. He'd never really given me an answer. This time, he did. I don't remember what it was (bless my brain for shitting out the tougher stuff) and while it wasn't nice to hear, I felt like I'd drawn a massive line under the whole thing and could crack on with the rest of my life.

9. Be proactive. I divorced him. I pushed us to sell the flat. I got a part-time job to add to my full-time job. Do stuff. Stop letting stuff happen to you.

10. Realise you can do anything now. You totally can. No matter how good that relationship was, you still had to run shit past your partner. Just out of decency. Not any more. YOU, YOU, YOU. This period is glorious.

11. Only text him or her after the hour delay. Give your brain an hour to catch up with your heart. Brain's in charge for a bit as heart is in pieces, scattered around your insides. Some of it is wedged between the outer wall and your bowels. Leave it be for a while.

12. Seek help and shoulders for crying on from anyone who'll offer. You'd be amazed who wants to help. Let them.

13. Get some cock(s)/fingers/tongues inside you. Fanny/cock/arsehole is still alive and well. Get it some non-emotional attention.

Chapter 14

Moving Back in with My Parents

I WALKED OUT of the only flat I'd ever owned (had a mortgage on) and turned right. We were getting a divorce. It was his decision but accepting it was one of my better ones. I turned right and he turned left. Not just metaphorically; my parents' home was to the right of our little flat and his whatever/whoever/who cares was apparently to the left. I walked through a park with a small box of the last of my things and cried all the way.

The decision to move back home was an easy one. I couldn't afford, and more importantly didn't want, to live on my own. I knew I needed a few months of cuddles, and who better to fall back on than the cushion of my family who had loved me for twenty-nine years, not just the paltry eight the ex-husband had managed. I asked them and, thank God, they said yes.

So I moved back into the bedroom I'd moved out of eight years earlier but, wow, had I acquired a lot more shit since then. I've always been a hoarder. Not documentary level but I did have several years of *Empire* magazines that I gave to him as I didn't have anywhere to put them. The deal still stands that if he sells them I want half the money.

I unpacked and slotted books back on shelves and knickers back in knicker drawers. My dad asked me if I wanted my Phillip Schofield posters back down from the loft and he meant it. I didn't. And no, it wasn't easy. It took a while for us all to adjust. At first, they wanted to know where I was going and when I'd be back. I was a teenager again, though one with the wrong name on her Boots Advantage card and a seemingly always-wet face.

I intended to stay for a few months, but in the end it was more like two-and-a-half years. There were times when I felt frustrated and trapped, like a kid again but not in a playing Guess Who? by myself, saving the world as a woman called Jackie, never really giving a shit about riding a bike, playing all of the songs from *The Sound of Music* on a recorder awesome sort of way; more in a 'help, help, I want to get out but what is out there for me anyway?' kind of way. But without my family I would not be doing stand-up now. Without them (and a counsellor)* I wouldn't be fixed enough to embark on another relationship and subsequent marriage.

But walking through the park that day, I was broken. A small box of tat and a slow, slow walk. My phone rang; I answered it. In a happier time, it seems I'd put myself on the returns list for Linda Smith's show at the local theatre. A ticket was available; did I want it? The slow legs thought no, definitely

---

* To read more on the benefits of counselling, see Chapter 18.

no: these big red eyes and tissue-filled hands aren't ready for being out in public and definitely not alone. But a tiny spark of my former positive self thought, Maybe yes? Maybe it's just what I need? A nice distraction.

And wow. I sat alone in a crowd of excited comedy fans. No one knew how my insides hurt. They probably thought my face was always that puffy – or didn't look or didn't care. And I laughed. Of course I did. It was Linda Smith, the first female comic I'd ever seen live. I walked out and my life was just as shit as when I went in, but I'd had a breather, a release, a bloody good laugh. And now, when I think about other jobs I've had and how much more worthy than stand-up comedy they were (getting people into work, helping people find the right benefit), I think of the lift I got from Linda Smith and hope I can do the same for others.

HOW TO BE CHAMPION

If you move back in with your parents, be grateful. You are fucking up their retirement when they were planning to have sex in the kitchen and only wear clothes on Tuesdays.

Expect to be treated like a child again. It's inevitable and sort of understandable. But you can play on that by crying to get more Arctic roll or getting your dad to clean the dog poo off your shoe. Also, pocket money.

Chapter 15

So Many Proper Jobs

SO, YES, I am incredibly proud of the jobs I've done. For my second stint at the Jobcentre, people rang us from home on what they call 'warm phones' in Jobcentres to make a claim for benefit. As well as being on the phones, I was a first-aider for the office. I went on the little course where you learn how to kick a Stanley knife away from the foot of a ladder and how to put a giant man in the recovery position. The latter is all about using his own size as leverage, something I've found useful since when sleeping alongside a snoring husband. I like helping people and I like controlling situations. Working out the table plan for my fortieth-birthday party was one of the best things I've ever done, and I've sat between David Tennant and Jeremy Piven in Jonathan Ross's green room and had a sex dream about the Rock.* So this role seemed perfect for me.

---

* In the sex dream, the Rock gave me some kittens. Yep, that was it. I'm sure things would have progressed had my forty-two-year-old bladder not woken me up.

on the course – recovery, Heimlich, mouth to mouth, kick away Stanley knives, turn giant men over, sandwiches. The adrenaline I get at a gig when someone announces 'Sarah Millican!' is huge but still only 2 per cent of what I felt when I was needed in an emergency. (Actually, just announcing my name doesn't necessarily mean I'm about to walk on stage – I could be at the doctors. I'm so used to applause following my name said aloud that every visit is a disappointment.) Doctors, nurses, police and firefighters must be built of sterner stuff than me. I don't think every time they're called to an emergency they mumble, 'Oh, shit,' and run up multiple flights of stairs farting all the way.

The civil service is full of women; that's one of the reasons why I miss them so much in comedy and why I create women-filled spaces like Standard Issue, for example, and a little new-material gig I run. Groups of women are wonderful. Yes, they can be catty as fuck, but they will also keep you busy while you wait for pregnancy-test results to come in, make you a cake on your birthday and hug you in the photocopy room when your heart is breaking. On one lunch break, I saw some jeans in the sale, but when I got to the till they charged me full price. I got back to the office a bit gutted, as I probably wouldn't have bought them at full price, just at the price written over it in red. The rallying women in the office suggested I go back to the shop after my shift and complain. They should have charged me the lower price. Buoyed up by how convinced they were that a happy ending was nigh, I went back, complained and won! See, that's what office women can do for you. Get your tenner back and give you a spring in your step.

Once, as part of some internal training we had to do an assertiveness test. My results were horrifically low. I was surprised and absolutely deflated. I wanted to be, and thought I was, assertive, but this course categorically said NOPE. Seeing how gutted I was, one of the girls tried to pump me up and said, 'You were assertive when we made you take your jeans back.' Read that again. You were assertive when **we made you take your jeans back.** *

Not everyone ringing the service knew which benefit they wanted to make a claim for, and it was part of our job to work it out before taking them through the system and sending the relevant forms out. Sometimes they had a rough idea. The main benefits we dealt with were Jobseekers Allowance, Incapacity Benefit, Income Support and sometimes Bereavement Allowance and Disability Living Allowance. My favourite requests were for Incomespasticty benefit, which is a portmanteau of Income Support and Incapacity. And Incaptivity benefit, which is mostly for pandas. One woman rang up asking to make a claim for Bereavement Allowance. She had been separated, but not divorced, from her husband for twenty years and had read in the paper that he'd died. I loved the chutzpah of the woman.

---

* One of my first telly performances was on Richard and Judy's teatime show. Richard recounted the story of my first gig and said I was rubbish. I shouted him down, forgetting I was on the telly, and the next day I went in to work to see my desk decorated with balloons and posters made by the girls that said 'I wasn't rubbish, Richard!' I bet if there'd been an assertiveness test right then I'd have refused to do it and told whoever set it to fuck off and stop wasting my fucking time.

We each had a desk protector, a durable black rubber mat, and under mine I'd keep a piece of paper listing the following: '8.30 8.40 8.50 9.00 9.10 9.20 9.30 9.40 . . .' It went all the way to 5.00 or 6.00 depending on what time I finished that day. I would tick each ten-minute slot off as the time passed. Sometimes, if a call was particularly involving, I'd get to tick two off. I always felt a bit untapped in these jobs, like I was destined for something less demotivating and more creative. I just didn't know what. Yet.

Looking back now, I was clearly depressed. Partly the divorce and partly feeling trapped in a job I didn't like while beavering away at my writing each evening. On the Metro in to work I used to listen to Chris Moyles on my little pocket radio. The laughs I got while listening to him were sometimes the best part of my day. I was lucky enough to be able to tell him that once. I don't listen to him now, though, as someone on his team does an impression of me and it all feels a bit shit.

I was moved to a desk just outside the manager's office. The rest of the place was open plan aside from Hilda's (formidable woman) office. The walls to the one private office were not soundproofed, so they needed to fill the two desks outside with people she could trust not to pass on anything they may have heard. That was me and a girl called Lizzy, who I'd spoken to a bit but not much. She very quickly became my best friend and has been ever since. She is golden. Only two people were ever needed to cover the phones between 5 and 6 p.m., and it was often Lizzy and me as we liked working hard and being paid overtime. On those days, at 4 p.m. we'd drink a can of Red Bull each and take a Pro Plus just to 'liven things up'.

Lizzy and I were both moved to CRU (Compensation Recovery Unit) in Washington, in different offices but the same building, so lunch breaks were a joy. I never really got my head around this job. I just sat beside a patient woman called Edith who attempted to train me.

When they were looking for jobs for us, Lizzy and I said we didn't care which department or office we ended up in as long as were in the same building, so CRU suited us fine. I think you can get through any job if you have someone you can roll your eyes at.

This was my last proper job. There was something excellent around the corner.

HOW TO BE CHAMPION

There is no substitute for hard work. I'm never keen when successful people say they're lucky. It's mostly just being good, focused and working your arse off. When I won my newcomer award at the Edinburgh Fringe, as I was working my way through the crowd to get outside so I had enough signal to ring Gary, the brilliant comic Jo Caulfield stopped me and said, 'Well done. You've done the driving.'

And if all else fails, remember this quote by Tim Notke: 'Hard work beats talent when talent doesn't work hard.'

Chapter 16

Pre-stand-up Stand-up

HAVING BEEN A very quiet child, head in a book, very few friends, it must be odd to those who knew me then that I now do stand-up comedy as a job. Until my first gig, I'd performed in front of a group of people only a handful of times.

- I was Mary in the nativity in reception but had no lines. Patriarchy gone mad. I had to sit down as well because Joseph was a short-arse. I was five and had to be encouraged by Miss Charlton to cuddle the baby Jesus. My arms were loose and the baby Jesus was slipping. I clearly hated kids even then. Or maybe it was the religious bullshit I could smell. She kept saying, 'Cuddle him. Cuddle the baby Jesus,' and I reportedly complained that he had pen on him. Snobby, child-hating atheist at the age of five.
- I was the narrator for the nativity when I was ten. I auditioned for the Angel Gabriel because 'she' got to go up a ladder. They said I had a good speaking voice so I was given the narrator role. I wore my sister's thick blue cowl-neck

dress, which was far too hot for the occasion. I must have looked forty. I was in the third year, and the show performed by third- and fourth-year juniors was an evening performance, while the first and second years had a matinee. I was pulled out of my lesson because the narrator for the matinee had stage fright. Luckily the nativity is generally the same across the board, no matter what your take on it. I banged it out. No fear.

- In the first year of senior school the drama teacher, a terrifying woman called Mrs McCue, decided we'd do *A Christmas Carol*. Because most of the boys had little interest or were a bit crap, my friend Kimberly got the lead role, finally redressing the balance of my silent, sitting turn as Jesus's mam. I wanted to be involved but didn't want a big role – I mostly liked being there and watching it all. I've never been great at learning lines (your own show that you've written is a totally different deal) so probably good that my role, Third Child, only had the one: 'Here's Martha, Mother!' Which I nailed each time in my little mob cap. The narrator of this one was a very well-spoken girl who had moved into the area. She did a great job, but it wasn't until the final dress rehearsal that the teacher noticed she pronounced 'melancholy' like an adverb. M'LAN'CHLY.

- I talked to someone I knew on the Metro once about how I was taking my granda's books back to the library. I distinctly remember the people all around us laughing along at what I was saying. Sort of my first gig.

- On a team-building day (shudders), while I was working for the Jobcentre, we were put into groups, did some exercises and had to report back our findings at the end of the day to everyone else. The rest of my group bottled it and pushed me to the front. I did it. It was a very dry subject but somehow I managed to make a whole room of civil servants laugh.

My love for Live Theatre, my favourite theatre, which is on the Quayside in Newcastle, is strong. I spent many a night there just after my divorce, keeping myself occupied and soaking it all up. I did a six-week play-writing course with Jeremy Herrin and Gez Casey that put much fire in my belly. I'd love to write a full-length play for Live Theatre some day but time hasn't allowed it so far. I used to get involved with their scratch nights. The idea behind them was that you'd send in five to ten pages of something you were writing and, should it be chosen, it would be read aloud by proper actors in front of an audience. It was a total thrill. I was always leaning towards the funny and because of that mine always got picked, and I'd sit there, in a cabaret-style table alongside people I didn't know and hold my breath. Hearing your words, which sound so flat on paper, brought to life by wonderful, wonderful actors is amazing. The actors would act, the audience would laugh and I would skip home. Jeremy Herrin, bloody lovely man, would gather votes in at the end for people's favourites, and I invariably won. Not because I was the best writer but because I had made folk laugh. And often my conversation between two pensioners was slotted in after a tense seven minutes of nuns in a war. Comedy wins.

Creative writing was my way out. It was my release from a heartbreak I was beaten down by. From jobs I hated. I used to regularly say to myself, 'I'm going to write myself out of this shithole,' and, eventually, over many, many years, I did.

But back then I was a bit lost. I think I was looking for something, but I didn't know what it was. I was working six days a week, killing every spare minute I could. Shutting it all down. Reading self-help books. And then one day, during my lunch break at work, I booked myself on a bloody performance workshop. I have no idea why. It was for people who had written but never performed. Before then I had written a film column for the free paper, a few short films, a few short plays and I hadn't performed at all save the previous examples. I had written but never performed, so I qualified. What if that ad had said 'For those who've eaten meat but never killed a cow?' Or 'For those who've done frontsies but never up the arse?' I could have been on an entirely different course. Though not that second one. WINK. Tried it once, wasn't as nice as having a shit, didn't bother again.

There was a gap between booking the course and doing the course so I forgot all about it. I just got on with work and all the crying. I had days when I felt like I could do nothing; I was just broken, my whole future (and indeed my hole future) gone. I had that 'what the fuck am I supposed to do now?' feeling that I'd only previously had when confronted with a massive running spider or when I once trod dog shit all over a friend's house and lied that it wasn't me. I'd go to work, but outside of the actual job I was barely functioning. I was convinced I would, at some point, run out of tears. I never did – the numbskulls controlling the tear ducts must have been knackered. I remember my sister once stroked my hair for three hours while I lay on her bed crying. But I had some of my best-ever sleeps during that time. Crying is like having a wank in that regard: some effort, small amount of cleaning, relief-induced kip. Smashing.

I also had days when I felt like I could do anything – I felt pretty much invincible. I'd never experienced this feeling before. I think most of us live our lives somewhere between the two: between can't do anything and can do everything. I called them my She-Ra days, inexplicably, as I'm more Wonder Woman era. I'd wake up full of energy, ready for the day. Awake. Properly awake. If someone had said, 'You have to climb this mountain,' I'd have asked for time to pop to Millets for the right socks and then given it a bloody good go. I signed up to this course on a She-Ra day.

The day came along and I was excited and nervous. It was a half-day workshop in Gateshead run by Kate Fox, the poet, stand-up and all-round brilliant woman, followed by a performance that evening at Caedmon Hall. Talk about being chucked in at the deep end. It was a very practical course: less about what you'd say, more about how you'd say it. We were encouraged to bring something we'd written so mine was a monologue about the breakdown of my marriage. Cheery, hey? You have to remember that this wasn't stand-up. It was just a monologue. Just me trying a thing I'd never tried. And in my new-found freedom the possibility of anything was sexy. I knew I had potential, but in what?

Most of the others on the course were poets who wanted to become performance poets. We walked around, weaving in and out of each other, saying words out loud. The sort of thing I hated but really needed to do. Kate had created a very safe space where no one would be anything other than supportive. Poets are, in my experience, a smashing bunch. Gentle, generous, interested. It was a great environment to be myself in. My new self.

And we did a show that night – God knows how. To a lovely, receptive crowd, I read my monologue aloud. The paper I held shook with the aftershock of my crazy heartbeat. That's why if you see me do new material now, I read it from a notebook or index cards. Books and cardboard do not shake like paper does. Luckily I stopped there and didn't end up with a plank of wood or a brick with my notes scrawled on.

I read the monologue and parts of it were brutal, and parts, it turns out, were hilarious. I went into the ladies' loos after my set and jumped up and down in a cubicle. I'd done a thing I was terrified of and it felt amazing. What was so terrifying about standing in front of a roomful of people and telling them about your personal horror? The scariest thing in the world had already happened. I was at rock bottom. It turns out people laughing at something you've said feels like nothing else. And not your friends, but people who don't know you, who have no obligation to laugh at you, who have paid to be entertained. I jumped in the loos. Then on the walk back to the Metro, I rang my dad and simply said, 'I did it.'

My family must have seen a turning point in me then. For me, it was a thing ticked off my list. Never to be done again. No need. Done it. Four months later I rang Kate – out of the blue, I suppose. I just rang her and told her I wanted to try stand-up, and she said, 'I know,' like she'd been waiting for the call. She got me a gig and offered to meet me there before it to give me some more tips. The gig was at the Cumberland Arms in Byker and run by John Cooper. I had five minutes on stage. I went straight from work and realised on the way that I'd forgotten the page of jokes I'd written. It was the bits from the monologue the crowd had laughed at and a few more I'd written since. I had no time to go home so I just decided to busk it, remember what I could and see what happened. Kate, as promised, met me at the pub before the audience came in. I stood on stage, mic in one hand and cable in the other, as I'd learnt on the course. With no idea what to wear, I'd brought a Marksies batwing long-sleeved black top and jeans.

The way comedy gigs usually work is that the new people go on in the middle, and this was no different: the opener, then the newest in the middle, and the most experienced/best at the end. John, the booker, was MC and Ben Schofield was opening with the late Mark Rough closing. When I went on the audience sat there, a lot of arms folded, and for the first two-and-a-half minutes remained much the same. I remember silence but maybe it was less harsh than that. Then I did a joke about my dad being the voice of doom and my life changed.* The room went from silence to a roar of laughter. A big woof of recognition, pity, acceptance and 'poor bugger' – but laughter all the same. And at that moment I realised that even though then husband didn't love me, fifty people upstairs in a pub in Byker did. Or at least liked me. A lot.

---

* To read the joke, see Chapter 17.

Turns out no one cared about the batwing top. That's one of the things I love about stand-up: no one cares what you're wearing. I can do a full tour and get a couple of people on social media asking where my dress is from and 219, 998 people who don't give a shit. As long as I was funny.

Ben Schofield came up to me after the gig and said, 'Are you willing to travel?' I said yes and he gave me the number of a Manchester promoter to contact for a gig. I smiled and, as he walked away, I deleted the number. I wasn't going to travel for this. Was he mad?*

I left my leather gloves at that gig, and when I mentioned that to comic, sometime *Night Owls* host (Metro Radio's late-night phone-in show) and all-round good egg Steffen Peddie, he offered to drive by the pub to see if they were still there and then give them to me the next time we gigged together. What an adorable man. That was after meeting him once. I thought he was trying to get in my pants. Turns out he was just a nice bloke.

My second gig is significant as it was where I met the love of my life (if you don't count the dog, which I shouldn't but sometimes do). It was at the Cornerhouse in Newcastle and run by Warren Speed. The opening act was supposed to be Nik Coppin, but he'd been replaced by a bloke called Gary-something.

---

* Can I just remind you that I have since done shows in Australia and New Zealand?

HOW TO BE CHAMPION

If there's something you really want to do, work out how to do it and get cracking. Sometimes vocalising what it is you want to do makes it all seem so much more feasible. My friend Annie and I used to make an annual list of what we wanted to achieve that year. And the rule was that it had to be achievable goals. So we couldn't say 'I want a sitcom on the BBC' but we could say 'I want to write a sample sitcom script and get it on the desk of someone at the BBC'. She also added in domestic stuff like 'new carpet for the living room'. Whatever it is you want, write it down, and doing it with a friend is a great idea. Then, at the end of the year, look at the list and see what you managed. You'll be surprised – we had usually ticked off at least half. Pinpoint what it is you want, work out how to get from where you are to where it is, and just get started. There's no magic involved. Be focused and work hard.

Chapter 17

My First Proper
Ten-minute Set

AFTER DELIBERATING FOR six months I concluded
that I wanted to give comedy a proper go. Had I been living
on my own with two jobs and no flexibility or money, that
door would have slammed shut. But my outgoings were low,
so I dropped a few hours at my civil-service job and started
to get a lot of trains and sleep on a lot of sofas. And my
family supported this. Not once did they question why I was
telling strangers about the breakdown of my marriage for no
money (to begin with) in a batwing top from Marksies (I wish
someone had questioned that bit). They just let me be me,
finding the new me, whoever she was when she crawled out,
heart slowly mending, tear ducts fucking knackered. They'd
let me be me when I tap-danced on the tiles around the coke
boiler, when I read a poem from behind a curtain, when I
showed them my new dance in the garage: why would this
be any different?

By this point, I'd written a stand-up set that I thought was strong enough to enter in the new-act competitions. A comic whose opinion I valued said I wouldn't do well in competitions as I was too conversational; I didn't agree. I entered Funny Women initially, and came second. But I wanted to see if I was good against any comic, not just other women, so I entered So You Think You're Funny? And came second. HAHA. I also entered the BBC new-act competition (came second) and the Amused Moose, which I won. I dropped my Moose trophy on the way home from the final and it came apart from its marble base. My dad said, 'We're going to fix that and then build a cabinet.' I never got it fixed.

This is the set I used in those competitions.

I've just got divorced.

When we split up, someone said it was like a bereavement. It's one of those stock phrases that roll out of people who've never thought of peeing on their husband's toothbrush and not telling him. 'Plenty more fish in the sea', 'Time's a healer' and, my own personal favourite, 'I never liked him'. That was my mam. I still get the 'How are you?' head tilt. 'How are you?' I just want to get this straight. It isn't like a bereavement. If he'd died, I'd have got my mortgage paid. And I could've danced on his fucking grave.

When we sold the flat we left carpets and blinds, but there was one pair of curtains that he wanted to take. They're green fleur-de-lis and not to my taste. He's had them for ten years. I worked it out. Through three flats and a house, two girlfriends and a wife, these curtains have prevailed. I suggested to him that maybe it wasn't such a good sign that he could commit longer to a pair of curtains than he could to any one woman. And his response was, 'But they're lined.'

So I moved back in with my family. You need to know a little about my family so you know what I'm dealing with here. My dad has a heart of gold but is the voice of doom. When we were trying to sell the flat and no one had been to see it for a bit, my dad said, 'What if no one buys your flat?' Which, to be fair, had been whirling around in my head too. But what answer did he expect? Oh, we'll probably just stay married. That'll sort it. Then when he still hadn't found a flat, days before completion, my dad said, 'What if he never finds a flat?' Again, Dad, thanks for your support. But the best one by far, when he surpassed himself, was when I was sitting on the floor sobbing uncontrollably, with snot coming out of every hole in my face, and he said, 'You're bound to be upset. You've lost everything.' Then he left a little pause and said, 'You've got nothing left.' As if I hadn't understood him the first time.

Not long after I moved back in, we went out for a fancy meal to celebrate the fiftieth anniversary of my mam contracting polio. Thank God for blank cards cos you cannot get balloons with that on.

Since moving back home, I've reverted to acting like a teenager. I grunt instead of giving a full coherent answer, I sent 1,652 text messages last month (my personal best) and I had a stand-up argument with my dad about how I couldn't catch flu if I wasn't wearing a coat because flu is a virus. That ended with my mam shouting, 'Under my roof, you'll wear a coat,' which wasn't really the issue. I also caught myself finishing an argument with my older sister with the words, 'Mam, tell her . . .'

I've decided to only wear sexy underwear from now, even for Asda, so I've been doing out my knicker drawer. Anything that looks like I bought it in grey or lemon but I know was actually white when I got it has gone the journey. I've been buying knickers with writing on. 'Treat me like a princess', 'Lucky pants', and my most provocative to date say 'Kiss me' and it obviously means 'down there' but is too polite to say cos they're from Dorothy Perkins.

I like the idea of knickers with instructions on and I'm currently trying to track down a pair that say 'Mean what you say' and another that say 'Clean your own fucking sick up'. And apparently a pair have been spotted locally that say 'I'd do anything for love' and on the back 'But I won't do that'.

I bought some that say 'He loves me, he loves me not'. My friend said that she needs some that say 'I love him, no, I don't, well, he's nice'. Mine would say 'Why hasn't he texted? Should I text him? Again? What'll I say? Do you think he's just busy? All day?' My knickers would have to be huge. I was doing some research on the Ann Summers website and on there are a pair of knickers that bypass all pleasantries, body-language reading and signal-sending to suss out if someone's up for it. Unzip your trousers, hitch up your skirt and flash your drawers that read 'It ain't gonna lick itself'. Fantastically classy. So they're on order . . .

I thought, what with dating again, I'd better get back on the books at the family planning clinic. I didn't want to tell my dad I was going to family planning so I said I was off to 'sit with scallies and be frowned upon for having sex out of wedlock'. They've changed the name to 'sexual health and contraception clinic'. Presumably that's because most people who go aren't actually planning a family. They're just trying to avoid having an abortion and the clap.

I said to my dad before I went that this'll be the first time I've been to family planning without a boyfriend or husband in tow. My dad said, 'That's because you're free-lance now.' Presumably that's code for slut. I'm a freelance shagger and my dad approves. How cool is my life?

When she was doling out my two months' supply of condoms (I'm single so she gave me twenty-four; married people just get three and one of them's a spare in case you're thinking of having an affair) she asked if I wanted any flavoured ones. Well, the only thing I'd want a condom to taste of is cock, but apparently no one's cottoned on to what a brilliant idea that is and I wasn't keen on their two most popular lines, Lambrini and Greggs pasties.

Chapter 18

Counselling

I'M A BIG believer in counselling. I think it works for me, as a chatter. Unbelievably, I wasn't put off by that first horror appointment, and during the first week of being made surplus to requirements in my own marriage, I made an appointment for the doctors. Mine wasn't available so I saw a locum who wrote down that I was depressed and suggested anti-depressants a little too easily. I suppose locums are the supply teachers of the medical world. Something to keep you quiet and then disappear into the night (doctor's surgery car park). I asked if I could have counselling and she put me forward for it.

The truth was, this appointment was three weeks after that godawful day and I was doing okay. Not brilliant, but a lot better than I was. That was due to a few things. Firstly, I rang the Samaritans. I expected it to be like when you ring the bank with a bit of music and some options. Nope, they answer super-quietly and they just let you talk. I remembered a friend who'd worked for the Samaritans for a while who said that often they had men ring in and •does wet fleshy noise with mouth and cheek• which I took to mean wanking, though she never clarified. So surely my sad crying about the end of my marriage has got to be easier to listen to than that. I'm sure people ring sex lines to sad cry about their marriages. Maybe they're sometimes interchangeable.

The lady didn't say much but let me talk, which, that day, was what I needed. It was the day after that I realised I wanted someone to talk back. While waiting for my appointment, I decided to fall back on my friends. A lot of people had said 'I'm here if you need me'. Some I wouldn't have expected it from. And then some I definitely thought would help disappeared. Not physically, maybe, but they certainly tiptoed out the back door of my crying room never to be of any help ever again. It's very interesting, and the old adage of finding out who your real friends are certainly rings true. Some are genuinely helping you clean all the shit off your fan, getting wet wipes out of their bags and checking the fan is switched off at the wall, while some peel away doing little retches in their hands. And your friends stay in your new formation – they don't revert back to pre-shitstorm. I think when they slink away while you're eating trifle with your hands, they know not to bother coming back. If you're not there when I'm eating trifle with my hands, don't come back when I'm eating it with a spoon.

I made a list* of the friends who stepped forward and there were fourteen. Fourteen people who didn't mind me ringing them for a cry. I found crying every morning really cathartic.

---

* I love a list (as you may be able to tell from this book).

It made the day – having a shower, getting the Metro, being at work – much more feasible. So for the three weeks before my counselling appointment, I rang a friend every day before work. I put them on a rota so as not to bother them all too much. God bless friends. Crying and moaning is so good for you. I'd come off the phone feeling empty but awake with a little more fight than I had twenty minutes before. Sometimes when I cry I feel great afterwards. Like I imagine people feel after a run. And you don't need special shoes to cry – though sometimes wellies might come in handy.

Another thing that helped was going to the pet shop. There was one in Gateshead town centre and I'd go on my lunch break and put my hand up at the glass while sobbing. It must have looked like I was visiting a hamster in prison.

When the appointment came round I was nervous but also hopeful that this was something that would help. I wanted to talk it out, learn how to cope better, learn that I was valuable, and ready myself so that, if someone nice came along, I would be less broken and weepy. The lady gave me a questionnaire to fill in and the answers ranged from 'I strongly agree' to 'I strongly disagree'. The questions included things like 'I have planned my own funeral'. I filled it in and handed it back.

She skimmed it and looked up. 'It's a very low score,' she said, in an arsey way. A low score meant that you were doing okay. I was furious. She was dismissing how I felt because I wasn't suicidal. Also, by the time this fucking appointment came along, fourteen friends, my family, the Samaritans and a whole bunch of assorted rodents had done a lot of work on me. I responded with, 'You seem disappointed. Do I not win the car?' We should have just stopped the appointment there, but we carried on for another fifty minutes, with her desperately trying to get me to cry, and me resisting for as long as I could. It was like a precursor to my appearance on *Who Do You Think You Are?*. I left that appointment thinking, Counselling is shit, counsellors are shit; this is not for me.

I cancelled the second appointment.

Then I reasoned it out. Haven't I had bad doctors? (Told one I'd had a period for five months and he told me to come back when it was six). Dentists? (One I had made some shocking decisions leading to numerous lengthy root-canal appointments with a specialist.) Hairdressers? (The bleached fringe that fell off in the sink, the nana perm.) Opticians? (He wore glasses.) Maybe this woman was just a bad counsellor and good ones also existed. Like the gynaecologist who put a coil in, the dentist who cured me of my dentist phobia, the hairdresser who makes me feel wonderful every time she's done snipping and colouring. Oh, and the optician who told me I didn't have to wear them for disco dancing.

As it turned out, working for the civil service had its advantages. There was a counselling service free of charge. I got in touch and my amazing manager offered to have her lunch at the same time each Wednesday so I could use her office for my counselling appointment. I didn't mind the rest of the office knowing I was having counselling. I've always been pretty open about it to pals. The way I see it, I get my car checked regularly, why wouldn't I do the same for my brain?

I considered the first counsellor a 'no ball'. Doesn't count. Start again. Which I did, and she was great. I think I must have

139

been an anomaly for her. At a time when most people get pissed and shag around to make themselves feel better, I was standing on a stage in a Marksies batwing top talking to strangers. And she helped with that too. She would often suggest that things I said might be material. Remember the gag in my ten-minute set earlier about lined curtains? She suggested I try that as a joke. And was right. She was very supportive of this newfound creative outlet and confidence builder, and even asked me to perform at her wedding reception. I suggested she come to a gig first so she could watch me talk about how great divorce is. She came, she retracted her offer, I laughed.

Things that I've had counselling for:

1. Getting over a marriage
2. Living with my parents again
3. Starting a new relationship
4. Burn-out
5. Reactive depression
6. Anxiety
7. Dealing with being recognisable and the oddness that goes with it
8. Family illness
9. Stress
10. Family relationships
11. Touring and being away from home a lot
12. General upkeep of mental health

It has always helped. Sometimes I just need someone to gabble at. Sometimes I need pointers on how to improve. Don't give me a fish; teach me how to understand my brain, please. If you're considering it, go for it. Obviously it depends on the individual, but I've found that it works for me. I have a theory that all of us are fucked up, but those of us who've had counselling are less so.

HOW TO BE CHAMPION

I am not a counsellor. But if you think it might help you, give it a go. For others, medication is the key. Try things until something works. There is help out there. And love to you.

Chapter 19

Things My Dad Taught Me

YES, YES, HE taught me loads of standard things, as did my mam. They're the reason I can brush my teeth, wipe my arse and tell the time. The following, while not as everyday, are still locked in and ready for use.

1. How to kill a dog. I don't mean any dog. My little rescue dog Tuvok hasn't gone from the frying pan into the fire. Sure, Dogs Trust, I've got a fence and, yes, we'll get his knackers taken off as part of the conditions of his adoption, but you don't mind if I practise my dog killing on him as well, do you? No, this was a self-defence thing. During my childhood, the front page of the *Evening Chronicle* always seemed to feature a big scary dog that had savaged a bairn. So my dad, being the pit ninja that he was, thought it prudent to teach me how to deal with such a situation. In case you want to know, it involved putting an umbrella through its collar (thank God for the two-finger rule, right, guys?) and twisting it 'til the head popped. I think he

actually said 'til it died, but I was a kid so I've chosen to remember the word 'pop'. Of course, as someone pointed out, what if it didn't have a collar on? Well, then I'd need to put a collar on it really quickly. Probably carry a selection of sizes with me at all times. What if, the same pessimistic person asked, you didn't have an umbrella. Imagine me as a bespectacled nine-year-old; of course I had a bloody umbrella. And spare pants in case I fell in a river.

2. How to stay safe in London. My sister and I went to London together when I was sixteen and she was twenty-one. There was an emergency alert at the Tube station and we rang our parents (from a payphone) to let them know we were okay, as we were sure it would have been splashed all over the news. Nope. If anything we made them more worried. I was very excited when we got off the train at Kings Cross to see a bookshop as we walked out of the station doors. A nice little independent bookshop. My sister did what she always did when I asked to go in a bookshop: rolled her eyes, reluctantly agreed and logged that I owed her one and would probably have to traipse around a big Marksies later on. We walked through the door, parting the vinyl strips hanging down, thinking, London is weird, isn't it? Loads of men in here. Hmm, London men are so cultured. And then I saw that all the books had tits on the cover. Instead of just running out of the shop, we sort of styled it out. Both with big red faces, we continued to look around before I announced,

'Nothing I fancy,' and we left. Lesson learnt. London is weird and pervy, and vinyl strips are a sign. My dad was a bit worried we'd be trapped underground as it hadn't been long since the horrific Kings Cross fire, so he taught us how to get out of a tunnel. He showed us which lines were live, how to follow a draught and that water always finds a way out. So at least we'd know where not to wee and how it would ultimately be helpful.

3. How to get out if there was a fire at home. Smash the double-glazing windows – I think the fact that they were weak at the corners came into play – tie the rope that can be found in the bottom of Mam and Dad's wardrobe (don't ask – please don't ask; I didn't and I'm so glad I didn't) around one of the middle parts of the bay window and slowly lower yourself out. I'm sure in extreme situations I'd be able to do this, but I remember my attempts at rock climbing at school. If I didn't actually wet my pants, it certainly came out the lips and loitered there 'til Stuart Cowie lowered me back down. I think I only got six feet off the ground. I faked a laughing fit so I didn't actually cry. Good tip, that.

4. How to do triple anal. I can't remember the circumstances during which I asked my dad about triple anal. I imagine it was something I'd heard about when talking to comedians. I was also stepping back into the dating world and nervously asking around for what people did now. I couldn't get my head around triple anal, and seeing as my dad is a dad,

and dads know everything, I thought I'd ask. How would you get three cocks up your arse? As he was an engineer he worked it out. He said it depends on the circumference of the aperture and the size of the cocks. He worked out, using a pen and paper, that the best way would be to tie the cocks together. At which point I reminded him that the cocks would, ideally, be attached to men. We deduced that maybe it was all in a row like a painful conga.

HOW TO BE CHAMPION

Listen to your dad. Unless he's a dick. Some of them are – mams too. But if you're lucky enough to have one or more good parents, listen to them. Who else would I have asked about anal sex, eh?

Chapter 20

Not Drinking

I DON'T DRINK. Well, I drink pop and juice and copious amounts of tea. But not booze. I haven't always been a spoilsport, party pooper and designated driver. I used to drink. College was my prime going-out time. Saturday nights, funded by Saturday days working in WHSmith, out on the town with my own money, hard-earned by nailing a till or tidying magazines violently so that those just reading them would bugger off. Guessing who needed a bag, working out which book the old lady wanted when she asked for the one with the blue cover for her niece. I loved spending money I'd earned, even if it was on whisky and McChicken sandwiches. Yep, whisky. They'd ask which one I wanted like I was some kind of expert. I could hardly say the one that will make my arms warm and give me the confidence to talk to people. That one. So I'd say Bell's or Teacher's like I gave a shit. Anything but Jack Daniel's, which tastes like perfume. It's the Earl Grey of the pub.

I dabbled in Mirage and lemonade when it came out. We'd go to the Venue, South Shields' ultimate wine-bar attraction.

The main rumour about the Venue was that if you didn't use your own straw with your drink you'd get clap from the glass. If we could only get to the bottle bar, I'd have a Hooch, but mostly it was whisky. In the Bizz Bar, another of South Shields' ultimate wine-bar attractions, there was a button you could press to be in with a chance of getting a cheaper drink. I often won a treble whisky for the price of a single. Maybe I thought it was cool to drink the drink of an old homeless man. Who knows? I know that I often went out with a tenner, got a bit giggly drunk and then had to choose between a taxi home or a McChicken sandwich. The McDonald's in South Shields hadn't long been open and it was still a novelty. Whenever we were in, we'd wait for someone, anyone, to walk upstairs with their tray of food only to come straight back down a few minutes later. It was only the toilets upstairs, with no sign saying so, and that was the best laugh we had. You know, while other people were having sex, that's what we did. Laughed at people taking burgers to the loo.

I once had my drink spiked by a friend's husband, I think. He was a bit like that. I'd had hardly anything to drink, yet the next day I vomited every fifteen minutes for five hours. He'd bought me a cider, which I never usually drank so wouldn't have been able to tell if it tasted weird. My mam got the emergency doctor out, who gave me an injection in my bum. I mentioned it to my friend the next time I saw her. She said he once spiked her drink with speed and that she didn't mind so much as she got loads of hoovering done.

I used to sometimes drink fizzy wine while sitting on my friend's living-room floor because 'you can't fall off the floor'.

The occasion that made me realise alcohol perhaps wasn't for me was when I was invited to a do at the Dorchester in big fancy London. It was the year 2000 and I was working in the audiobook industry, and we had been nominated for an award. I hired a dress, and as we were waiting in the gold foyer who walks in but Liam Neeson with two pensioners and loads of shopping bags. Now, they were probably just his mam and nana, but I like to think they'd won a competition. Upon successful completion of an Uma Thurman word search, Betty and Ena from Gateshead had won tea at the Dorchester and a shopping trip with Liam Neeson. At the party, I drank far too much free champagne and showed my roots by getting so excited by the pudding that I took a photo of it. I ended up being sick on the squirrels in Hyde Park. Well, not actually on them, because they're really bloody fast. One door to drinking closes, another opens on pudding photography. I have quite the collection. I like showing them to people. I mean, I don't have kids but I imagine it's very similar. 'I'm so proud of them', 'It's amazing to think I used to have them inside of me' and 'Look at his little ICING'.

It wasn't just that occasion. I was starting to get bad hangovers on not-much booze. A glass of wine gave me a headache or even sickness the next day. And you know how you feel awful but then pick up and, by the next weekend, you've forgotten and you drink again? I just stopped. The after-effects weren't worth the fun times. I lost half days, sometimes full ones. I've also had to clean up pissed people's sick and that's no fun. Going out with someone who comes in at 5 a.m. and voms through three rooms and just leaves it is enough to put you off for life: scrubbing rented flat's carpets, trying to work out if that's a tomato skin and realising yes, it is, when it rolls up as you scrub.

I started drinking booze again when I got divorced. Actually, no, when I started dating again. The thought of talking to, flirting at, knockering with, fannying under someone new was so horrific anyway, but the thought of doing all that on Fanta was worse. So I had a few drinks and a small fling. I stopped drinking as my hangovers were as bad as before. I also went on the pill and came off just as quickly due to all the songbirds in my fanny.* I've never been great on the pill. I told my doctor that I didn't think the fling was worth it. To which he replied, 'None of us are worth it,' and I think he is right.

HOW TO BE CHAMPION

If you don't want to drink, don't. When people asked why I wasn't drinking, I used to say, 'I'm on big tablets.' Now, if they try to push me into having a drink, I just say, 'I don't respond to peer pressure.' If I did, I'd have had sex a lot earlier than I did.

---

* Come on, guys; thrush, not nightingale.

Chapter 21

Things I'm Good at Doing on My Own

I can play on my own

I always excelled at things you do on your own. Which was good because I was once prescribed Fiddlesticks* by a doctor because my eyes were sore due to blinking too much. That's right, a doctor. Well, that's what it said on his van.

I also loved playing with my View-Master, a small, red slide-show contraption through which I could watch a much-abridged version of Disney's *The Fox and the Hound* in about forty-two images, only changing the reel twice. Literally seconds of fun.

---

* Fiddlesticks was a bunch of multicoloured plastic sticks that you held upright then dropped. The aim of the game was to remove one stick at a time by flicking it with another, without moving any of the other sticks in the pile. And to think kids have laptops and mobiles now. If you gave a kid some fiddlesticks these days, they'd use them to stab a pensioner.

And I could play quietly. My dad worked shifts and was often asleep in the room next door. Developing the ability to be quiet meant I was a model neighbour when I lived in flats, and it made wanking at my parents' house a cinch.

I can play with myself on my own

And I was good at that too. Eventually. I didn't go pro 'til after my divorce, when I went to Amsterdam with my best friend Lizzy. When I first got divorced she bought me a toy mouse from *Bagpuss*, which, when you squeezed its hand, sang, 'We will find it, we will bind it, we will stick it with glue, glue, glue.' First step, fixing mouse; second, vibrator. We stood in a sex shop in Amsterdam and she fanned her arm out at the wall of cocks and said, 'What do you fancy?' like I was in the crisps aisle in Asda. Before then, if you'd asked me (and I don't know why you would have), I'd have said, 'No, I don't masturbate.' But if you'd asked me how I cleaned myself in the bath, I'd have said, 'Thoroughly.' I didn't know where to look in the sex shop so I just stared at the floor, which was a glass cabinet full of fanny and cock utensils. I was trying to act like it wasn't my first sex shop, but my cover was blown when I clocked one item and shouted, 'That's what they do smear tests with.' Who sees one of those and thinks, I want one of those for home?

I can travel on my own

When I started doing stand-up and was still working for the civil service, I used to come in to work each day with a little pully suitcase and leave that night on the train to do a gig somewhere, sleep on a sofa, and then get a train back to work the next day. One day, an older colleague came up to me. You know the sort; she's probably only sixty but she's had the same desk for two-hundred years and no one remembers her looking any younger. She asked me where I was going that night, and when I said 'Sheffield' she said, 'On your own?' It's a major part of the life of a comic, but only then did I realise how out of the ordinary it is to some.

As I couldn't drive, I used to get the train everywhere for gigs. This was before Google Maps, so I'd sometimes carry seven or eight *A–Z*s in my case for a long stint away. At home I had a shelf of forty *A–Z*s. I know, it's hard to believe – like saying cocaine used to be worse for you than sugar. Or if you couldn't think of the name of that actor in that programme, you just had to wonder about it until the library opened.

A lot of my memories of when I first went to the Melbourne Comedy Festival are of me doing something on my tod/bob/lonesome. Thanks to selfies, I can still have permanent reminders of those things. I have never and will never hand my camera or phone to a stranger to take a photo of me. I know they would run away with said phone/camera, or continue through the aquarium at a faster pace than me, probably taking better pictures. I once had my phone stolen in Paris when I was ignoring a beggar. He came towards us in a restaurant, knowing we'd ignore him, and, while we were averting our gaze, he lifted my phone. But fuck him; I was insured and had a more restful holiday because of it.

I've stayed on so many sofas over the years while touring I got very good at figuring out people's showers. It's similar to what it must be like to be promiscuous. I have been in more men's showers than I have their beds. I'm getting better at figuring out how the knobs work.

Very quickly, I had to get good at being on my own, both at home and at new work. I think it's important to find out who you are again at the end of a long relationship. And that blossoming certainly helped my stand-up. While I was telling the audience who I was, I was learning about myself as well. I see it as a regeneration of sorts, like *Doctor Who*.*

HOW TO BE CHAMPION

Most board games can be played on your own with the benefit that you always win. You're both a winner and a loser at the same time.

Masturbation is excellent. Sometimes it's fun, sometimes it's medicinal (if I'm tired but not sleepy), and sometimes it's just because someone wore a mesh vest on *Strictly*.

---

* This line originally said, 'like *Doctor Who*, but where women are allowed a go.' But between the writing and the publishing of this book, it was announced that a woman *is* being allowed a go. Hooray! Go and fucking kick Dalek arse, Jodie Whittaker.

Chapter 22

Friendships

I'VE HAD MANY best friends in life. As a nine-year-old, I wrote about one of them in the Junior Hamster Club newsletter (my first published work). She was called Honey and sat in my hand. Another was just a piece of wool with a pretend dog at the end.

When you get older, it's harder to make friends in general and damn near impossible to find a new best one. They've all been stuck together since tap class or primary school, or are best friends with their mam, which is weird.

I made the grave error of having a husband and best friend who was one and the same. HUGE mistake. When one leaves, they both do. It's tricky to say, 'Hey, I know you don't love me anymore, but who will I moan to about work, dance at when I'm happy and set the world to rights with over a pot of tea and a box of fondant fancies? Oh, you don't care. Okay, thanks, bye!' NEVER AGAIN.

So, post-divorce I was on the lookout for some cock and a new best friend. Definitely separate things. I wasn't actively looking for the new best friend (WINK), but in some small way every conversation I had with a woman was a sort of audition.

After making me laugh in a job that was slowly draining the life out of me, I have been best friends with Lizzy – bezzie mates, if you will – for twelve years, during which time we've both been through a fair amount. For me, the brokenness of a surprise divorce and the oddness of fame; for her, learning to walk again after an accident that left her paralysed.

Not long after her accident, we were chatting and she asked how I was. I had a migraine but I said to her, 'I'm never going to complain to you about such nothingy things.'

And she said, 'You have to be able to moan to me, otherwise how will we be friends?'

So while this amazing, strong woman taught herself to walk, I continued to blether on about heavy periods and hard gigs, and hopefully made her laugh too.

She is the straightest, most honest person I know. She is the only person I'll call while in the bath. She is the person who told me I'd 'get used to' the smell of dog shit. She is excellent for advice and for crying to and laughing with. Nowadays, our walks are slower as we have to pick up dog shit (I only retch at the poorly ones).

Besides Lizzy and a core few, friendship is an interesting concept and one I'm struggling with a little at the mo. Who are your friends? Are you as important to them as they are to you? Maybe they're further up your list than you are up their list. Is a friend someone who you meet up with a lot because you always pay? Is a friend someone who comes round to your house but never invites you to theirs? Is a friend someone who has eaten your home-cooked food but you've never eaten theirs? Is a friend someone who comes to your wedding but doesn't invite you to their birthday party? Are they nice to you in case you can do something for them?

I think a friend is someone who asks how you are and means it. Someone who checks in with you to make sure you're alright. Who texts you when you sound unhappy on Facebook. Who clambers on your knee when you're upset (that might just be the dog).

I meet up with four glorious women in London when I'm down there. We have a long chatty lunch and all go our separate ways. The last time we met up, there was a Tube strike and torrential rain and the trains were all buggered. Three battled the bloody Tube strike and found alternative ways to get in. One was coming from Reading and her journey took twice as long as it should have. One couldn't get a bus, as they were too rammed and not stopping, so walked for fifty minutes in the rain, which soaked through her trousers and meant she had to buy some leggings en route. She also had the lurgy. And I drove for five hours. We kept each other up to date on arrival times and then one sent this message 'We must love each other very much to fight our way to each other like this.' It made me do a little cry. Truth is, it hadn't occurred to any of us to turn around and go home.

I'm not sure if it's age or the way things are at the moment, but a lot of my friends have stuff going on: ill parents, no work, too much work, knackered from kids, knackered from work, relationship stuff. Maybe it's always been like this and we didn't share as much before, but now there's always a lot to chat through and listen to and maybe offer help with. I am a giver and a taker of this.

Twice I've befriended a woman via the dislike of a third woman. The first was in a car on the way back from a gig in Crawley. I hadn't realised that getting a lift back to London means you get dropped off in Trafalgar Square. In Manchester someone will drop you at your door, not at a major tourist attraction with no idea how to get back to where you're staying. The comic who was driving dropped me and another comic, Juliet Meyers, off at Trafalgar Square, but dropped the head-liner off at their door. I was a bit lost. I didn't know how to get back to my sofa for the night at 1 a.m. Juliet showed me the night-bus stands and helped me work out which one I needed, all while we were comically bitching about the other two. We've been great friends ever since.

The second time it happened I was in Melbourne, about to do a stand-up set on live radio in front of an audience. It was very noisy and I wanted somewhere quiet to pace a little and focus before my spot. Felicity Ward, another comic, had thought exactly the same. The third woman in the quiet room, let's call her The American, did not seek silence. She was loud and asked which part of Ireland I was from. I glanced at Felicity and rolled my eyes. It was a risk. She could have been super-pals with The American. She was not: she rolled her eyes back. The American left the room, and Felicity and I started chatting and haven't really stopped. She gives the best answer to the question 'Are you hungry?' Her 'I could eat' has resulted in 11 a.m. curries.

Immediately after my divorce, I got myself a beautiful bright-red coat. It signified a lot to me: a willingness to stand out, to show myself to the world again. It made me feel amazing. I'd worn dark clothes for a long time. Who knows why? Depression, bad body-image, they all matched, you don't have to separate them for the washing machine, they take a spillage very well. But I went out and bought a bright-red coat. Around the same time, I overhauled my knicker drawer and bought loads of CDs. I think I was making a fresh start. Finding out who the new me was, what she liked, what size knickers she was, etc.

I spoke to a few pals before writing this book about the stories I should tell. Quite a few of them remember the time a sad girl wore a red coat. Like in *Schindler's List*, but obviously a lot less sad.

One of the times I met my friend Juliet in London, at Victoria station, I was early so I just stood outside WHSmith (where I always feel at home). I saw Jules appear from the crowd and walk in my direction . . . and then veer off. How odd. I felt sure she had seen me. She was making a beeline for something and that something wasn't me. It was a bright-red double postbox. A double one. You know, the ones with a slot for stamped and then one for franked. Yes, she 'didn't have her glasses on', but she still thought a giant red DOUBLE (FFS) postbox was interchangeable with me in my bonny red coat. Friends who can still make you laugh while insulting you are precious.

I've always been of the opinion where friends are concerned that you have to be ready for them all to disappear at any time. But how many friends do you really need? Facebook's limit is 5,000. I think a good, solid six.

HOW TO BE CHAMPION

Be a good friend. It's the best thing you can be. But only with those who would reciprocate. One-sided friendships are draining and hard. Friends are like family for adults.

Your best friend can totally be a dog.

Chapter 23

The Six Men I Have Loved

1. Shakin' Stevens

Some might call him a poor man's Elvis (my mam, herself a big Elvis fan; she even had an Elvis pillowcase as a teen), but for a long time Elvis was to me a poor man's Shaky. 'This Ole House', 'Green Door', 'Woahowoah Julie', 'Lipstick, Powder and Paint' – all classics. If I had never heard 'This Ole House', I wouldn't have known what shingles were when my mam got them. And thank God her doctor had time to fix them. I identified a lot with 'Green Door'. 'Don't know what they're doing but they laugh a lot behind the green door' reminds me of all the fun I've been sitting outside of. My sister and cousin once shut me out of the bedroom we were all sharing so they could have a midnight feast. They'd saved apples and Polo mints so it was going to be great. I was stuck on the landing so I made crying noises on the stairs 'til my mam, who was chatting with my auntie, asked what was wrong and the plug was pulled on the whole thing.

Shaky was my first real crush. I vaguely remember dancing in front of the telly when I was about five during his performance on *Top of the Pops*. I didn't understand anything about telly so I thought that every time he looked at the camera he was looking at me, and I danced HARDER. He followed me a few years ago on Twitter. For all the times Twitter is an arsehole, the days he and Jason Donovan followed me are worth it.

2. Phillip Schofield

My main love during my formative years was Phillip Schofield. Still the longest relationship I've ever had, and I've been married twice. My love for him is well documented. There was a time when I cleaned my parents' house to make money to spend in Athena on posters, prints and postcards of the broom-cupboard god. I sent him a photo of my bedroom bedecked in Athena's finest prints of his life when he lived with Gordon the Gopher.* He sent it back. Signed. Whenever a BBC envelope plopped on the doormat, I'd get so excited my mam would make me run up and down the hall to get it out of my system.

He said 'happy birthday' to me on his radio show once. I'd sent in a shop-bought birthday card that had a hamster on the front. I signed it as if it was from me and Hilary Hamster. He read it out then said to his listeners, 'I love reading your cards and remember, you don't have to try to be funny.' Crushed. It

---

* I'm sure you NEED to see this photo. It's in the photo section. Flick to it now if you like. I don't mind.

was my first joke and it didn't work. Maybe the fact that I do stand-up now was all just a bounce-back from that. I WILL MAKE HIM LOVE ME. I once got a letter off his mam. I can't remember what it said exactly but something like 'No, I don't know why he hasn't got a calendar either'. The last thing I sent him was a Valentine's Day card that played the theme tune to *Love Story* when you opened it.

3. Kevin Robson

Just a boy at school, but a kind, funny one who said he was a feminist when I didn't know what that was. He helped me in woodwork once. By that token, Kenny Nesworthy should be here too, who once helped me figure out my double-barred shoes. Kindness goes a long way.

4. Kirstie Alley

Bit leftfield this, but as I didn't go to university I didn't get to dabble like everyone else. Lectures, piss-ups, touching your first cock/labia/both. Instead, I had a manageable infatuation with Kirstie Alley, star of *Cheers* and the *Look Who's Talking* films (I saw the second one five times at the cinema). I used to cut out the two-line description of *Cheers* from the Newcastle *Journal*, even if it didn't mention Rebecca, her character. I also collected stills of her from the *S & P Parker's Movie Market* catalogue that I Blu-Tacked to the inside of my wardrobe doors alongside the blurry pic of Jason Donovan from the balcony at the Mayfair, the North East's former ultimate music venue attraction. I have no doubt that if I'd had the chance to go to university, I would certainly have collected photos of Kirstie Alley there too. 'She collects pictures of Kirstie Alley' should be a euphemism for lesbianism.

5. Then Husband*

6. Now Husband

He was on at my second-ever gig and was the funniest person I'd ever seen. The first thing he said to me, as I came off stage, was, 'You rock.'** Things I love about him include:

- He first complimented me by saying, 'I'm very impressed by how little you sweat.'
- When I have thrush he goes to the chemist to pick up fanny tablets for me, so I don't have to be embarrassed.
- He makes the best baked potatoes I've ever had.
- Before I could drive he scooped me up from many a random gig, even if it was massively out of his way.
- I once overheard him explain to our then kitten Chief Brody that the microwave was a telly for dinners.
- He also hates cheese and has a good work ethic.
- We have three pets, even though he is massively allergic.
- He is Solihull's ultimate comedian-husband attraction.
- Home only feels like home when he's in it.

---

* He's had enough airtime.
** And, to be fair, I do.

- He's listened to every word of this book multiple times. He is champion. He is my champion.

'You Rock' is engraved on the inside of our wedding rings. It's how I feel about him every day. He rocks and is my rock. Verb AND noun.

7. The Dog

Technically my second dog, if we count the six weeks of biting we had with Roy the Yorkshire Terrier when I was about nine. You know, the one that disappeared to a farm in the sky (or something) during a sleepover at my friend Rachael's. Or Waffles, my imaginary dog that to the naked eye was just me pulling a length of pink wool around the house and yard. Probably shouldn't count him. Commander Tuvok is the love of my life. No human will ever be as pleased to see me as that little sausage. Or the rest of him.

HOW TO BE CHAMPION

The people you love can come in many forms. Men, women or dogs.

Chapter 24

Holidays

GARY AND I had been together for a while when we decided to go on holiday to London – the first time we went for fun rather than work. We wanted to go to the Planetarium as we're both interested in the night sky. Actually, Gary knows a lot about the constellations, as I discovered on our first trip away as a couple. For this story Gary's version of what happened will be in brackets. We went to stay in a log cabin (chalet) in the Lake District and had a wonderful time. He was living with a flatmate and I was living with my parents, so a few days of just us was amazing. We'd brought a disposable barbecue with us and Gary lit it rather lethally (very safely) on the steps of the log cabin (chalet). We were caught by the woman who ran the place, who asked us not to light a fire on a wooden house. Fair enough (bit dramatic).

One night, we went out for a walk in the pitch dark where he saved me from a badger (bear). We looked up at the sky, which was so clear we could see millions of stars. He asked if I knew much about the constellations; I said a bit. I'd done a project for fun when I was a kid. Not a school project – for fun. That's the sort if kid I was. I stood in front of my mam and dad's living-room window with my binoculars and made a note of what I could see while the double-decker buses rushed past. What an odd (excellent) kid. I'd forgotten most of what I'd learnt by the time we went on this holiday in the Lakes. I only know the North Star, Orion and the Plough. The classics. So I was excited to learn again and stood with my arm around my love while he went through them one by one. 'That's the North Star,' he said. I thought, I know that one.

'That's Orion.' I know that one.

'There's the Plough.' Right, that's me done. Everything from now on is learning.

I listened intently, excited. There was a pause. 'There's another plough,' he said. Then I realised he knows the same three constellations I know. But he does know all five ploughs.

There was a visitors' book in the log cabin. They're always a treat: a good way to find nice pubs nearby, but can also be hilarious. Our favourite entry said: 'We've thoroughly enjoyed our time here. Would definitely come again. Lovely walks, accommodation very clean and the Dog and Duck do an excellent steak on Thursdays. Our holiday was only marred by the sad death of the people's princess, Princess Diana. So three stars.'

Back in London, in the queue for the Planetarium, it became clear that the only way you can get through to that bit is by doing, and paying for, Madame Tussauds too. So THAT'S why there's always that massive queue. Frustrated astronomy nerds forced to look at Tom Cruise and whichever actress is stood beside him at the moment. We paid, we queued and, as happens with us, if something's shit we make it fun. Not that Madame Tussauds is shit. As far as rooms full of lifelike waxworks of famous people go, it's the best there is. That's just not our cup of tea.

As we walked through briskly, an old Indian man came up to us and asked why there were two Nelson Mandelas. He was a great man but it seemed odd. Then we pointed out to him that the Nelson Mandela standing between Brad Pitt and John Travolta was actually Morgan Freeman.

Gary wanted to have his photo taken with Captain Jean-Luc Picard and Albert Einstein, so we nailed those two, but in the world-leader room he decided he wanted a quick picture with Hitler. You know, for a laugh. The room was almost empty so he got in position, arm around his shoulders, like pals on a night out. I took a pic. He started to release his arm. 'It's all blurry,' I said, so I took another. 'Too dark.' I took another. 'You moved.' Another. 'You blinked on that one.' Another. The room was starting to fill up, and Gary was getting agitated because of the people looking and judging him for wanting a picture with Hitler. Eventually, I said, 'That was a good one,' and with relief he unhugged Hitler and we swiftly moved to the next room. Not before I told him I'd taken nine perfect pictures of him with Hitler. Ha.

We pop to London every now and again to see a show. Sometimes we drive straight back; one time we did a matinee and got a train either side. On this occasion we were there for a couple of days. Precious days off work together and away from home with no responsibilities. No animals to feed, no poos to pick up (hopefully). So, we went to see a big musical. Everyone I know had seen it and said it was utterly brilliant. We were excited. We sat in our stupidly expensive but tiny seats; the man beside me lost the armrest to one of my fleshy saddlebags. About twenty-five minutes into the show I was bored. Bored, bored, bored. I had to work out if Gary was bored too. I leaned over to him and whispered, 'How many out of ten so far?' He whispered back, 'Six?' And I knew he was the same as me. When the interval began, again I leaned over, like the temptress that I am, and whispered, 'We don't have to come back after the interval, you know.' His face lit up like I knew it would. Like a naughty bairn.

So we picked up our things and walked out. I didn't want anyone to think we were leaving, though, so I made a bit of a song and dance about 'fancying a tab', even though I have never smoked and neither has my husband. We came outside 'for a smoke' then realised neither of us had a lighter, so we went off into the night looking for a shop that sold matches. We didn't find one. What we did find was three hours of walking, talking, laughing, banana milkshakes, lamb cutlets and selfies of us in front of London's major tourist spots Buck House, Downing Street, Trafalgar Square. It was a bit like the film *Green Card*, where Andie MacDowell and Gérard Depardieu fake a past together with photos of them on skis and in sombreros. We had probably one of the most romantic nights of my life. This isn't the only time we've done this, either. We recently walked out during the interval of a play. Our code word now is simply 'Cigarette?' and we disappear into the night, or, in this instance, a nice French restaurant in Soho where we ate steak and dolphiny potatoes and googled act two.

Life is too short not to enjoy yourself when the opportunity arises. These musicals and plays weren't shit. Clearly not:

tickets were hard to come by and people were raving about them. But art in all its forms is subjective. Comedian Chris Addison once said that people are too afraid to say something is not their cup of tea. He's right. It always has to be shite or fat or an ugly cunt or not funny or looks like someone terrible on *Jeremy Kyle*. When someone says I'm not funny, if I can be arsed to argue, I'll say, 'That is factually inaccurate. It is my job and I am successful. What you mean is, you don't find me funny, and that's totally allowed. For example, I don't like you but I'm sure someone somewhere loves you. Even if you haven't found them yet and are losing all hope.' Something like that.

HOW TO BE CHAMPION

Holidays don't have to be expensive and fancy. I mean, they can be, but some of my best holidays have been cheapo ones. Just go with someone you can spend a lot of time with. And also, don't feel obliged to spend every waking moment with them. I like to bugger off on my own for a bit every now and again.

If it's somewhere you go regularly, keep all the coins for the next time you go. Excellent comedian Alun Cochrane was once very impressed that I had a Euro purse. I was ready for chips in Ireland straight away.

Chapter 25

Getting Married a Second Time

I WAS NEVER one of those girls who dreamt of their wedding. Sure, I had dolls I dressed up, but I also had an imaginary library. Back in the days when you could leave your kids to wander off in a shop, my mam and dad would find me sitting cross-legged in the book department. Years later, my dad caught a lady shouting at her son who was sitting among the books in a shop. He told her his daughter did that once and she's a writer now. Presumably I hadn't started doing stand-up yet or he would have made her come back to the house to watch a clip of *Michael McIntyre's Comedy Roadshow*. He once wouldn't let a plumber leave 'til he'd watched my *Live at the Apollo* set.

So, I was not a twirling pink princess of a girl; I wore trousers, glasses and liked reading. You could say I was a tiny Alan Bennett.

When I was little, I decided I would probably have kids but

didn't want to get married,* and seeing as you only get given children if you lie beside a man in a bed every night, I made my mind up to get married, get a baby and then get divorced.

I'm so glad that when I was twenty-nine and crying on the floor of my mam and dad's house neither of them reminded me that divorce had been on my To Do list. Right underneath becoming a vet and having as many rabbits as they did at Flamingo Land, Yorkshire's ultimate theme-park attraction. Also, thank God I didn't have a baby. It would have been so unlikely given that I hate kids. You have to make a pretty big boob to end up with something you've always hated; like somehow running a cheese factory or a spider ranch. Actually, I'm not too bad with spiders since I moved to the countryside; we have to sort of tolerate each other. The only ones I kill are the fast silent ones and, given that we've just had wooden floors put in, that's very few.

Always pretty career-focused from my teenage years onwards, I was never sure how my life would pan out roman-tically. So no one was more surprised than me when I said yes to a proposal from a man I'd known ten weeks. Well, maybe my parents. And my friends. Remember my date for *Speed* was 30 September? I went back to that café where it happened only a few years ago. I'd walked past it and been nervous of going in for the memories it held. I took my friend Tom for moral support, plus he's gay, so at least I knew it couldn't happen again if it turned out I was just irresistible in this one

---

* You know, boys smell. Men too.

tiny café. The rest of the world, very resistible. And me and it were fine. It was just four walls and a lot of cups. It didn't even feel weird. It was all very quick, but this was how it worked, wasn't it? My parents met when my mam was fourteen and still in a vest. My dad was sixteen with a plaster on his nose that my mam read as 'dangerous, sexy, probably been in a fight', but was in actual fact covering up a massive spot. You met someone who was the perfect fit, married them, done. It seemed so simple.

The breakdown of my first marriage made me hate the word forever. And Frankie & Benny's, perhaps unfairly. I have since been back to Frankie & Benny's, albeit a different branch, and have not got divorced again, so I'm pretty sure it was not their fault.

After that, I didn't see the point of marriage. I was in the 'just a bit of paper' camp. In the 'I don't need a document to know I love you' gang. But while I do think that 'I will not be dictated to as to when I will be romantic to my partner', I do still clap when I get a Valentine's Day card.

I don't believe in The One. That concept disappeared for me when I got divorced. He was supposed to be The One, but he clearly decided I was 'a' one. Like in *Jaws* when they find 'a' shark but not 'the' shark. Plus, I've got a better shark now who makes me laugh every day and knows my favourite kind of notebook. I've found the man I want to grow old with and sit beside on the sofa for another forty years, shouting at the telly. We do that now, obviously, but what I'm saying is I don't want it to end. I have found A One that I am very happy with. When he moved in with me I told a friend that we wanted to end our days together. He assumed we had a suicide pact. I meant oven chips and an episode of *Frasier* at 1 a.m. before bed.

That man is Gary and in the beginning we lived in separate houses for seven years. At various stages we were living anything from 80 to 200 miles apart, but as we were both travelling for our jobs it was doable. We spent a few days a week together and a few days apart. It was, in many ways, perfect. Friends who lived with their partners were jealous. You get cuddles and the bins taken out but then also long baths and Sandra Bullock nights.

It's very hard for perfect to get better. It's hard to want to change perfect. But we did. I moved and my new place only felt like a home when he was there. It was just walls and a roof the rest of the time. He brought it alive. When he left, the light dimmed a little. We made a decision: he moved in. And it was better than perfect. It was a slippery slope from there to realising I wasn't as against marriage as I used to be. That is if the slippery slope was sliding into a big vat of awesome. Think custard or gravy.

We didn't need that piece of paper, but we quite liked the idea of it. God knows, I've always been a massive fan of stationery. As we chatted like adults about marriage, it wasn't any less romantic. On the contrary; I found making plans about becoming a team a proper turn-on.

And that, to me, is the main difference between living together and being married. I don't do sports analogies as I don't understand most sports. When someone says 'He hit it out of the park', I always think, Well, someone will have to get it back – that mustn't be good. But it feels like now we're wearing the same kit. I might be Centre-Forward (guessing . . . netball?) and he might be Goal-Attack (no idea, someone help me) but we're both trying to get a ball over the H (definitely rugby that, phew).

It was an excellent wedding and the best day imaginable. I like being his wife. Girlfriend feels too new, and whenever I hear the word 'partner' it always makes me think of early PE lessons when the teacher would tell us to 'get a beanbag and a partner'. If only relationships were that simple. I wandered around with a beanbag all to myself for years (who says I can't do sports analogies?).

I work harder at this marriage. I know I do. And I believe in forever again not because relationships are easy, but because some are worth fighting for.

Also, if I die first (unlikely, but I can get dramatic – particularly before a general anaesthetic or flight), he has promised not to go out with anyone for two years.

HOW TO BE CHAMPION

If a building has unwanted sentimental attachments, exorcise them with a big slice of cake and an excellent friend who doesn't want to marry you.

Chapter 26

Tips on Making a Relationship Work

THESE THINGS WORK for me. Your partner (life or beanbag) is a different person, I hope. Please bear that in mind. Not everyone wants a bag of meat.

1. Buy them a bag of meat. When it's my turn to do the food shop I buy surprise meat. Like a steak when we were planning a pie. Who doesn't love a meat upgrade? I once bought my husband a bag of meat for Valentine's Day. Nothing says 'I love you' like chops and sausages. He was giddy.
2. It's very easy to compare relationships. But try not to. I had a friend who compared sex between her ex-husband and a one-night stand. That's a bit unfair; the one-night stand broke a lamp. The first would know that he would have to fix that fucking lamp.
3. Every once in a while, I offer to change the cat litter. Each day, we split animal duties into cat food/water/litter and

walking the dog. Traditionally, in the olden days, men would do poo jobs, but these days, because of feminism, women have to pick up poos as well. Plus, I don't mind emptying the trays. I am weirdly proud of what my cats have produced. 'She's her mother's daughter', etc.

4. I beat him* to making the first round of tea. This is rare, as I'm sure the kettle is sometimes on before his eyes are fully open, like a thirsty newborn hamster.

5. I buy tickets to a band or singer he likes. This is tricky as most of his bands are dead, and a visit to a famous grave is not as clappy as a concert. The most recent singer I surprised him with was 1970s folk artist Vashti Bunyan. I even went to the church (the venue) with him. And I enjoyed it too, even if the tuck shop turned out to be a harvest festival display. Too many Corn Niblets – that's how you know.

6. I try to get ahead of the game on his favourite authors and TV programmes. I bought the latest book by his favourite writer on the day it came out, and he hadn't even realised it was due. GOLD STAR. And when I casually mentioned that I'd series-linked the new series of *The Walking Dead* and he replied, 'Oh, when does it start?', I knew I was about to get another big tick.**

7. I say things like 'my favourite flowers are . . .' or 'my favourite chocolate is . . .' Anything that will give him

---

* As in I get there first.
**Tick, you dirty bugger.

a heads-up is a good idea. Partners are often pissing in the dark when it comes to present buying. Did I tell you Gary once bought me a Mr Potato Head? It doesn't matter what the occasion was, as there is no occasion when that is appropriate because I did not meet Gary in my childhood.

8. When we first met I cut his toenails a few times as I thought it was an intimate thing to do. Wow. I've since shaken off that responsibility. And my nightmares have lessened, which is good. I suppose this tip is: don't do anything you don't have to do in the early days in case you have to do it for FIFTY YEARS.

9. Do whatever feels right. Marriage isn't for everyone. But it is for some.

Chapter 27

My Favourite Room in the House

I ALWAYS LOVED nature as a kid. Whether marvelling at rock pools with my dad or collecting caterpillars with my granda, I was permanently wide-eyed and probably a bit grubby. And it wasn't just animals. I was still beaming when planting seeds or identifying flowers. The *Observer*'s guides to garden birds and to wild flowers were well-thumbed, with all of that knowledge being filed away in my brain for future school projects or a chance to confidently put my hand up to answer another question and lose another friend.

In fact, my strongest memories are of nature. Like the day my family went to Farway Countryside Park,* East Devon's ultimate farm-based attraction, got lost because someone turned

---

* I've just learnt the proper name. I always called it the Country Faraway Park because it's Devon and Devon's far away, right?

the signs around, and waited in the rain while my dad went off to track down the car. He took ages to come back as he'd rescued a deer from some barbed wire on the way. What a hero.

Or the time my mam said yes when I asked if I could breed frogs (I've realised since that they do most of it without our help). It was the first time I'd heard the word 'brainwave' when my mam announced, 'I've had a brainwave. Let's have a pond.' Some kids wanted to go on holiday to America or be a princess; I was happy stealing sticklebacks from the local pond to plop into my modest watery hole. I remember twirling in my older sister's bedroom, telling her about how I was breeding frogs now. She didn't understand how amazing it was so I likened it to her getting all of Lady Diana's clothes. Then she understood.

Or the time I planted seeds for lupins in our garden, went into the garage for the watering can, came back through and couldn't remember where I'd planted them. They never did come up.

Then I did GCSEs, A Levels, college, first job, second job, fell in love, got married, third job, fourth job, started writing, divorced, comedy, fell in love, more comedy, bought a house. During the last twenty-four years I have barely thought about wildlife apart from when killing a spider or running from a wasp.

But Gary and I moved to the countryside and, while happily not in the middle of nowhere (chocolate can be purchased after a fifteen-minute walk), I am in amongst it. And the seven-year-old in me skips with delight when I see any birds or animals in the garden, or spy new flowers bursting through. I have a greenhouse and just ate my first courgette I've grown from seed. I came into the house holding it aloft, singing the well-loved Christmas carol 'The First Courgette'. I still have no idea what I'm doing, though. My gardener friend surveyed my potted twigs last January and said, 'You know tomatoes don't grow back, don't you?' To which I smugly replied, 'We'll see,' as if I knew something he didn't.

Before we had a garden, we'd seek grass elsewhere. We both lived in alright flats with balconies. I'd moved from my parents' home to Manchester, where it rains 92 per cent of the time. Why did no one tell me how pointless it was to have a balcony? I moved to Manchester for a few reasons. It's a great city where I'd spent some time doing gigs as the comedy scene there is bustling and full of absolute smashers of comedians. Geographically it made sense to be further down, more central but still in the North. Almost everywhere is far away from South Shields but two hours or less in a car from Manchester can get you to Liverpool, York, Birmingham, Nottingham, Hull, Leeds, Bradford, Sheffield . . . the list goes on. Plus, I noticed a shift. As the train pulled into Piccadilly station, there was a warm home-like feeling. New comedy home. New home. In the six years I lived there, I only ever went on my balcony if I didn't feel well and needed fresh air quickly. Gary's balcony was out of action due to neighbours who thought 'outside' was their room and would play antisocial levels of shite music at all hours. And yes, it does matter that it was shite music. If it was Wham!'s 'I'm Your Man' playing on a loop, I'd be dancing for the first thirty-six hours for sure.

So we'd go to the park, and lie on the grass and nap. The only thing that distinguished us from dead bodies was a tartan blanket and the odd fart. In fact, Gary once knocked a jogger off his rhythm with one of his farts. The man was running expertly when a well-timed parp caused a wobble before he righted himself, unsure of what had just happened. We knew and tried to do it again on several occasions.

Sometimes we'd go to Sutton Park. It's massive and a wonderful place with huge fields, cows, ducks, rabbits and nooks and crannies where you can be alone. There's also a dedicated place for children and middle-aged men to fly their noisy model airplanes, presumably so they can be as noisy as they like without having to worry about other people complaining. Of course, some of those middle-aged men broke the rules and just flew their children's toys wherever they liked. One time Gary and I were having an hour in the park, lying on a blanket, my leg looped through my handbag strap because, you know, people. And I heard it. Like a wasp in my ear. A fucking remote-controlled airplane. First of all, we checked to see if we were near the special noisy whirring middle-aged-men place. We weren't. They were on our patch. The quiet, please don't bother us, yes we're napping place. Furious that our silence was broken, that our nap was looking unlikely, that our hour of quiet in a crazy busy week was ruined, I sat up. I thought, They'd better be fucking kids. I looked around and spotted the culprits, pretty far away. Grown men in hi-vis jackets. In the daytime in a park. Hi-vis jackets. Good. It meant I could vis them. Without a word to Gary, I got up and started walking in their direction. Just walking. Trying hard to make angry heavy steps but trainers on grass always sound pleasant.

In a straight line between us, desired peace and them – men older enough to know better – I walked. The sort of furious walk you do when you know why you're mad but you're not sure what will come out of your mouth when you get there, as every part of you is just concentrating on walking with purpose. What I did say when I got there was a lot more casual than I'd expected it to be. They barely made eye contact before I blurted out, 'Could you *be* a bit more anti-social?' As soon as those words hit the air, I was worried I hadn't Chandlered it up enough and they'd start shitting in the field as proof that, yes, they *could* be more anti-social. Neither hi-vis twat said a word to me. So I turned on my heel and walked in the same way back to my alarmed and I'm assuming turned-on husband. But brilliantly, exquisitely, they won. Because for my entire walk back, they hovered their remote-controlled plane a foot above my head. It was hilarious.

So now we have a lovely garden. It's my favourite room in the house. It's either a place to lie and look at the sky and listen to the birds, or it's the most beautiful ever-changing painting we can see out of half of our windows. I love being outside and up to my elbows in soil. Fresh air, manual labour, rosy cheeks. Plus how wonderful it is when seeds you've planted start to grow. My friend Juliet said it's like the slowest-ever firework display.

I've even picked damsons from a tree in my garden. As a woman who prior to this house only ever had a yard full of bins, this sentence is alien to me. Like when I asked my husband if he'd managed to get 'my special muesli' or when I decided I needed a washing line. I don't think I have changed since moving to the countryside; it's just that a dead middle-class housewife sometimes uses my voice. I know I haven't changed as the muesli thing is probably a phase and I would still rather have a Chunky Kit Kat and a cup of sugary tea. I have no idea what to do with my damsons. I'm not even sure what they are. I googled them and they seem to be smaller horrible plums. Or massive shit grapes. Somewhere between a bollock and a haemorrhoid, then.

I haven't tried them as I read that they have an 'astringent' taste, and I'm pretty sure that's what I use to take my make-up off. Also, my husband is convinced they'll be full of maggots due to either a childhood memory or a horror film, I forget which. So I picked them and, contrary to expectation, I was not wearing a sundress and wide-brimmed straw boater. Rather, my nightie (Marksies, T-shirt material, too short at the back) and some trainers (pulled on fully laced; I miss Velcro). I held a damson to my ear, wondering what maggots sound like when sitting in a shit grape. Nothing. The maggots were asleep. It WAS early.

I asked Twitter for suggestions as to what I should do with my damsons. Les Dennis said jam, Nigel Slater said crumble, my friend Ruth once stirred stewed damsons into a cake batter and said it was delicious. All agreed that they were bitter raw, but once warmed through with a huge amount of sugar were very edible. So would haemorrhoids be, I'd argue. The one I had, I only saw once with a mirror and it looked like a well-chewed Hubba Bubba.

And though most people I know are aware of damsons, but like me don't know what they are and can't resist doing a rubbish joke about them being 'in distress', I know something that would blow their minds. I've heard a rumour that, as damsons are cheap and abundant, they form the basis of most cheap jams. Bung in a couple of the more showy fruit, like a strawberry or a raspberry, and there you go. Damsons on toast all round. So while we're all shouting about how we don't know what they are, we may have had them on toast this very morning. I feel so ashamed. I have no evidence if this is true, but I will happily now think of damsons as the quiet heroes of the jam world. For now, they are in my freezer, in a drawer alongside ice pops and unlabelled plastic tubs of brown, waiting for a time I can make a cake.

But perhaps I have changed. Thinking about it, my levels of cleanliness have dipped and I don't get freaked out quite so much by creepy crawlies. In the past if I'd felt something crawling through my hair, maybe a fly, I'd have screamed the place down. The other day I had my hair up in a bun and I felt something just wriggling around in my hair, and silently, with the flat of my hand, I squashed whatever it was into my hair and carried on with the dog walk.

I know I live in the country because I can hear birds. That's how I know. Don't get me wrong, there are other signs: the local pub has hanging baskets, there are often no pavements, and sometimes outside just smells of shit. But if you can hear birds, you're probably at least in a park or near the beach (or a pet shop or the tip). You're somewhere excellent, is what I'm saying.

I've always been fond of birds. As a kid, I loved budgies: I had three of them and they were all I could really draw. I still know the Latin name for them (*Melopsittacus undulatus*). So when my mother-in-law bought us a bird table for the garden I was thrilled. There were three hooks for food and a water bowl. Oh yes, they got a choice: sunflower seeds, generic bird seed and meal worms. It took them a while to trust us, which I assumed meant they'd been hurt in the past and needed time to heal. Maybe the previous owners had hung realistic paintings of fat balls up and the birds were made to look foolish as they slammed into them, gobs open.

But then they came. In no time there were tits aplenty, jays, wood pigeons, arsey magpies, rooks (or crows; I still don't know which) and a pied wagtail we called Barry. It went a bit crackers, with sometimes nine or ten birds feeding at once, like a scene from *The Birds* with our eyeballs played by fat balls. Soon we were adding bird seed to our big shop. Oh, and just so you know, it isn't 'tuppence a bag', Julie bloody Poppins.

So, essentially, we rented wildlife: we put food out and watched the best telly channel there is. We told each other when we'd seen a new bird, and I showed off my bird-recognition skills to my husband. It's nice to have new ways to impress a man after twelve years together.

But then, in mid-September, it all stopped. I know birds fly south for the winter (bloody Londoners get everything), but I didn't think they all went. On the same day. Like they'd arranged a coach trip. For example, I know robins are still around as they're on Christmas cards. We binned the food in case it was stale, we washed out the containers and refilled them. Still nothing. For three weeks our garden was silent and sad. We assumed we had a predator lurking and I tentatively wandered about the garden looking for anything skinned and bodybuilders in combat gear. Then I remembered that's The *Predator*, not A predator.

Thankfully, some of the birds are back. It isn't a squawky chaos any more but we have enough to keep us happy. I think they all went on holiday and a few Shirley Valentined it.

Our most recent visitors were a group (gang, I like to think) of a dozen partridges who had clearly lost their way and ran around the garden close together like a group of old ladies who were late for church. As my fella said, 'Isn't it great when you see a new animal in the garden for the first time?' Like the frog I thought was a jumping leaf, the stoat (which is the best in my accent), the hare who stopped for a photo and the buzzard that I saw without witnesses or glasses (might not have been a buzzard).

I came out of the door one day and there was a poorly looking bee on the front step. And only that day I'd read what you're supposed to do to revive a poorly bee. If you don't know what to do, you make some sugary water, dip a cotton bud in it and you offer it to the bee. The bee has a little drink and off it flies and you've saved a fucking bee. So I had to google how you make sugary water. I'm not very good in the kitchen and I thought, If this needs a pan it can fuck off. Turns out it's just sugar and water. Who knew? All of you. So I made some sugary water, dipped a cotton bud in it and offered it to the bee. Now, looking back, I think the bee might have already been dead because when I poked it with the cotton bud and pulled the bud away, there was an antler stuck to it.*

---

* Is it antler? Yeah, antler.

I was sitting in the garden last summer with my family, who had come down for a few days. We were drinking cups of tea in the sunshine and having a smashing time. Then we started to get bothered by wasps and I thought, I wish I had one of those wasp catchers. I don't know if you've seen one. It basically looks like a bottle, and you put jam inside, the wasps come in, they eat the jam and they can't get back out the neck. HAHAHA. I didn't have one of those but I thought, I'm quite practical, I could probably improvise one. So I had a dig around in the garage and I found a tea-light holder because luckily I've got friends who don't know me very well. What the fuck am I going to do with a tea-light holder? They've been in my house; they've seen the switches and how I turn on the electric lights. Why the fuck do I need to light my house by fire?

So I got the tea-light holder, which was almost exactly the shape I needed: it was a bottle with a removable bottom. Who wouldn't want one of those? I took the bottom off and put a bit of jam in. I used the good stuff because I think wasps know. I put the bottom back on and placed it in the middle of my family – like a really fucked-up version of spin the bottle – and it worked. The wasps came and had some jam. And then they flew back out again because the neck was too wide. My husband looked across and said, 'What you've created there is a wasp pub.'

'Thanks for the jam. We've got loads of energy now to sting your family.'

Since getting a garden, I've learnt I'm a bad plant mam. I'm a good cat mam, a good dog wife mam, but an awful, awful plant mam. In the winter (I think I'm a fair-weather gardener)

I treat the back garden (greenhouse, raised beds, my domain) with the same utter disregard I poured over all hobbies as a kid. The problem with declaring something your 'domain' is that no one else goes near it, even when it starts to look like *Jumanji*. Yes, I'm still talking about my back garden, though I appreciate you could apply the metaphor to the 'front garden' too.

One thing I did do was grow great big fuck-off sunflowers, but that was more driven by competition with my husband than the urge to garden. We both planted seeds: mine in the greenhouse to get them going; he wanted to put his straight in the ground. I didn't stop him. I'm a bad wife. Hey, it's a competition. I'm not an idiot.

His didn't come up. We assumed birds got them. I laughed in secret. Mine were doing pretty well three weeks in when he decided to plant some more seeds (batch two) in the greenhouse. I have no idea how this happened, but his grew taller than mine. I still win though because his first ones are in some blackbird's tummy.

The plants that I like the best when I'm busy are the snowdrops, crocuses and daffodils because they've got my back. You never hear them asking to be watered or just dying off willy-nilly after a year. Every year, when they pop up, I can almost hear the opening bars to Destiny's Child's 'Survivor' as they push through the earth flicking the Vs at all the shit plants that don't have the get up and go to come back.

Daffodils are my favourite flowers so to have them grow themselves in my garden without any work for me is awesome. I also love tulips but, as it turns out, so do rabbits, who ate the buggers practically as they were being planted. Maybe I feel a kinship to bulbs. I didn't get much attention for years, but I powered through with my big yellow face. This is a terrible analogy.

Two very exciting things have happened in the garden recently, and neither have anything to do with plants. Firstly, for my fortieth birthday I got a washing line. I had asked for it. The very domesticated me rubs up weirdly against the very feminist me, but I reckon feminism is about women being equal to men and I'm pretty sure men are able to hang out washing, even if, in my experience of living with them, it's been in the washing machine for four days and smells like mouldy bins.

My washing line is actually one of those spinny ones, which I had always resisted as I thought they moved on their own and I couldn't get my head around where you'd plug them in. I've very quickly become that person who declares it 'a good drying day', pays attention to weather forecasts and runs out with a washing basket at the merest hint of rain. I understand why they run. I once had to bring in a duvet cover that had been hanging out in the rain for hours, and I could barely bloody lift it. It's worth noting that since the last time I hung clothes out (when I lived with my parents), my knickers now need three pegs each.

In the summer, in between driving to gigs and writing jokes, I have tea breaks with choc ices on the grass. I fell asleep in the garden the other day. No need to worry about sunburn: I was face-down, though I inhaled my fair share of ants. Summer Sarah has outside activities now. And not just Swingball on her own (much easier) and supersoaking plants. Her greenhouse isn't empty in the summer and a reminder of hobbies she hasn't started yet. There are food and flowers growing from seeds, and the local wild rabbits are stuffed full of her strawberries and pansies. So much so, she's considering planting some Gaviscon seeds for them, poor buggers.

The main reason I've been in the garden recently is because that's where we empty the dog. The first two weeks we had him, he had kennel cough so we could only walk him in the garden. It gets a bit samey after a while so I started listening to music while I did it. My husband says that one of his favourite images of me is my dancing to 'Return of the Mack' at 6 a.m. while wearing a big yellow raincoat, wellies and pyjamas.

In the beginning, picking up warm poos with only a tiny bag is fucking disgusting. We were both retching on the lawn while the dog looked up like, 'And these are my well poos. Wait 'til you get a sniff of my poorly ones.' So, while we got used to the smell, we'd leave the poo for the other parent to pick up next time with a pretty accurate description of where it was. We called it Battleshits. It's not like that now, though. I've been known to be so keen as to accidentally pick up another dog's poo at the same time. Nothing more disconcerting than a clay-cold turd.

The dog had many accidents in the house at first. He'd been in kennels for a year where presumably they just wee and poo where they are. A friend stayed in our spare room one night. He saw the cream carpet and said, 'Oh, should I take my shoes off,' and I thought, An hour ago there was a turd there. I wanted to tell him to keep his shoes on (but didn't).

When we replaced the carpets, Gary suggested we get one where the pattern is yellow-and-brown splodges. I said, 'That's what we've already got, love.'

HOW TO BE CHAMPION

If you wear black nail varnish no one can see the crap up your nails.

Poo bags come in many different colours but I always buy the black ones rather than the purple and pink ones. I just didn't want anyone to stop me thinking I'd been to a kids' party: 'Oh, that chocolate cake stinks . . .'

Oh, and tomatoes don't come back.

Chapter 28

Millican's Law

SOME CALL IT Millican's Law. Russell Kane calls it Millican's Maxim. I call it the eleven o'clock rule. When I started stand-up I was twenty-nine and hadn't learnt a new thing in years. I said to my husband the other day, 'I haven't learnt anything new in years,' and he took it as a slight on our sex life. I said (a) it's not up to you to bring in new things, (b) I'm forty-two, I'm already doing everything with my fanny that I'll ever do, and (c) you could start shouting facts out with every thrust.

I very quickly fell in love with doing stand-up. Every part of it: writing jokes, trying them out, being backstage with other comics, booking my diary, working out travel logistics, performing to all sorts of different crowds, sleeping on random sofas, working out how to improve. The travel logistics are such a major part of the job, especially as for the first few years I couldn't drive. So, can I get home after the gig? Am I spending the entire fee for the gig on a cheapo hotel? Or is there someone on the bill whose sofa I could sleep on? Do I know anyone in Cambridge? Where is Gary? Gary was often my knight in shining Clio. Because it was lit and populated, I'd sit in a train station in the middle of the night while he drove from his gig to scoop me up and take me to his or mine. I LOVE working out the travel logistics of a tour. I think if the comedy thing ever went down the swanny I'd become a sat nav.

I wanted to learn from everything I did, but I realised that sometimes the previous gig would impact the next. So if I struggled at the previous gig, I'd walk into the next one thinking I wasn't any good. I needed to be able to shake that off quicker, to judge every gig as an individual thing. So I developed a rule. As I'm such a cautious person, I'm great at rules. I've never cheated on a partner, killed a person or flushed a sanitary towel, and only once have I kicked a dog turd under a bush. Sorry, Nottingham.

The rule was designed for me but has been adopted by many comedian pals who in turn have passed it on to the next generation. Oh yes, there's a next generation. The other day, a waitress in Wagamama said she was a big fan of mine; I smiled and thanked her for the kind words. She then said she'd been a fan since she was a kid. While I was crying and checking my hands for liver spots, I realised that I have been doing stand-up for twelve years and, as she was twenty-two at most, yep, she could have been a fan since she was a kid. But why was a ten-year-old watching a woman talk about fannies and saying fuck a lot? She was very polite and never judged how many sides I ordered so I think she turned out just fine.

The rule, while made for comedians, can also be utilised by anyone anywhere who has a thing they need to get past. You must be strong and stick to the rule. If you are the sort of person who cheats, murders, flushes, and kicks turds under bushes A LOT, I'm not sure this is for you.

The rule is this: if I've had a bad gig – this could be that I wasn't good, they weren't good or for whatever reason it just didn't work – then I can only be sad, furious, frustrated and annoyed about it until 11 a.m. the next day. Then, at 11 a.m., I need to shake it off. Because if I go into the next gig thinking I'm shit, I'll die. Equally, though, if I nail a gig, I can only be smug, thrilled and kissing my guns until 11 a.m. the next day. Because if I go into the next gig thinking I'm king of the world, I'll die. Comedy is about being in the moment, and carrying baggage – good or bad – can ruin things. And this rule totally works. I've been known to put my alarm on earlier just so I can bitch and moan or dance and clap for longer.

The rule can be adapted too. For example, when you're at the Edinburgh Fringe you can be doing five gigs in a day and be on stage any time from 11 a.m. (I was once introduced at that time by my good friend Steve Day with 'Gateshead Library's loss is comedy's gain'; I'd never worked at Gateshead Library but my outfit said I lived there) to 3 a.m. (the one time I played Late 'n' Live: I talked while they stared or slept; it was awful and I was placated afterwards with a glass of ginger beer). You then don't have time to wait until 11 a.m. to shake off the detritus of the last gig. So the eleven o'clock rule is then adapted to half an hour after coming off stage. If you see comics standing outside venues having a short cry or a small dance or shuddering, that's what they're doing.

If you're not a comedian, feel free to adapt this for yourself. Bad day at work, argument with your partner, annoyed with a friend, dog seems to love your partner more than you – feel your feelings 'til 11 a.m. the next day and then crack on with life. It's empowering and positive and absolutely works. And the dog WILL love you more than he loves your partner, even if you have to keep sausages in your pockets to start with. You know it's just because you change your clothes more often and the dog thinks your partner smells of dinner when it's just stains on his T-shirt.

Chapter 29

Life on the Road

IS IT WEIRD that I like living on the road? There's a lovely rhythm to being on tour that I don't get in any other area of my work. A routine, I suppose. Outside of tours, every day is different. I'm writing a thing, going to London for a telly thing, trying new jokes out at a place. But a tour ticks the boxes left unticked when I handed in my notice at the civil service. It's the uniformity, the sweetness of knowing where you're going every day and that every day is mostly the same. There's a real comfort in having spells of that.

Having said that, I like a good gap between tours. My first two pretty much ran into one another and I felt like I was going a bit mad. Things change at home when you're away a lot. When I went to Australia for a month, Gary (we didn't live together at the time) moved into my flat to look after our first cat, Chief Brody, who wasn't allowed in the bedroom at night as he nibbled toes and jumped on bums and we needed sleep. I thought it was good to have a rule from day one that the bedroom door was shut at night and he was on the other side. I made sure I left a light on for him as he was scared of the dark, or at least mewed a lot until a light went on.

When I came back from Australia, I walked into my bedroom and there was Brody, spread-eagled on my side of the bed, with a look of, 'And you are . . .?' He had also developed a habit of sitting beside the fridge whenever the door opened. Odd. Until I saw Gary drop ham for him. (I am definitely bad cop where our animals are concerned. I make sure they've eaten their food before treats. If Gary was in charge of the world we'd all be living off biscuits and sausages. We often say that, based on how we treat our animals, if we had kids they'd be fat and in prison.)

Sometimes I return from tour to find the house has changed too. I was away for a few days on the last tour only to come back and find out we had a mezzanine. I asked where Ripley was (our little girl cat) and Gary said, 'She's on the mezzanine.' I'd been gone four days. Four days and he'd built a new level. I said, 'Where's the mezzanine?' Turns out he meant the landing.

When I get home I empty my bag of dirty washing as soon as I arrive. I call Little Dog* into the room. He loves dirty pants and socks so he looks up at me like, 'Is it my birthday, Mam?' or 'Did I win a competition?' I empty my bag of worn underwear and, instead of rushing at it, he calmly circles it, taking it all in. Like he's a posh man in an art gallery pretending he knows what art means. He then thoughtfully selects a sock

---

* Little Dog is Tuvok's other name. These are just two of his many names.

or two and one pair of pants. Whether it's because they're the most pungent, we, the observers, can only guess. He places one sock in the spare bedroom for later and carries the others to his bed for a good sniff. This is one of my favourite things about coming home.

You can get used to hotel living. Sometimes I live 'like a boy', which means I balance the new toilet roll on top of the empty tube rather than actually slotting it onto the holder. I once dropped a bit of a Twirl on hotel sheets and didn't spot it until I'd slid down and caused a two-inch brown smear. I had to leave the chocolate wrapper out near it so the cleaner didn't think it was ANYTHING ELSE. Good tip, that, for next time you shit the bed. I regularly carry a bottle of Halloween fake blood around with me for when I have my period.

The little dog had a leaky bum when I was in Norwich on my last tour. I did my best with tissues but he doesn't half growl when anyone tampers with him at that end. He ran back into the hotel room, jumped on the bed and sat bolt upright, bumhole kissing the duvet cover. I was so panicky about the stain that I dropped my Cornetto. There was only one thing to do: apologise to the staff on the front desk, explain what it was and hope they believed me. Sorry, my mistake, there were two things. And I chose the other one and flipped the duvet over. And replaced my Cornetto.

When I take him out on his late-night walk, he gets so excited that I have to carry him out of the hotel or he'd bark everyone awake. When I pop down for breakfast I leave the telly on for him, and if the keycard system means the power goes when I pull it out, I fashion something else to shove in its place. I've made my own Do Not Disturb sign before too. Sometimes you check in late and there isn't one, and you can't be bothered to ring down to ask someone to bring you one up. You just want a cup of tea in the bath and then bed. In those instances I rip out a page from my least-favourite notebook of the seven I've probably got with me and make a Do Not Disturb sign. Nothing says Do Not Disturb more than a homemade sign scrawled in angry glittery gel pen. It's like the craft project of a mad man.

When you live on the road, hotels are your life, but obviously it's not like being at home. I once had a very heavy period in a quite posh hotel. They clearly wouldn't cater for that: sanny bin, red sheets, wellies. The bathroom pedal bin was only big enough for two cotton buds and one sharpening of a lip liner. So you work around it. I filled it so full with giant, full night-time (for through the day too) sanny pads that the lid was half-open like a sad crocodile. I dripped pink juice on the bath mat, and no matter how hard I tried the towels got a little on too. None on the sheets, though, as I lie on a bath towel and sleep on my side for damage limitation.

When I left the hotel I piled the marked towels and bath mat in the bath to illustrate the blood bath I had just survived, and placed the singular paper bag with a lady in crinoline on top. She looks a bit like the one on the old Quality Street tins. Maybe that bag is just for your brightly coloured wrappers. Do you think the same lady modelled for both?

'What's this session for, Mr Johnston?'

'This is for a large, sumptuous tin of chocolatey delights.'

'Oh, how marvellous. What about tomorrow's?'

'It's for, erm, well, it's for, err, it's to do with a letter from Aunt Flo.'

'Oh, the postal service? Charming.'

Mine has always been more of a package from Aunt Flo. That needs signing for. We should update those bags; why are we still so embarrassed about periods? The bags should depict a woman going about her normal day, doing her job, maybe looking after kids, all the while haemorrhaging pint after pint of blood and making sure none of it is seen or smelt by anyone nearby. You know, so the human race can continue. Failing that, the bags could just be bright red with the words 'Shark Week' on them. That's my favourite euphemism.

I like a bath in a hotel room. You have to ask for one, as these days, to save space, they just shove a shower in and you can't steep your ragged arsehole* in that when your IBS has been horrendous because you've eaten badly because you're on the road. In one hotel in Bristol, when I asked if my room had a bath, the man on the front desk proudly exclaimed that there wasn't a single bath in the hotel. As my face didn't match his beam, he then threw at me the entirely irrelevant information that every room had an iMac. I said, 'Unless that has a BATH APP, I'm not really interested, flower.'

It was 1 a.m., much too late to start looking for another hotel, so I just went up to the room. I love a bath to wind down after a show. Some people get drunk and take drugs; some go 'looking for pussy'. I've tried that, but I only ever

---

* Sorry.

find them crouching under warm cars and my knees can't take it any more. I like a bath and a cup of tea, preferably at the same time. Maybe a book, too. Bliss. I've stayed a few times in a posh hotel that didn't do kettles. You had to order a cup of tea from room service, which would take ages and cost a bomb. So I bought a travel kettle instead. It comes with little cups and a tiny teaspoon. Some decaf teabags from the tour kit, resealable bag of sugar and some travel UHT milks stolen from various venues and cafés, and I'm ready for any tea-based emergency, which, given that I'm English, is all emergencies.

Refusing to give up, and having a bit of a *MacGyver* brain that I put down to having an engineer for a dad, I placed the bathroom glass over the plug hole in the shower to see how high I could get the water. Obviously I had to stay inside as opening the door would have ruined it. I got it a foot high and sat in it like a TV rape-victim (they always show rape victims sitting in the bottom of the shower when they should show them talking to an understanding police officer who can help them put the fucker away). Sitting in a foot of water is not an entirely unpleasant experience but it did ruin my book.

I once did a short run of gigs in Wales, and it was so remote that you had to tell the train conductor which stop you wanted to get off at or they'd just speed through it. And when I say 'speed' I mean anything but. I checked into the hotel, which was more of a B&B. I hate B&Bs; they're like staying in the house of a rela-tive who hates you. I was once chastised because I changed my mind about having breakfast and hadn't told them. The breakfast finished at 8.30 a.m., and that's like 4 a.m. for comedians so I slept through. When I checked out I was asked why I'd changed my mind and shown the laid-out dining table with breakfast presumably just for me. The toast had a tea towel laid over it. I couldn't work out whether it was to keep it warm or if the toast had died. Or was being shushed like you would a budgie. In Wales, this hotel room had no en suite, which is the very minimum I require. The toilet was two floors up, past lots of other rooms full of apparently permanent residents. I wasn't keen on walking so far with my nightie on and didn't want to wake myself up by putting my clothes back on. But then I noticed, on the side of the sink in the room, a loo roll. So I did what they expected me to.

The main things I love about touring are:

1. Doing my job. I love my job and I'll be doing it loads. •beams•
2. My audiences. They are a joy.
3. Hotels. I love my home, sure, but I know what all of the buttons there do.
4. Figuring out how to angle the mirror so I can watch the telly from the bath.
5. Spending time with friends (who are also my support acts).
6. Watching Little Dog enjoy a service station like it's an actual destination.
7. Killing time in random places. I'm good at it these days.
8. Chips. We're allowed them whenever the tour is visiting the coast. Or if we just fancy chips.
9. Backstage preparation. I love the tea and the eating and the make-up doing. All with a dog on my knee.
10. Being back on the road. Doing what I love the most: making people laugh.

Right God, I always loved this top. It hid a multitude of sins. At the Lincoln Comedy Festival, 2008. (*Ped Briggs*)

Below My first Edinburgh Fringe poster photoshoot. The photographer was Andy Hollingworth, who brought the squirrel himself, trying to get across that I was 'Not Nice'. I've since done about forty photo shoots with Andy. He always makes me feel so comfortable and knows all my best angles. Over the years, he has helped me develop my four facial expressions, which is three more than I had. (*Andy Hollingworth*)

Right When you get nominated for an Edinburgh Comedy Award, you do a photo shoot with all of the other nominees. Can you see how much I love approval from others? I am hugging my award. I went on to win the newcomer award that year (2008) and got nominated for the main award two years later. I quite rightly lost to Russell Kane. His show was so good that I cried when he won, which my agent took as losing sadness and patted me on the arm. (*Geraint Lewis/Edinburgh Comedy Awards*)

Left The photo shoot for my second tour, 'Thoroughly Modern Millican', was one of my favourites. I was very clear about what I wanted. 'Can I look like I'm in *Downton Abbey*? But be holding a dog in a bonnet that looks nonplussed?' FOR NO REASON AT ALL. (*Andy Hollingworth*)

Below left The first time I ever thought I could look glamorous. Turns out I rock a 1950s headscarf. This was for my 'Typical Woman' Fringe show, and the poster was inspired by Rosie the Riveter and won some award for best poster. Oh, and some lesbians messaged me to say they thought my arm was sexy. (*Andy Hollingworth*)

Above right Our little girl, Ripley. A rescue cat, eats off the floor, is a ninja at hiding and the sweetest animal I've ever met.

Far right My little man, Commander Tuvok. I took this photo, but it looks like it could be a poster thanks to his canny little face and, you know, spring. He is one of the loves of my life. I sometimes just cry at how much I love him.

Below right The time I got to put pants on Tuvok (for medical reasons) will always feature in the top-ten days of my life.

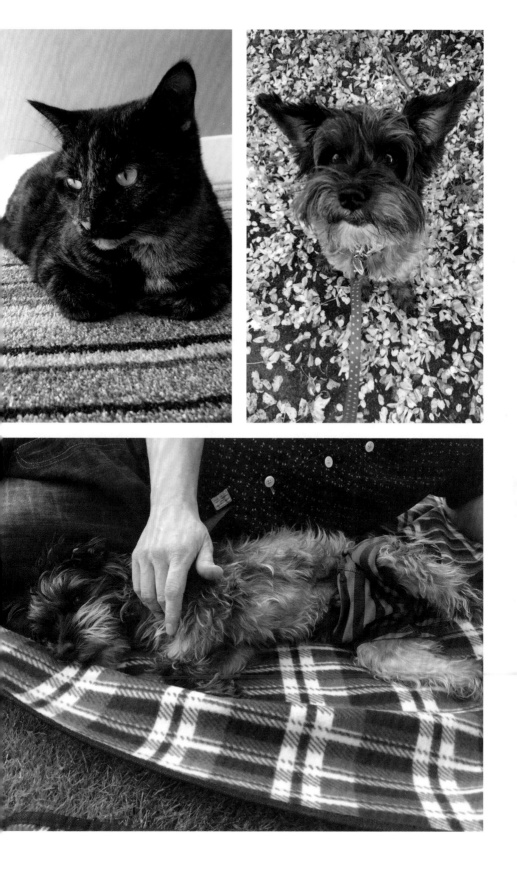

Above We met! We met! And he hasn't had a restraining order taken out or anything! What a lovely bloke. *Puts posters back up*

Below It's bad form to ask another guest on a chat show for a photo so I held back when I saw Oprah. But then she asked One Direction for one so I figured she'd opened that door. I'm not sure why, but during this photo she was pushing down really hard. It's very possible she just has a heavy head and was grateful for the rest.

Above right I was nominated for two British Comedy Awards in 2010 and lost both. I was nominated again in 2011, this time for King or Queen of Comedy, which is a public vote. I was working at 'Rock with Laughter' at Birmingham NEC with Graham, Dara and Jimmy (and Marti Pellow, Gabrielle and 10cc). There was a small camera crew buzzing around, but Graham was also nominated so that didn't give any indication. I got to give Graham his award and then I relaxed a bit. If I won, Jimmy was to present me with the award. While Jimmy was onstage, and therefore unavailable, I saw the camera crew panic and grab Dara, who looked straight at me and I knew. I was thrilled. Public vote awards always mean more

Turn to page 229 to find out what I was hiding behind Jimmy in this photo from *The Big Fat Quiz of the Year 2014*. (*Brian J Ritchie/BFQ Limited*)

Looking thoughtful for *Who Do You Think You Are?*. Acting is not in my skillset so I'm especially proud of this. (*Wall to Wall Media*)

Oh, my *Deal or No Deal* episode is one of my favourite telly experiences. I was surrounded by people I love who'd been bussed to Bristol from pretty much everywhere. What started as a funny, chatty quiz show very quickly turned into an incredibly emotional experience. I was playing to raise money for Macmillan Cancer, and when I turned to the audience for advice on whether I should deal, two women who didn't know each other but were sitting together both told me that they had cancer and I should play on. I cried from then on for about forty-eight hours. Such incredible strong women, and an experience I'll always remember. (*Endemol UK Ltd*)

Right On stage for *John Bishop's Christmas Show* in 2015. Thirty minutes before this, I had fallen down some stairs and cracked my jaw. I was picked up by my agent like when nanas lift buses off their grandbairns and taken back to my dressing room for a ttle cry and make-up redo. I did my set and later met Kylie, who was funny and great. My ace friend Tom Allen and I did 'WE'RE TALKING TO KYLIE!' eyes at each other when she wasn't looking. (*Ellis O'Brien/ Lola Entertainment Ltd*)

Below and below right The year after my BAFTA experience, I did what I'd promised o do in my *Radio Times* article and wore the ame dress again. I was touring and couldn't go to the ceremony, so I wore it to my show in Buxton. I walked out and got a standing ovation, which are a lot rarer than people think. It's the closest I've come to crying on stage. On the right is my ginger tom Chief Brody and a present I got from a member of the Buxton audience. So I got a BAFTA in the end: a Buxton Award For Tremendous Attitude. I fucking love my audiences.

I get asked to do brilliant things in this job, and when *Stylist* asked if I'd interview Anna Kendrick after a screening of *Pitch Perfect 2*, I said yes immediately and had THE best time. Here is me high-fiving the woman herself (she was a smasher). (*Joel Ryan/Universal Pictures International*)

Live at the Apollo in 2016. Thrilling and terrifying every time. I always panic that when I walk out through all that smoke I'll just keep going and end up in the audience. (*Ellis O'Brien/Open Mike Productions Ltd*)

Let's give you a glimpse into what happens backstage before the show, while you're having your wees and getting your drinks. We get into the venue and, during the soundcheck, one of my team (tour manager and support act/friend) will ask if I've played there before. I will whisper that I'm not sure but sometimes I accidentally do that into the mic. I often ask the venue staff if there's a ghost in the theatre/town hall/arts centre/corn exchange. There always is.

I hang up the two outfits I have brought with me. The one with the fewest creases by 7.30 p.m. is the one I wear. I never iron. Sorry, everyone, I hate ironing. I *think* I have an iron at home but I have no idea where it is. If my body heat or fat doesn't push the creases out then, guess what, guys, I'm going to be creased.

Before the show, I sign a box of tour programmes. I try not to get distracted while doing this, as if my mind wanders, so does my Sharpie. Towards the end of the last tour I was a bit homesick and missing my cats (we call them our mittens; I have no idea why). My mind was drifting and I glanced down to find I'd signed a programme 'Love, Sarah Mittens xx'.

I put my make-up on. I love putting my make-up on, and I'm now comfortable enough with Team Tour to pluck my tash and beard in front of them. They don't notice or give a shit. Sometimes I straighten my hair, or clag* a whole bunch of heated rollers in. Sometimes it's just clean and brushed. I don't always do the back. The same way I sometimes only

---

* 'Clag' is North Eastern for 'put' or 'shove'.

shave the bottom front parts of my legs. I recently found a patch behind my right knee that had been left to nature for many years. It seemed a shame to trim it back. God knows what wildlife lost their homes that day.

HOW TO BE CHAMPION

Micky Flanagan gave me some touring advice once. He said treat yourself well: nice hotels, a tour manager if you want one. I think because you spend so much time away from home, the nicer you make it, the more likely you'll do it again. So, I take the dog, stay in nice hotels and eat chips whenever I want.

If you're in a hotel that has magazines, make sure before you check out that you've moved them from beside the loo to beside the bath. 'Oh, I love a read while I'm ~~pooing~~ washing.'

A well-placed Twirl wrapper can disguise a skiddy. But only on soft furnishings – bed, sofa, that sort of thing. No need to balance one on the toilet seat.

Chapter 30

I Don't Want Kids

I AM A forty-two-year-old woman, and whenever I tell someone that I don't have kids they assume one of four things: infertile; selfish; haven't met The One; in denial. It works the same with alcohol. When people learn that I don't drink (well, a pint of shandy every other year and a mouthful of champagne if I have to toast the happy couple) they expect me to be a recovering alcoholic. Or pregnant. I recently posted a photo of a mocktail on Instagram. I love a mocktail. When you don't drink you get so sick of coke and orange juice that something fruity in an adult's glass fits the bill nicely. I got a lot of comments implying that I was pregnant. The public have never seen me drink booze. Have I been pregnant for years?

Nope. I'm not a reformed alcoholic or pregnant; I work a lot, drive a lot and a glass of wine makes me sick for twenty-four hours. Allergic? Probably. I'm not bothered enough to find out. Similarly, I may well be allergic to children. Is there any allergy test for that? Do they rub a tiny claggy hand on a square of your arm and observe the results? No need. Put me on a bus and watch my neck go red.

A lady once stopped me in the street in my home town and asked if she could take a photo of me with her child. The toddler was eating a saveloy dip (a North Eastern delicacy). I didn't know what to do, so I said yes. Somewhere there exists a photo of me looking deeply uncomfortable beside a buggy, inhaling the wonderful smell of the child's sausagey treat. What a snapshot of South Shields. The kid is looking at me like, 'Who the fuck is this?' And I was thinking exactly the same, but 'what', not 'who'.

Since I realised that kids weren't just dolls you were handed as soon as you got married, I've never wanted them. Well, that's not technically true; there was a five-minute period when I considered it. I had a baby-name book for writing purposes; I used to write short film scripts and how else would you stumble across the excellent name 'Pearl'? It was during my first marriage, and I thought MAYBE for five minutes. I picked two names out of the book and went in to see then husband who was playing kicky-fighty games on his PlayStation. He was an adult, by the way. I didn't marry a teenager. I wasn't allowed to play against him on the PlayStation any more because I always won. He said I had no skill, but I think my ability to pick one kick or punch for my *Tekken* character and just press the button loads and really fast was very effective. It's also my wank strategy.

He stopped playing his game. I told him the two names I liked if we ever had kids. He said he didn't like them and I thought, I'm not going to bother, then. And I haven't considered it since. Genuinely. Hate. Kids.

I DON'T WANT KIDS

Some of my friends disagree when I say I don't like kids: 'Yeah, you do.' Like if I don't then I must be some sort of monster. One reminded me that his son drew me a picture once. I said, 'It doesn't mean I kept it.' It was rubbish, a waste of a magnet. When in a restaurant or café, I usually select a seat away from families as I like quiet and I don't enjoy the face some mothers do when their child does something amusing. It's all a bit 'look what I did'. When that happens, I am always tempted to pull out my GCSE results. It's all relative though, isn't it? I was in a pub with my fella last week when an old couple came in and were directed to the table beside ours, before the octogenarians requested to be moved 'away from the kids'. We looked around. Yep, it was us.

I don't have children because I don't want children. There, I said it. It's not because I can't. The same reason I don't eat cheese: because I don't want cheese. No one tells me it'll be different if I have cheese of my own. And that they didn't like cheese to start with but grew to love it as soon as they'd shat some out of their fanny.

I don't want children because I like my life. I have no responsibilities but me and some pets. I have freedom and the ability to stay out later for an impromptu curry. Though we can't stay out all night. To be fair, having a dog is very similar to having a child. Just looking at his face makes my heart swell with love, and I am responsible for disposing of his shit. See? Same. It's just we can leave him on his own for four hours. So he's better. A better baby.

I have a full life doing a job I love, with great friends who buy me birthday socks as they know I rarely get home to do my washing. I have a good family and a man who means the world to me. I love eating out, hoover only if someone is coming and the only things that grow in my house are the contents of my fridge. I'm happy to say I hate kids. They're noisy and want all of the attention. That doesn't suit me, as I want all of the attention, please. A man on Twitter recently accused me of being like Hitler for saying I hate kids. That's a little extreme. And how bad would those baby showers be?

I have no idea whether I am fertile. A while ago I was at the doctors and asked about the possibility of having a fertility test. If not, I could relax a little on the protection front, being in a long-term relationship. My doctor said such a test exists, but you can only have it if you've been trying for a baby for eighteen months. The daft side of me considered going back to a different doctor in the practice and pretending I'd been unsuccessful for eighteen months, but then knowing my luck, I'd end up accidentally on IVF. I'm too polite.

I suspect I am not fertile given that I have polycystic ovary syndrome (PCOS), something I was checked over for when I was twenty-two but wasn't diagnosed with until twelve years later. It's like my body caught up with my brain. When I was twenty-two I had unexplained pain, and an old male twat of a doctor lifted up my nightie to see how hairy my belly was and decided it wasn't PCOS from that. I should go back to him – I think I now have PCOS on my chin.

For my PCOS, I take Metformin, which all pharmacists think is for diabetes because I'm a bit fat and always look like I'm thinking about chocolate. I take great pleasure in telling them I don't have diabetes yet. Like when I was put on tablets for migraines that were normally used to treat bedwetting; I laughingly told a chemist that they were for migraines but 'the bedwetting has cleared up lovely. HAHAHAHA.' She smiled and said, 'Oh, that's good,' and I can't go in there any more.

I've had one pregnancy scare in my life. Urged to by excited women at work (they had no idea), I took a tube of wee to the doctors. When I rang to get the results, the receptionist said, 'I'm sorry to have to tell you . . .' before the news that I was not pregnant. How dare she presume what would be the good and bad news. It was like *The X Factor* but before *The X Factor*.

'I'm sorry to have to tell you . . . you're through to boot camp!'

'I'm sorry to have to tell you . . . you don't need an abortion!'

The women at work did not understand why I was worried about maybe being pregnant. They hadn't listened when I'd said I didn't want kids. They hadn't noticed me making cups of tea when someone brought a baby in. Or not giving much of a shit when they told stories about their kids. My supervisor backed me into the kitchenette to tell me it was going to be the happiest time of my life. But I had to tell her that I didn't want kids and that, if I was pregnant, I would probably have an abortion. She walked away from me silently as she didn't know what to say. Someone much more on my wavelength is my best friend. Whenever our periods started we would say to each other, 'I'M EMPTY!'

These days, the possibility of having your own kids no longer ends at forty. As people tell me, I could change my mind at sixty and still have a small chance of becoming a mother thanks to science. Well, science can fuck off. I suppose this works for some women and all power to them, but it's not for me. I love sitting down and drinking tea now. What makes you think I don't want to be doing that full time when I'm old? The only bum I'll be wiping then is my husband's. And he'll be doing mine. We'll try to make it sexy.

Two friends and I have agreed that if we survive men (not all of them in some kind of *Sex and the City* apocalypse – our men), we will retire to a hot tub in the Lake District, England's ultimate lake-district attraction, and quack at ducks and eat chips and dips until we pop off.

I don't think that I am selfish. I am an okay daughter, a generous and warm friend and a corking wife, if a little needy and huggy at times (who isn't? Robots, that's who). My parents never ask about grandchildren, regardless of the fact that they are constantly asked by friends why they don't have grandchildren yet. YET. Such an assumption. As they say to me, 'We brought you into the world to run your own life. We've got our lives. You have yours.' My parents believe we (them, me and my sister) are all adults. All equal. I once asked my mam if I could have a key to their house. She said, 'As long as I can have a key to yours.' I do not have a key to my parents' house. There's no need, anyway; if they aren't in, I'll find them in the Metrocentre.

In denial? Do you know how hard it is to prove to someone that you are not in denial? That's not to say that I don't have maternal instincts. I do, but they are seemingly directed towards everything except children. Adults, animals, my car. I am the friend who wants you to text me when you get home. I am the one who asks if you have your keys if you are known to often forget them. I had to leave my first car, Thelma the Micra, an extra day at the airport once due to a cancelled flight. I was concerned that she'd think I had abandoned her and that with every influx of passengers in the car park, she would look up and scan the crowd for a grumpy bespectacled lady who eats far too much strawberry bubble gum and still hasn't found a good way of disposing of it while driving. Is that . . .? Is she . . .? No? Oh. Like a little kid at the school gates.

Maternal pangs strike worst of all with cats. Some women like cats. Deal with it. I had to give up my first couple of cats in my divorce (circumstances prevented me from taking them with me) and, while they were probably having a great life being stroked by younger women (I imagine), I missed them badly. I always hoped I'd get a new cat some day. One that would refuse to be petted by anyone under thirty. For an eight-year period there was YouTube and cats on hoovers, cats on printers, cats in boxes. I now have two cats and a dog and feel like an actual mam. We call them the bairns. On the drive home from picking up Chief Brody, our first cat, I commented to Gary that it was like watching a really long YouTube video. I was half-expecting an email from YouTube asking if I was okay.

Sometimes I think babies look nice, but that's because they are on Facebook and are two-dimensional and silent. I had one passed to me recently and it didn't cry or wriggle; it just looked at me with a face that said 'You don't do this much, do you?' I held it until its mam took it back off me. People think that because you're a woman, you instinctively know what to do with them. What if I dropped it? What if it cried? I could not guarantee that neither of these things would happen. I've dropped my phone loads and I love that. You should be able to get a protective cover for babies. A rubberised shield with anti-glare film and a power dock so you could still charge it. When you're a beginner you don't know how to do the passes. You just have it put on you then taken off you. You have to communicate 'I'm done' with your face to a parent or you'll never get rid of it. Also, fuck me, it was heavy. I had no idea they were that heavy. Like one-and-a-half fat cats. No wonder mams have got arms like navvies.

I like the idea of having something that loves me unconditionally but would rather it was my family and friends and partner than actually creating a whole new person. Is there really no one else in the world who would love me unconditionally that I have to make my own? And anyway, that's what pets are for. They rely on you for everything and you read that as love. Well, that's what I used to think when we just had two cats, but now that we've got a dog I know it's definitely love. He wags his tail when he hears my voice; he has rested his little soft head on my big squishy belly without judgement. Though he does sometimes sniff my jeans and decide not to sit on my lap.

I think if we get any more pets, I'll make sure they're old rescue ones. You want your pets to be old when you are. No pensioner ever buys a kitten; they go to a shelter and adopt a cat with a similar walking speed and grouchy disposition as themselves. Maybe if I did change my mind about kids when I'm older, I could adopt a forty-year-old son and be motherly towards him four times a year (my birthday, his birthday, Mother's Day and Christmas).

Friends who have changed their mind did it when they hit their thirties or when they settled down with a partner. I am past that age group and I'm pleased to report that, aside from calling animals in the garden our pets, I have not moved on maternally. I won't change my mind, much as I'm unlikely to decide I want to start wearing heels or sign up for paragliding lessons. When you hit forty you are who you are and who you will always be.

The outside may get saggier and greyer, but the inside stays the same, I think. And what I am is a woman, a comedian, a wife and a mother of three furry babies. My friend, who is in the same camp as me, has started referring to actual babies as 'skin babies'. Fur babies and skin babies – it makes total sense to me.

So who's going to look after me when I'm old? That's a question you get a lot. Well, maybe I'll be lucky enough to be able to afford help. But I have befriended some younger women who are likely to outlive me, just in case. If they can open jars five years after my hands cannot, I will still be able to have jam. And you can get squeezy jam now, anyway.

I am not childless unless I am also cheeseless. I am a woman who has made the decision not to have children and I am entirely happy with it. I tend to think that, if you're of child-bearing age and having regular sex, it's quite the achievement not to fall pregnant. YAY ME. •swings bloody jam-rag above her head•

HOW TO BE CHAMPION

The same as drinking: don't let society or your family dictate how your life should be. Kids aren't for everyone. And 'I'm on big tablets' works just as well as a reason.

After holding someone's baby, don't say 'it's lovely' when passing it back. Parents are very keen on you knowing the gender of it.

Chapter 31

My Love of Stationery

STATIONERY IS STATIONARY. I'm not daft; I know the 'e for envelope' rule when spelling the word. What I mean is that, for me, stationery is calmness, a constant. No matter what has been going on in my life, pads and pens always make me happy. They're a shortcut to joy. I'm sure other people are cheered by purchasing clothes and jewellery, but when I want to treat myself I wander into a stationery shop and breathe out. Plus, I've never been too fat for a ringbinder.

In times of stress and success I turn to biros, pencil cases and, in a weaker moment, some crayons. I've been in Paperchase, Ryman, WHSmith, Staples and a little independent one near me where the old ladies on the counter use their brains to add up instead of tills, to cheer me up on a rubbish day, celebrate good test results and because it's my birthday. It's like alcohol, but with more wonderment and possibility, and less vomiting and ill-judged kissing.

I once revisited the pubs I used to frequent as a twenty-something with two old friends and was thrilled when I saw a member of the bar staff wandering around Kirkpatricks (South Shields, classy pub but horrible Miss World staircase to the loo) selling highlighters. I did think it a little odd, but I hadn't been on a pub crawl in ten years. *Clearly this is what they do now.* Turns out they were illuminous shots of booze. I glanced around expecting to see lots of similarly disappointed faces, but no – everyone was shiny and hammered and not even thinking about pens. Idiots.

Stationery is a fail-safe present for friends and family to buy me. My husband has even learnt what the optimum notepad is like (soft cover, lined and not too thick as I never fill them because I get too excited to start a new one).

A new notepad marks a new start. Anything could happen between these pages. It's a Monday morning. A 1 January. A first date or day one of a new job. And for me it IS my job. I'm a lot less computer savvy than my spectacles and social awkwardness at parties would have you assume. I downloaded two Louis CK specials and one by Maria Bamford and then couldn't find them on my laptop. Never found them. No clue.

My stand-up shows are entirely written in a collection of scrappy notebooks. I don't trust computers; they're all full of excuses. 'Oh, sorry your work has disappeared but your iCloud was damp/I thought you wanted a blank page saving/I'm an arsehole and I hate you.'

My notebooks are like someone you know rubbing your back: 'It's okay, I'm still in your handbag/on your bedside table/in the car. Here, have a clean page for all those new cock jokes.'

And breathe out.

HOW TO BE CHAMPION

Late August/early September is a great time for buying stationery as all the new back-to-school ranges are in the shops. You're welcome.

Chapter 32

Who Do You Think You Are?

MY FAMILY HAS always been proud and supportive of my unusual career choice. Indeed, they were proud and supportive when I got my first job at WHSmith and sold *Shields Gazettes* in a nylon skirt, when I wrote for the local free paper for free, when I sold all of my Sindy dolls via the boards at Asda, and when I left a perfectly good civil-service job to tell jokes to strangers for money.

So when my parents said there was one programme they'd love me to do, I was all ears. Ears that were nervous of *Family Fortunes*, *I'm a Celebrity* or *Jeremy Kyle*, but listening nonetheless. I suppose the latter does uncover new family members just the same. But at least with *Who Do You Think You Are?* the family members are all dead.

I only ever had my mam's dad and my dad's mam growing up, and I didn't know much about the family tree beyond that. My nana introduced me to crinkle-cut chips. Rumour had it she crinkled her own. She also pickled her own onions but used normal-sized onions so you'd get a jar with three in, like a tube of tennis balls. She also made bilberry pie and let me pick her sweet peas. I have in recent months started making pies, and last year I finally got sweet peas to grow and flower. I love the smell of them so much. My nana also had the biggest boobs on anyone I'd ever seen. And she let me tear her Yellow Pages up, which was much less impressive than when strong men do it; there's a photo of me just taking a page out at a time while knickerless on her living-room floor.

My granda had a greenhouse in his spare bedroom. Well, he grew plants in there and I sometimes helped. He used to spray bluebottles to death in his little house and leave them like a warning on the floor. My sister and I did his housework for a while and his Hoover looked like it had been sent back from Beamish – you know, the North East's ultimate open-air museum attraction – for being too old. We hoovered up the graveyard of flies with the Hoover from our house for fear of breaking his antique.

Every Christmas Eve, we'd go to his house for tea, and my sister and I would look forward to going to the nearby paper shop because the lady wore baubles as earrings. My granda would make everything from scratch and it was a wonderful feast of a picky tea. His potatoes deep-fried in batter were amazing. One year, as he was getting older, my mam suggested he didn't go to all that trouble and she'd just bring some bits from Marksies instead. He reluctantly agreed. On the day, as my mam was unpacking the bags, he asked how much he owed her for the food. She knew he didn't have much so just said a fiver. He was pleased and surprised by how cheap Marksies actually was despite its reputation for being pricey, and gave her a fiver every year after that to do the same.

One year before Christmas when we asked him what he wanted off Santa, he said, 'Don't waste your money on me. I don't need anything.' We decided to ignore that, which is a good job as when my dad brought him round at 7 a.m. on Christmas Day he opened the living-room door (if it was shut, it meant 'he'd been') and excitedly asked, 'Which one's my pile?'

A tradition in our family was that when you turned sixteen Granda took you to the pub. Sadly he died when I was fifteen so I never got the chance.

My parents had had a go at tracing the family tree but hit a brick wall, so a team of professionals with more than a pensioner's grasp of the internet and access to some helpful ladies in a library seemed like the only chance of answers. When the production company asked me, I felt I had to accept. They ask if they can start researching you, and if, after two months, your history is all pretty standard, they leave it alone. Thankfully, my past had some sparks of interest and so off I went for a fortnight into the unknown. I was told we were going to be somewhere very cold. They don't tell you where you're going or what they've found out until you're at an airport or in front of an expert with the camera rolling. Makes total sense but when the make-up artist Kat and I got 'cold-weather training', we knew it was going to be somewhere really cold. Russia? Canada? Gary said that the cold-weather training was probably just for the start of the show when I chat to my parents in South Shields. Cheeky bugger.

The cold-weather trainer told me to wear Spanx, as cotton knickers would make me colder. Something to do with sweat freezing. Or better still, he suggested, just go commando. He sat back all proud of himself. I told him in quite graphic detail how heavy my periods get and asked if I was just supposed to stick the fanny pad to my leg? Little did I know that we were going to end up in temperatures of around minus 26.

At the start of the shoot we travelled from my home to South Shields to see my parents. My mam had asked me not to include one of our relatives in the show. I explained we'd mostly be looking into the dead ones; it wasn't *Surprise Surprise*. They filmed my parents and asked what they thought we might uncover. My mam was convinced there was money because someone in her family had a piano. My favourite thing of the whole trip happened that day. My mam and dad were sitting around the table after being interviewed, and the sound man needed to record some 'wild sound', which is just what the room sounds like without anyone talking. All locations have a different sound so he needed us all to be quiet while he recorded just a minute of that room's version of silence. To identify the recording he held a boom mic in the middle of the room and said, 'Wild sound. Sarah's parents house. The back room.' At which point my dad leaned into the mic and said, 'Dining room.'

It turned out we were going to Canada, and at the airport the production team gave me some salopettes to try on in the airport loos. I tried on five or six pairs and none would shut around my belly. They told me not to worry and that we'd get some during our stopover in Toronto. We tried several shops in Toronto. I was too fat for snow. Even blokes' sizes wouldn't fit. Jesus. I knew they'd want me crying during the making of this programme but I had no idea it would start in the fitting rooms. We eventually found some that would do up – in a shop called HogTown. Rude.

The crew were great but regularly whispered in the corner about what the next day had in store. As Kat pointed out, it felt like they were always about to bring out a birthday cake. So after that, every time they came back over from whispering, Kat and I would start singing 'Happy Birthday to You'.

The trip was fascinating. I found out that one ancestor was one of the first divers, and another worked in the fur trade in Hudson Bay and lost both of his feet to frostbite. Such incredible stories.

Over the two weeks I walked in waist-deep snow, fell asleep during a very expensive helicopter trip (my excuse was that the beautiful scenery was 'very samey'), waved at some kids on Orkney, cried in various countries, recorded an interview a second time as the first time all they could hear was the expert's terrified heartbeat, helped get twenty-six pieces of luggage and equipment off a million planes, found out they use rivers as roads when they're frozen, searched for a phone in the snow (and found it!), fell in the snow, farted in a diving outfit, shouted, 'Get in the fucking helicopter!' and googled ahead when they wouldn't tell me what was happening the next day. Google had nothing. Of course Google had nothing, otherwise the show would be called 'Who Googled My Ancestors?'

The schedule was punishing, the expedition draining but it was extraordinary. Thank you, BBC. You've made a comedian's parents very happy. Technically my job, but we'll skirt over that.

HOW TO BE CHAMPION

Never listen to a man telling you what kind of pants you should wear.

Singing 'Happy Birthday to You' is always fun. Especially if it's no one's birthday.

When someone dies, put up photos of them in happier times around the house. We had them everywhere when my granda died: on mirrors, back of the toilet door. That way, the image you had of them old and potentially ill is replaced by, in my case, a picture of me standing wearing a hat out of a cracker, beside my granda who is beaming in a brown cardigan.

Finding out about your ancestry is fascinating. What I took from it is that their strength and determination are just sort of in me. It feels like I have strong characters sitting on my shoulders and we're ready for anything.

Oh, and a bag of shopping from Marksies does not cost a fiver.

Chapter 33

Sometimes I Hate Myself

ASK ME HOW I feel about my body and my answer changes daily, maybe even hourly. At this moment in time I'm okay, but that's because I'm not near any reflective surfaces.

Last night, at a charity gig, a photographer who did not smell great, but was a volunteer so I felt bad for even thinking that, went through a huge amount of photos he had taken of me on stage. He did a nervous giggle when we got to the end because I hadn't okayed any of them. I asked him to pick two he liked and show me them. He did, they weren't hideous, I signed them off. For someone who often hates what she looks like, I have to have my photo taken a lot.

At the time of writing, I have photo shoots coming up for this book and my next tour. I'm dreading them. Not because of the shoots themselves, as I control them very carefully, always using photographers I know, whose work I love and who I feel comfortable with. I always have the same make-up artist too. Kat is someone I trust and like and who knows how to make my face look its best. Someone who would mention my eyebrows with something like, 'Ooh, you've got a couple of stray hairs, can I get them?' rather than, 'Oh God, I'll have to sort your eyebrows,' while visibly wincing at my face. That has happened. More than once. Wincing. Like I'd plastered myself in dog shit and forgotten to tell her. It's almost like being pretty isn't my fucking job. Or anything I'm obliged to be. Sorry if my eyebrows are too bushy for me to be funny on a chat show. That could only happen if my eyebrows were so ginormous they had grown into my ears, mouth and brain. Otherwise, honestly, who cares? Ah, some of the public care and comment on it at will.

I've had some very odd experiences at photo shoots in the past. Because you're a comic, you get asked to do weird things that the photographer or whoever is running the session thinks are funny. Some things I have been asked to do for photo shoots include:

- Jump in the air.
- Peep out of a telephone box.
- Wear handcuffs (I refused).
- Wear lens-free glasses as the brilliantly impressive photographer couldn't take photos of me in my glasses because of the reflection. I've had my photo taken a million times and this has only once come up. My dad can take a photo of me with an iPhone and you can't see the reflection.
- Stand with my hands on my hips (classic Millican pose).
- Dress up like *Downton Abbey* holding a pug in a bonnet (my idea).
- Stare wistfully out of the window on a train – for *Who Do You Think You Are?*

- Eat a muffin (my idea).
- Hold an axe over a child's head (my idea).
- Sit in front of a squirrel on a plate (my idea).
- Laugh in a fake-fur coat outside (I did it inside).
- Hang on a coat hook by a backpack on my back.
- Drink from a mug (another classic Millican pose).
- Sit with my legs up and to the side with my arms out (very odd).
- Dress up as Rosie the Riveter (my idea).
- Hold an ice cream on a windy day.
- Shrug (like I'm thinking, Who's this cunt?).
- Throw my notes in the air.
- Pop out from behind a door.
- Wear unflattering smocks because I'm not a size 10 so we'd better hide it all. The sort of thing your mam would put on you when you were five and you'd decided to get your paints out.
- Be my husband's legs (I was happy to do this – and I got to sit on a gym horse).

A couple of these photos are in the obligatory photo section of this book.

The reason I'm worried about the upcoming photo shoots is because however I look and feel about how I look on those two days will be in print on the cover of books and tour posters for years. Literally years. And on the internet for all eternity.

When I look at my face right now I'm annoyed that I didn't put make-up on when I got out of the shower. Not the whole shebang like mascara and lip liner. Just a small amount of tinted moisturiser that takes down my rosacea a little and makes me look less tired. Sort of levels me off.

I first started wearing make-up when I had horrendous acne in my teens. It came on quite suddenly and we were never sure if it was an allergic reaction or acne. There were spots all over my chest, all down my back, on my face and through my hair. My mam took me to the doctor. Our nice lady one wasn't available so we saw one of the blokes, who suggested I put calamine lotion through my hair every day. Calamine lotion, FFS. I think my mam saw the terror in my eyes that I didn't want more things to make me stand out. Permed, soft, white hair. I would have to go to bingo to blend in. We then went to see the lady doctor who put me on some mild antibiotics, which vastly improved it in about two days. Amazing. Someone did warn me, like in a fairy story, that I was only delaying puberty and I would get all of those spots whenever I stopped taking the pills. HAHA – I took those pills for twelve years and braced myself when I came off them but nothing happened, weird stranger who foretold my spotty future. Those magic beans you gave me were shit, as well. And I'm not eating that apple.

I think there have been a number of contributing factors to not seeing myself in a very positive light:

- Being laughed at for what I was wearing/my hair/my face/ my glasses.
- That French teacher helping kids learn adjectives by saying in French that I was fat (I wasn't, but even if I was . . .).

- A man at the marketplace, when I was thirteen, saying that if he'd bashed me in the face with a big metal pole it wouldn't have made any difference.
- Social media. Every time I'm on the telly I get vitriol. I tend not to reply these days as I read somewhere that a troll's main aim is get a reaction. I suppose some of these people are trolls, but a lot are just people who think you need to know that they didn't like what you were wearing. The hardest bit about doing a telly job is finding something to wear. Something that is suitable and looks nice isn't easy when you're not a size 10. As the majority of shops don't want you in their clothes, you are restricted to four or five places. Telly cameras can't handle certain patterns, like stripes and spots. So you find a dress you like, with a pattern the cameras can handle, and which looks okay when you sit down in it. I used to do a quick scan to see what the public could hate about it. Not any more. Fuck that shit. If I like it, and it won't go strobey on the telly, I'm having it. I get shite no matter what I'm wearing so why not just please myself?
- Reviews in newspapers and on websites describing my physical appearance when it is not relevant. I've been described as 'homely', 'sturdy', 'dumpy'. Why is this relevant? Are you laughing? Are the audience laughing? That's one of the reasons I love live work. The public in a comedy audience don't care what you're wearing. On tour, I try to look 'okay'. I don't overly dress up and I won't just wear jeans. Somewhere in the middle. Because I want them to listen to what I'm saying, not notice what I look like at all. Because it isn't relevant.

- Women's magazines showing us how we are supposed to look. Am I beach-body ready? I've got a book and no socks on, so yes. Whenever I'm at the hairdressers, I take a photo of the magazines they give me to read with me flicking the Vs in the foreground and send it to my pal Mickey, who edited *Standard Issue* magazine. She loves it. I will not run my life based on a simplified, limited idea of what a woman is. I've never had a pedicure, I don't wear high heels, I don't know what shape I am, I buy whatever shampoo is on special offer and I don't care what size tits are in fashion right now.
- Women on the telly largely being tiny (see below). I nearly ate Amanda Holden once. I feel like fucking Hodor whenever I'm near another woman on telly. But oddly, standing beside a bloke I look pretty normal.
- Going shopping for clothes (see below).
- Getting my hair done (too many mirrors).

I always think I look massive on the telly but fine round Asda. Backstage after a telly recording once, I had my photo taken with the executive producer of the show and her wife. They stood either side of me, sort of tucked behind me. I asked what was going on and they explained to me a brilliant way to look smaller in group photos. They were both about the same size as me, maybe a little bigger, and they said the best thing to do is, firstly, make sure you're not the one standing in the middle. Then proceed to tuck half of yourself behind the person who IS in the middle. And this is exactly what they'd done. In the photo, I was standing face-on, full-on. They were each coquettishly tucking a boob behind my back.

The next time I had my photo taken, I thought I'd give it a try. It was on *The Big Fat Quiz of the Year*. They take the photos before the show as the recording is generally five hours long and they don't want photos of tired, crabby, shiny comedians. I was at the front, on one side of Jimmy Carr, who had Mel B, the Spice Girl, on his other side. Mel B was, as expected, wafer thin. I thought, If I don't make myself look smaller, compared to her I'm going to look like a fucking wardrobe. So I did it. I tucked a boob behind Jimmy Carr. And because I love the man and thought he would like to know, I told him. I said quietly, 'I'm just tucking a boob behind you, Jimmy,' and he said, 'Oh, good Lord.'

Going shopping for clothes is something I've got better at. I blast all four shops that consider me worth clothing then go home. I'm a size 18 and I sometimes think being a 14 or 16 is worse as you can ALMOST get in clothes in loads of shops but not quite. If I walk past Topshop and see a pretty dress in the window it's like I'm passing an art gallery. Oh, that's bonny. Whereas if I was a size 16, I'd try it on and potentially be disappointed when I looked like the Michelin Man in a tea dress.

If you want to know how bad shopping can be, see the salopettes fun in Chapter 32. I once got cut out of a dress in Monsoon. I told the personal shopper it was too small but she was convinced it would fit. And it did. As long as I wanted to live in it. Even now, if I hear on the news, 'Monsoon kills eighty,' I think, I'm not surprised – I could barely breathe in that brown satin halter dress.

My problem with the way women are judged is that I don't think physical appearance is important. Vital that you're a nice person – good, honest, caring, interested and interesting – but the outside? Nah, mate. You can tell how keen I am on being judged in this way by the photo of me coming third in a bonny-baby contest (see picture section). I'm wearing flares, I look bored, my dad is telling me to smile at the camera – I am blatantly refusing. Still came third though, eh? •kisses guns•

Some folk think famous people need to take the criticism. Probably not you lovely lot as you've bought my book and like me already. But maybe a friend of yours, who hates comedy or women or Geordies or glasses-wearers or just me, has asked to borrow my book from you. You're surprised because you know they hate everyone who wears glasses, even Gok Wan (and who could hate him?), but you lend it nonetheless as maybe he's trying to change. That person may think that when you're famous, anything goes. Your head is above the parapet and you have to take it. And to these people I say abuse is abuse regardless of the situation. If I had a doctor who was a perfectly good doctor but I thought he wasn't as attractive as I'd like him to be, or his tie didn't match his shirt or the hair on his arms bothered me, I wouldn't tell him. Because (a) I'm a nice person, (b) I don't notice shit like that and (c) it doesn't matter. A lot of my body-image questions can be answered with 'it doesn't matter'. But I would like to like myself more.

I was fascinated to hear Claudia Winkleman say recently during a *Standard Issue* event* that her mam never allowed mirrors in the house when Claudia was growing up. What a

---

* You can listen to the podcast.

wonderful idea. That you have to concentrate more on your personality as your face and body don't matter. I think we had a normal amount of mirrors growing up, though the last time I stayed with my parents they seemed to have more. I'd go as far as to say too many. I know that because I watched a fat woman have a shower. You think that's bad? My dad told me he watched an old man have a shit.

I used to have what they call negative automatic thoughts: a mean thought would pop into my head very quickly and I'd disagree with it, which I suppose is a good sign. One example was when my fella and I went to a summer wedding, and I took a selfie of us in our glad rags on the walk from the car as the sun was out and everything was green and beautiful. In bed that night, into my brain popped: *Well, no one said anything so I mustn't have looked horrific.* (By the way, it's really hard to write this chapter.) My logical brain immediately retaliated with, *Of course you didn't look horrific*, because what is horrific? An extra from *The Walking Dead* is horrific, and I know I definitely had all of my innards tucked into my knickers and hidden behind a maxi dress.

I think you have to take your worth from yourself. If you don't look like people do on the telly, it doesn't matter. If you have nothing in common with the women and men in magazines, it doesn't matter. They're not the norm. Magazine women are put there to make us buy stuff. All it makes me want to buy is food. And fewer magazines. Fuck that, none. If you know that you are a good person, kind, hardworking, interesting and interested then go with that. Fuck what your hair looks like. Or your nails. The heels of my feet are covered in such hard skin that they make a noise on wooden floors. Do I dash out and get hard-skin-melting shite from Boots? No, I just think, If shoes become scarce I'll be fine. My husband once said that skin is nature's shoes. Sometimes I put slut-red nail varnish on so I look like a sexy hobbit. A year or so ago I took part in the *Guilty Feminist* podcast for my friend Deborah Frances-White. I really like her and she's got a good brain on her so I was happy to be a guest on her show. I recorded two episodes. One was about women's magazines. That was a piece of piss. I bought a few and was determined to cover them in skull-and-crossbones wrapping paper. I backed them, like we did with exercise books at school. I forgot how satisfying it was. But getting hold of the wrapping paper was tricky – I looked in all the likely shops and searched online. Nothing. Then I walked past a toy shop in Bournemouth and spotted it in the doorway. I bought so many sheets the lady on the till said, 'This must be for a very big pirate present.' I just smiled because it was easier than telling her I was giving women's magazines the covering I thought they deserved.

I listed what was in the magazines – 'How to fake a facelift' and other such bullshit. I compared it to what was on the home page of my *Standard Issue* magazine, which included abortion, *Game of Thrones*, a film review, kid tantrums, lady sheds, mental health and British Science Week. Because women are interested in everything.

The other show was trickier. It was about knowing your worth. I think when I said yes to doing the show I couldn't quite work out how I felt about it – it's a work in progress for me. I think better of myself than I used to. I think that's because now I allow myself to take my worth from me rather than from others.

A good example of this is an old review I only saw the other day. I wasn't looking for it; I try not to see these things. For the title sequence for *Who Do You Think You Are?* they make you do this thing where you turn and smile at the same time. And I can't. But until then I did not know that because nobody had asked me. Why would it come up? I was with my friend Tom and he said, 'Oh, remember those titles? I laughed out loud when I saw yours.' We tried to find them online and they are available. They're hilarious because all of the people who are actors were great at it. That's just a normal day for them, turning and smiling. All of the people who weren't actors, like John Simpson and me, were just shit at it. I urge you all to google it.

I had to do mine in public. We were out and about, and by the time I'd 'nailed it', as in done one that was acceptable to the producers, there was a crowd. So while we were looking for the clips I sort of fell across the review. Tom said, 'Don't read it!' but I thought it was ages ago and also it's different. If you do a stand-up show they can say 'it's shit', but I didn't think they could say 'your ancestors are shit'.

This is from the review of the show.

Sarah Millican has made audiences laugh with a piping Geordie voice and a dumpy figure. Seemingly designed to model printed floral dresses and wellies but she soon shows that she is not as daft as she looks.

Now, at the moment, are you aware of what this is reviewing? This is reviewing my physical appearance, not my ancestors. No mention of a diver there. Or the fur trade.

So then it says:

In Who Do You Think You Are?, *BBC One, discovering that her ancestor James Hoult, a marine diver, had by 1851, age thirty-four, fathered five children, she exclaimed, 'I'm thirty-seven and I've just got a cat.'*

That's fair enough. It's factually accurate for the time. I've since got another cat and a dog.

Perhaps it was because of her professional success, as we were told followed on the heels of a divorce after seven years of marriage, that she was so moved to discover of her ancestors' struggle to leave descendants . . .

Why watch the rest of the programme when you could just assume . . .?

So one minute she appeared comically out from a diving suit of the kind Hoult would have worn and the next minute wept as she learnt of his making a gift to seven children left orphans by a shipwreck. He was an all round good man, she declared with more loyalty than evidence.

It's quite harsh, isn't it? My favourite bit is at the end.

SOMETIMES I HATE MYSELF

But Malcolm, lost one day in the freezing waste, suffered frostbite so that both of his feet had to be amputated at the trading station. 'I expected that to be his end but amazingly he returned to Orkney, married and fathered five children of his own. I was unprepared for how protective I'd feel of my ancestors,' Millican concluded. Perhaps aware of her big new house with only the cat waiting for her return.

What the actual fuck? So what that review has done is said that I'm dumpy, I wear flowery dresses and wellies, and there's a dig in the middle about only having a cat instead of children because obviously kids are the be all and end all, and then the big empty house with just a cat for company. So I am worthless unless I am married with children. Sure, she's got feet, but that's it, right? And they're in wellies anyway. Doesn't she have any heels? OH, FUCK OFF.

From the same newspaper, by a different journalist as that guy hadn't written any more reviews of *Who Do You Think You Are?*, I found a review that was of a man's episode. It was Paul Hollywood. So I read his and at various points it says, 'It made for an absorbing and affecting hour of televison.' They call him a 'silver fox' and it made me wonder what is the female equivalent of a silver fox? There isn't one.

Meanwhile Hollywood, so exacting in the Bake Off *tent, and often the butt of co-presenter's jokes, came across beautifully. He was palpably proud of his forebears and touched by his grandfather's love letters home to his sweetheart yet never wallowed in sentimentality, turning away from cameras when he had something in his eye and retaining his dryly self-deprecating sense of humour. Good bloke, good bake.*

Now, this is not a dig at Paul Hollywood, he's a lovely man. But this never mentions that he is a little bit overweight, never mentions what he's wearing, what his family situation is like, whether he has a wife, kids – anything like that.

They didn't start by saying, 'Lonely, grey-haired, dumpy Paul Hollywood has made his career by eating bread and wearing boring blue shirts.' They're not trying to hide how they feel. They're not even trying to disguise their misogyny. I'm not attractive to them or a mother so therefore I'm worthless.

And then, of course, there is the *Irish Mirror*'s recent and brilliant story about my 'incredible weight loss'. Well, it started in the *Irish Mirror* and spread to the *Mirror, Sun, Express* and Newcastle's *Evening Chronicle*. In the story about my 'incredible weight loss', some photos of me were compared. The one to signify fat, past me was from a *Never Mind the Buzzcocks* in 2014, where, during the group shot, I had my arm around Lethal Bizzle (lovely man). The one to signify new, better, slimmer me was from a year ago, though they cited it as recent as I'd posted it up on my Instagram days before. My show *Outsider* was on Channel 4 so I popped up a pic of me backstage at the DVD recording with my dog on my knee. Please note that this photo was taken by someone who knows and likes me and I selected it for Instagram.

Now is probably a good time to tell you that I am fatter than ever, heavier than I've ever been, and give fewer fucks than ever before. The paper said my 'incredible' weight loss had been paired with 'freshly dyed brunette hair'. Yep, I went brown two years ago. Well done. Also, the photo they described as me looking 'healthier' was taken after two hours of make-up. And it was a selfie so the camera was up high for chins.

What led them to believe I was on a 'health kick', then? Oh yes, a photo of some satsumas on Instagram. I can only assume that they genuinely thought that before then I just ate nothing but cakes and biscuits. I'm sorry if I'm letting you all down, but I also eat fruit and veg, meat, bread – loads of things. One satsuma plus two self-controlled, more flattering photos equals 'incredible weight loss'. Hilarious. A photo caption in one version of this utter load of cack said 'not the woman she once was'. Yep, I definitely am. If anything, I'm more of that woman.

If a newspaper prints a story that you've slimmed down and implies that you're a better person now than fatty belatty from before, that is bad enough. You are the same person whatever weight, and no better if you're thinner. But imagine if that happens and the slimmer bit isn't true. That article basically said 'Sarah Millican is fat, isn't she?' But it's so ridiculous. That it's a 'news story' is actually hilarious. My reason for mentioning it here is so you can see what rubbish it is. I'm waiting 'til they see a photo of one of the cats for their 'Sarah Millican has a ginger baby and it's deformed' story.

So while battling these outside forces, I need to find my own worth.

Yesterday, I made a decision to try to help myself. To value the bits I like and ignore the bits I don't. I put the bathroom scales in the cupboard; I've started getting dressed away from the full-length mirrors that adorn our wardrobes (this house previously belonged to more confident folk). I'm going to do more of my big, fast walks. I'm going to remember that what I look like is neither here nor there. I'll let you know if it's working.

The photo shoots for the cover of this book and the next tour poster are both within the next two weeks, at the time of writing. I've got a wardrobe lady helping me get some clothes. I told her I didn't have time to lose weight. She told me just to get new bras. I mentioned in an email to her yesterday that I don't need what I call 'sucky-in knickers'. Take me as I am, kids. I'm not getting thrush or sitting uncomfortably so I look better to others. I'll pluck me tash (I'm not a monster) but I am human-shaped. And you'll have to accept me as that. I am the norm. A heavily lipsticked, hair-curled, top-ironed version of me. A me I like.

Small update: both photo shoots were an absolute joy. We filmed tits up, which is usually a phrase that means things have gone badly, but not in this case. Tits up meant I didn't worry about my belly or shoes,* three things I'm not keen on. My new bra worked a treat and my make-up lady is a hero. I chose the spotty top I'm wearing on the cover of this book because it's a bit clowny and reminded me of an all-in-one I used to wear for bed when I was about seven. A clown all-in-one complete with the collar and frilly elasticated cuffs and ankles. I loved it. Even on the day I was sick and puked

---

* Hate shoes.

in the sink. With the long-gone innocence of someone who trusts their bowels, I pushed out a fart while puking, only for something wet to hit the inside of my clown suit and run down. My mam loved my clown suit that day too, as the elasticated ankles saved her kitchen floor. I totally get how some people are scared of clowns.

For both photo shoots I worked with photographer friends and the rooms were filled with flattering light and lovely supportive people who like me. And I love the photos. I look like me but GREAT. The old crappy body image got a bit of a talking to that day. And to paraphrase Elbow, one day like this a year really helps.

HOW TO BE CHAMPION

If you have bad body image, remember that it is ever-changing. It comes and goes. Some days it's fine •kisses guns• and some days it's not. I worked out that it wasn't a case of finding the one thing that makes me like the way I look and then I'm sorted. Little things can nibble away at it and then one good thing can balance it out for a while. It's a work in progress.

Chapter 34

Ten Good Things About Being a Bit Overweight

1. No one expects me to give anything up for Lent
2. I never need to iron clothes as I just fill them out
3. I never lose food through a thigh gap
4. I'm comfy to lie on
5. I'm warm
6. Strong winds don't blow my car around when I'm in it
7. I never worry about putting a bit of weight on over Christmas
8. I'm not easy to tip over (some boys threatened to throw me into the canal at Deansgate locks in Manchester once; I encouraged them to try – they backed off)
9. Clothes shopping is in some ways quicker as there are only four shops
10. The dog rests his head on my belly in bed sometimes and 'I've never felt so accepted for who I am

Chapter 35

The Poo Holiday of 2011

GARY DOESN'T FLY so we've always had to be quite creative with holidays. This instance was just a few days in Brighton. I love Brighton. I never normally remember which year I did what, which is why this book is occasionally quite vague. I sometimes just remember things by hairdo. Blonde bowl cut then 'the perm years', short like my sister's, short and I've cut it myself to save money, blonde bob, Hollywood hair (when it was long and brown, but only Hollywood when a hairdresser or make-up artist had spent an hour on it; I just put it in a wet bun) and now. But this holiday has a name.

Most holidays are known by the place or who you went with. Some examples you could use: Spain with the girls, Cornwall with the folks, Malaga with that twat. This holiday's name is the Poo Holiday of 2011. The first instance of crap happened on our way down to Brighton. Simple, this was: stopped at the services for a wee, where I trod in dog shit as I stepped back into the car. Gary pulled in to a lay-by where I spent fifteen minutes meticulously cleaning the dog shit from the grooves of the left shoe of a very old pair. I used tissues, wipes and cotton buds. Then, when it was definitely clear of shite, I threw the shoe in the bushes. It took the full fifteen minutes of retching and de-shitting for me to realise they were very old battered shoes I should have binned ages ago. My husband couldn't believe what had just happened, but he was about to pay me back substantially.

Part two (of three) involved Jimmy Spices.* I blame comedian Carl Donnelly for this part, as he had recommended this eatery of wonder. Imagine every kind of food you can think of, all buffet-style. Of course, all Gary ate was meat. Meats from around the world, of course, but meat. Just meat. When we checked into our posh Brighton hotel we didn't think for a second that hours later we'd be scouring the room for something to unblock the toilet with. At one point he shouted from the bathroom, 'A coat hanger! Pass me a coat hanger!'

I shouted back, 'They're padded!'

We should have stayed in a Premier Inn after all. But this hotel clearly had what my husband describes as an 'eco toilet'. He would rather believe that all modern toilets are equipped for a lesser amount of shite due to the environment than admit he is older and fatter and eats more meat than ever before. We tried all the usual ways of unblocking the loo: a carrier

---

* I genuinely thought it was called Jimmy Five Spices because I clearly got the all-you-can-eat world buffet restaurant mixed up with that bloke Gazza used to knock about with, Jimmy Five Bellies.

bag, a small towel (these methods involve creating a vacuum and quacking the poo away). They didn't work. He tracked down a hardware shop and came back with a huge bottle of some kind of industrial fluid. Maybe it would dissolve the poo mountain. NOPE.

In the end, I suggested he ring downstairs to see if the hotel had a maintenance man. We had three more days there and I was going to need to wee and poo myself quite soon. I told him to make up a story about how he'd spilt something and mopped it up with loo roll then tried to flush the loo roll and accidentally blocked the toilet. I sometimes think he doesn't listen to me at all. He rang and said, 'Excuse me, but I've done a massive poo and it won't go away. Is there a fifty-year-old man you can send up to help me?' He just asked for a maintenance man, but his voice said an older bloke. Like a dad, please.

While I was clenching my arsehole mostly from embarrassment but also because I had something solid on the horizon, there was a knock at the door. No burly man – just a young, slight French girl holding a giant plunger. My husband, ever the gent, said, 'I can't let you see this but I will borrow that. Thanks, love.' He took the plunger and shut the door. Plunger worked.

Remember, this all happened on day one. DAY FUCKING ONE. By day three it was very obvious that something else was now blocked: the husband. Too much meat had taken us through poo mountain to a brick wall. Like the one Wile E. Coyote uses to try to kill the Road Runner. But on this one, he'd painted a big sore tummy. We tried everything: padded hangers, carrier bag, hand towel, industrial fluid. He even went to the NHS walk-in centre and asked for an arse plunger, or whatever the medical term is. At one point he had all of this in his system:

Prune juice (two bottles of)
Syrup of figs (one bottle of)
Grapes (some of)
Over-the-counter bad stuff as recommended by the doctor at the NHS walk-in place
Something else herbal from one of Brighton's wanky shops
Senokot (maximum dose)

I was surprised the amount of liquid didn't just force the shit out. I suppose it did – gradually, thankfully. We were a bit scared he was just going to go BANG. We had second-row seats for *Joseph and the Amazing Technicolor Dreamcoat* that night, and we were worried the poor bloke's coat was going to be just the one colour that night. 'It was . . . brown and brown and brown and brown . . .'

HOW TO BE CHAMPION

Don't eat just meat.

Cheaper hotels have more versatile hangers.

Give all holidays names.

Chapter 36

The BAFTA Article

IN 2014 I was nominated for a BAFTA for my television programme. I was up against Charlie Brooker, Graham Norton and Ant and Dec, so I was just going for a lovely night out. It went all to shit. Here is an article I wrote for my column in the *Radio Times*.

I am a comedian. You may or may not find me funny, but the fact remains that I am a comedian. This feels like a defensive start to a column but you will soon understand why.

Last year, I was nominated for a BAFTA. Me. The quiet girl at school. The awkward girl at college. The funny woman at work. A BAFTA. And in a genderless category too. Alongside the entertainment greats: Graham Norton, Charlie Brooker and Ant and Dec. It felt ridiculous but I was thrilled. I've been nominated for awards before (even won a couple) and it really is the best. If winning is chips and gravy then being nominated is still chips. Lovely, lovely chips.

On the run up to the ceremony, plans were made. This here smashing magazine asked me to present an award, someone asked if I wanted my hair and make-up doing, my fella took the night off to accompany me, my friend asked if she could come shopping with me for my dress. Yes, yes, all of this, yes.

My friend and I danced into John Lewis knowing that (a) they have lots of mini shops in there, and (b) I can fit into most of their clothes. Fancy expensive designer shops are out for me as I'm a size 18, sometimes 20, and I therefore do not count as a woman to them.

We knew which one was the right one as soon as I swished back the curtain and both my friend and I oohed. At the till, when asked, I told the lady it was for a wedding as I was too embarrassed to announce I was off to the BAFTAs.

On the day, my fella and I drove to London, parked, and I had my hair and make-up done while he read his book nearby. We got changed into our glad rags in the toilets of the hotel spa that was the pre-show base. I don't have any interest in shoes so just popped my comfy black patent leather Marksies ones on. He helped me with my new necklace and off we went.

The red carpet is very intimidating, though I garnered a few laughs when I replied to the 'Who are you wearing?' question with 'John Lewis' and 'Where did you get your dress?' with 'The Trafford Centre'. I had a few awkward photos taken by the wall of paparazzi. Awkward, as I'm not a model (I'm a comedian), have never learnt how to pose on a red carpet (I'm a comedian) and I have pretty low self-esteem.

My husband wasn't once asked who he was wearing, which he was disappointed by. Mainly because he was dying to tell ANYONE he was wearing an Asda tux. Not one of the cheap ones, as he likes to point out; it was £60.

The ceremony itself was a wonder. Everywhere I looked were the best in the business. Writers I'd admired, actors I'd cried to, comedians who'd made me laugh so much I got a headache. Amazing people being applauded for being bloody good at their jobs. I'd heard the phrase 'knees knocking' before but didn't know it was an actual thing 'til I presented the *Radio Times* Audience award. It went okay, I don't think I messed up, and I went back to my seat.

After the ceremony, we had a lovely meal (apart from one of the courses, which had soil on it, intentionally) with the *Radio Times* lot and then I bullied Stephen Mangan into introducing me to Matt LeBlanc. Night made, we went back to the car to drive home.

In order not to dilly-dally, my husband did the first stint of driving while I got out of my dress at various traffic lights in central London. Driving clothes on, I checked my phone. Loads of friends and family had texted the expected 'You were robbed', which I wasn't, but they're my friends and family so they're supposed to think that.

Then I went onto Twitter and it was like a pin to my excitable red balloon. Literally thousands of messages from people criticising my appearance. I was fat and ugly as per usual. My dress (you know, the one that caused oohs in a department-store fitting room?) was destroyed by the masses. I looked like a nana, my dress was disgusting, was it made out of curtains, why was I wearing black shoes with it? I cried. I cried in the car.

And that wasn't it. The next day, I was in newspapers, pilloried for what I was wearing. I was discussed and pulled apart on *Lorraine*.

I'm sorry. I thought I had been invited to such an illustrious event because I am good at my job. Putting clothes on is such a small part of my day. They may as well have been criticising me for brushing my teeth differently to them.

Yes, there were lovely messages from my fans between the hate, but the hate was dominant and made me upset at first and then furious. Why does it matter so much what I was wearing? Why did no one ask my husband where he got his suit from? I felt wonderful in that dress. And surely that's all that counts.

I made a decision the following day that should I ever be invited to attend the BAFTAs again, I will wear the same dress. To make the point that it doesn't matter what I wear; that's not what I'm being judged on. With the added fun of answering the red-carpet question 'Where did you get your dress?' with 'Oh, it's just last year's, pet'.

And so I was invited back to the BAFTAs. Nominated again, indeed. Sadly, I am working that night. But if you have tickets to see my show in Buxton on 18 May, you may see me making my point anyway.

I did wear my BAFTA dress for my show at the Buxton Opera House. And bless that audience. When I came out, they knew why I had on a lovely flowery dress and gave me a standing ovation. My first, and will always remain my most precious.

It's the closest I've come to crying on stage. I blinked back the tears and performed my show. And some little smasher dropped a present off at the stage door for me. It's a fairy's wand, the sort you'd give an excitable six-year-old girl so she could grant wishes at her princess-themed birthday party. Not the weirdest gift I've ever had. That would be an advent calendar where behind every door was a picture of me. Even Jesus just put himself behind one door. Attached to the fairy's wand was a label with the letters BAFTA, spelling out Buxton Award For a Tremendous Attitude. That wand takes pride of place on my bookshelf. Thank you, whoever you are.

HOW TO BE CHAMPION

Don't be mean on social media. I told a journalist friend of mine that if I don't like a film I've seen at the cinema I don't mention it on social media, as there's too much negativity and vitriol (I know what that means now) on there already. He said, 'Well, you're a better man than me.' I said, 'Of course I am, you're a journalist.' That's a bit mean. Some of my best friends are journalists.

Don't be mean to people you know and don't be mean to people you don't. You have no idea what someone is dealing with at the time. Be nice or be quiet.

Chapter 37

Standard Issue

IN 2014 I set up *Standard Issue*, a no-bullshit women's magazine, and Mickey Noonan, Kiri Pritchard-McLean and I had our first meeting. Months before I had wooed journalist Mickey over mocktails and tapas at Browns in Leeds. Weeks before that I had emailed a handful of awesome women I knew asking what they thought of my idea to set up an online women's magazine that was the antidote to what is currently available to women – diety, lipsticky, orgasmy shite. Weeks before that I had a conversation with Annabel Giles – model, TV presenter, novelist and excellent pal of mine – about how women disappear. And I don't mean that when women get to a certain age they feel invisible because they aren't the target of advertisers, they're not flirted with, they don't count. Although that is certainly true. I mean that if you're over a certain age in television, more so, and media in general, you don't exist. I felt bad that wonderful women with stories to tell and experiences to share and lessons we can all learn from had no voice. People were willing to listen but had no way of hearing them. It was on that drive home from seeing Annabel that the *Standard Issue* seed was planted.

Included in the initial email to Sara Pascoe – comedian, writer, pal and one of the first women I contacted – are these two paragraphs:

> *What I propose is an altogether new kind of women's maga-zine online. One for all women. One where no woman feels bad or inadequate when reading it. One with no celebrity tittle-tattle, no photoshopping, no calorie-counting, no cellulite-circling. Just honest, good and funny journalism.*
>
> *When I used to read women's mags (and one of the reasons why I stopped), it didn't feel like a safe place. It felt like with every page I turned there was a chance I was about to be made to feel inadequate. I'd like to make a safe place for women to read about everything that involves us, so everything.*

What surprises me reading this three years later is that that is exactly what we did. A line from Sara's response was like a call to arms: 'It's not enough to just complain; you create an alternative and show that it is popular and possible.'

How easy it is to complain. And I've done it loads. While standing in a WHSmith in a train station scanning the maga-zine racks for anything that might appeal but also not sink its teeth into my wobbly self-esteem. What if I'm not getting enough orgasms? I can sort myself out in less than five minutes. When is the right time to wear white jeans? I have unpredict-able and heavy periods and stress-related IBS, and I sit on grass a lot and have a dog that likes putting his paws on my legs to say hi. So white jeans for me would be patterned in no time. How will I get my body ready for summer? I shave my fucking legs. I shave my fucking legs and that is it.

I hate the celebrity bashing in women's magazines. WOMAN, successful at her job, whose very inclusion in this dishrag helps increase the sales and therefore pays our wages, goes on a holiday and dares to dress like you would on a holiday. Also, she eats food. Eurgh.

Oh, I've complained. I complained when my perfectly fine dress on BAFTA night was considered awful by people whose job it is to bully and state their opinion as fact. 'Women who have big boobs shouldn't wear big patterns.' You know that one, right, guys? Though shalt not kill, covet thy neighbour's wife or deign to wear a flower print on your generous jubblies.

Sara's words struck a chord. Don't just moan. Do something. So I did. I rallied my women troops, I wooed the best journalist I knew to be the editor and we got cracking. I thought making a brilliant magazine would be the hard bit. Turns out, no. If you surround yourself with excellent women who are all rooting for the greater good – in this case making women feel good, definitely not making them feel shit, giving them something ace to read that assumed they were bright, smart and interested in everything as a starting point – making a crazy-good magazine is pretty straightforward. And when you tell incredible writers they can write about anything they like, they get very excited. They step out of the pink prison of 'Spiralise yourself thin', 'Thirty ways to get him to notice you', 'Eye shadows to make you stand out in the office', and step into 'Why Bruce Springsteen might be the US President', 'Shit tips – help with IBS', 'Dealing with the death of a sibling' and a quiz on Sean Bean's TV and film deaths plus regular articles on mental health, realistic motherhood, women's charities and exceptional women in business. Just celebrating women in all of their glory. You know, how we can and do do everything. That. And not just what we look like while we're doing it.

We launched after six months of prep, and I had a little cry at 7 a.m. on 30 September 2014 when we went live. We did it! We grew in size and took on more staff who all worked from home dotted all over the UK. The email threads when a member of staff was ill or their bairn was poorly, of multiple supportive women offering to take their work on so they could go to bed or nurse their poorly sausage, always warmed my heart. Our following grew in numbers too. In the two-and-a-half years we were live we had 10.8 million page views from 2.8 million unique users. So many wonderful messages from people telling us that FINALLY there was something for them. We did a survey of our readers to see who they were, asking for suggestions and comments about why they read us. One that made me realise we were hitting the nail on the head was something I'll always remember:

'There's no shaming me for being unmarried, childless and a little bit fat.'

We were on the right track, largely down to Mickey, the editor, Hannah Dunleavy, our deputy editor, the assistant editors and our abundance of wonderful writers and illustrators. Those who had avoided women's magazines for similar reasons to me now had something that appealed to them.

Looking back, we were pretty green about the site making money. But we were also pretty green about making a magazine, and we did that. We thought that if we made a brilliant magazine people would read it. And if enough people would read it, we'd get people wanting to advertise with us. Sort of a 'if you build it, he will come'. We took on a woman to get some advertising revenue in for us. She got dribs and drabs but not much. In some ways we were an easy sell – very good stats, a lot of people reading, crazy-good open rate on the weekly newsletter. But we were tricky. We didn't want to write about how brilliant a certain lipstick was just to get money from the lipstick manufacturer. Feels like lying. It is lying. And we only wanted to work with pro-women companies – no diet-pill bullshit, etc.

We dismissed subscription because it wasn't inclusive. We were 'For all women'. That was our tagline. Not 'For all women who can afford it'. There have been times when I've had nowt – we've all had times like that – and the last thing you want then is for yet another thing to be unavailable to you. Especially funny articles that might cheer you up, inspiring articles that might help and columns about mental health that might make you feel less alone. What about a membership scheme? Where you can join for £10, £25 or £100 and get badges, stickers and maybe a tea towel? You can 'join the gang' and know that your money is going towards the running costs of a magazine you read and love. If you bought a magazine in the newsagent for, say, £3 each month, that's £36 per year. Surely people will pay a tenner. Not all, obviously. Maybe 10 per cent. That would have saved the day.

To give you an idea of figures, at the time of announcing that *Standard Issue* magazine was going offline and moving to a weekly podcast, we'd had 127,000 unique users in the previous month. Since we launched the memberships, we've had 1.5 million unique users. We have 2,000 members, some 0.13 per cent. Conclusion: it is nigh on impossible to get people to pay for something that is free. If the *Guardian* is asking for money, what hope does little old us have?

We approached some ad networks to help us. The first one involved a young bloke telling us he could definitely make us money if we ditched all of our principles. He didn't get a second call. Another seemed a bit like us, a woman running her own small company where the women worked remotely. She battled for us and got dribs and drabs, but not what we needed. She at no point covered the costs of employing her.

As the boss and payer of wages and bills, I needed to think of a plan B. It was never about making profit. It just needed to cover its costs, and it wasn't. *Standard Issue* magazine operated at a massive loss every month. When I was in Australia on tour, I wondered if, rather than jacking it all in, we could cut our cloth accordingly. I'm not great at giving up and there's a massive need for us. *Standard Issue* is vital, as a resource, an outlet, a voice and proof that some people want something else that has previously not been provided. So, what if we reduced the staffing and output but still existed? And weren't beholden to advertisers? And didn't have to say yes to companies we didn't think shared our ethos? And didn't have to write about loving lipsticks when the truth is I'm more of a balm girl? I talk too much for lipstick. And I'm not great at mascara as I rub my eyes a lot. I look like a make-up manufacturer's hungover, gothic nightmare.

What if we could still be bold and bright and smart and funny, just on a smaller scale? Subscribe on iTunes and PodOmatic to the Standard Issue podcast if you like excellent content for women, by women, about everything. We are there for you.

HOW TO BE CHAMPION

If something doesn't exist and you think it should, and you think you can, try.

Magazines are funded partially at least by advertisers who want to sell you stuff. So it is not in their best interests to say, 'You know what? You're fine.' Far better for them to point out what's wrong with you and then show you an advert that offers a solution. Trust your judgement. You're fine.

And subscribe to the *Standard Issue* podcast, of course. I'm so proud of what we're doing.

Chapter 38

How to Be a Comedian

I REGULARLY GET asked for tips on how to start doing stand-up and how to get good at it. So, this is what I've learnt from doing the best job in the world for twelve years. Here we go . . .

Being funny is not enough. You have to work hard. There is no substitute for hard work. Some okay comedians work their arses off and are more successful than lazy brilliant ones. I used to have a framed notice on my wall that I made myself. On the left it said, 'What have you done today to make you a better comedian?' And on the right, 'Just work harder.' It might sound a bit wanky but it worked for me. I don't believe in coasting it with a good twenty minutes. You should always be getting better, writing more and learning new things. The sign hung above my desk for many years. It was moved into my spare room, and when a comedian friend stayed once she thought it was a dig at her. Like, if you worked harder you'd be in a hotel, not on someone's fold-out sofa staring at a passive-aggressive sign.

I've always worked hard, no matter what job I've done, but much more so now, as when you're self-employed it's all down to you. If you have no work next week that's because of you. Yes, I am harsh too. And I also work harder when it's something I love. It's much easier then.

On the other hand, I'm not someone who subscribes to the idea that if you love your job it isn't work. It's easier, yes, and much more fun, but you still need to clock off and watch telly or lie on some grass. The attitude that work you love isn't work made me burn out. And that is no fun AT ALL. I was told by my counsellor to take three months off immediately, and because I just had to play my diary out, it was eighteen months later (including a TV series, full UK tour and a month in Australia) when I got that time off. It was messy. So, yes, work hard. Work really fucking hard. But it is still work and you also need to rest when you can – the odd day off, maybe a holiday. I'd say try to find a balance, but in the first five years of being a comic it's very full on. You've usually got a day job for a lot of that anyway. Rest when you can. Make another day busier to preserve a full day off.

Being nice to people – other comics, promoters, venue staff – is the only way. Some comedy clubs judge you on how nice you are to the staff as well as how funny you are on stage. So that's a good reason to be nice if you needed one, other than it's just nice to be a nice person. You know how some people need a religion and promised rewards not to be a twat? Like that.

Bitterness and resentment is unhealthy and can slow down or stop your progress. Stop looking where your peers are and concentrate on your own career. Back when *Time Out* magazine listed loads of comedy gigs, I'd buy a copy whenever I was in London and trawl through it. A couple of times another comic would point out a name and wonder aloud, 'How did SHE get that gig?' Whereas I would look and think, If he's doing that gig, he's about the same level as me, maybe I should approach that promoter. Same info, different outlook. Be positive. It gets you a little further because being negative holds you back. No one likes moaning Minnies but other moaning Minnies.

Generating material is so important. In the beginning, for every fifteen or twenty jokes you write, one will work. The more you write the better you get. There's no magic formula; just knuckle down and do the work. The more you write and try out new jokes, the better gauge you'll be and the higher hit rate you'll have. When I was working my ten-minute set up to twenty, I'd do ten spots of new stuff all the time. Of those ten minutes, one minute would be great, two or three would have potential but not be there yet, and seven would go in the bin. Now I have a higher hit rate but I still often get it wrong. We never know as well as a group of people what is funny and consistently so. Consistency is as important as funny. A joke that works every other time needs binning.

Harnessing ideas helps generate material. Every funny thought, idea, phrase, overheard snatch of dialogue, conversation you had with a friend should be written down to be tried out. A notepad is your friend; your memory is not. I'm not even sure if my phone is my friend. I once updated my iOS and lost six months' worth of potential jokes. I sometimes text ideas to myself or say them into the audio recorder on my phone. If I'm driving and have a passenger, they will text me the joke, which often means I'll be trying to reply to a text that simply says 'cock blocking monkey' or 'spider dogs'. The notes should be detailed. Who knows what the cock blocking monkey joke was but it sounds like a classic. I am addicted to stationery so for me carrying a notebook at all times is like a smoker having cigarettes or a child having a teddy. Harness every funny thought you have. It makes writing so much easier if you have a starting point.

Remember that university audiences aren't necessarily cleverer than you. When I started out I did a few university gigs and they always went badly. Having not gone to university, I thought they were so much more intelligent than me. And I was also talking about divorce and heartbreak in front of a bunch of teenagers, half of whom were virgins, the other half riddled. At a Lincoln Uni gig there was only one person laughing at me and that was the promoter, Shaun Almey, a gem of a man. He booked me loads after that but not for university gigs. Then, one day, my husband, who I've always taken stand-up advice from, told me to look at the students. Just look at them. Next time, I did. Turns out that, while some are smart, some are really not – just like normal audiences. I shook off my wobbly confidence about not being as smart as them, reframed my divorce jokes as advice for how not to fuck up your future and BINGO, did quite well at uni gigs after that.

It's not a good idea to churn your set early on. Get a bullet-proof ten and then extend it. I did seven weeks in a row at the new-material gig at the Chilly Arms in Newcastle to get from a ten-minute set to a twenty. I love a new-material gig. I do them a lot. Put new-material nights in your diary regularly to give you something to write towards. When you're on a bill with your peers, aim to be the best. When you're doing an open spot at a big club, aim to be the best.

Recording early gigs or those where you're trying new material is invaluable. Your memory will just give you a blanket 'It was great'. A recording will enable you to say that spontaneous ad lib again and again. After listening to the recordings of my new-material nights, I make notes of changes I've made and then try it again. This process continues until the joke either gets the response I think it should or goes in the bin. Most ideas get five chances. Some don't even get read aloud when I'm on stage and realise they're already shit (spider dogs). My audience is so lovely that when a comic at one of my new-material gigs silently disregarded the first joke on his list, a woman in the front row said encouragingly, 'No, no, no – go on!'

Ask advice from other comics, especially those you respect, but take it all with a pinch of salt. I always asked – gently, mind you – if a comic on the bill who I thought was good would watch me and give me some notes. Mostly they don't mind; they're nice people. And asking their advice is a teeny ego boost for them, and we all love that. Take the notes graciously and ignore the ones you think are shite. I was told by various people directly and indirectly: 'you'll never do well in competitions', 'women don't sell DVDs', 'you shouldn't talk to the audience'. I ignored all of those, but I also took a lot of suggestions that made me better.

Forums (aside from finding out about gigs) are a waste of your time. Write some jokes instead. I think forums are less a thing now that social media exists. They used to be where comics hung out online and were either very helpful or bitched about other comics under a pseudonym. I'm sure there are Facebook groups for doing that now. Avoid. Gossiping is a negative use of your brain cells. You need them for joke-writing, gig-getting and dealing with whatever happens on stage.

You get really good at figuring out people's showers. In the beginning, pre the B&B or Travelodge debate, you will sleep on a lot of sofas, sofa beds (if you're lucky), armchairs, floors and sometimes share a bed with other comics. I've shared a bed with a fair few – doing that in a cheap hotel can save money and be less miserable. Eating chips in an Ibis with a pal after you've died at a student gig is actually quite a laugh. No need to top and tail. Just don't fuck them if you don't want to fuck them.

Fizzy sweets do a good job of keeping you awake on long drives. Caffeine is the go-to keeper-awake, but on your way home, if you're tanked up on coffee or Coke, you'll never sleep. Tangfastics are especially good in that if you eat too many of them they make your mouth sore and your face explode. I also find singing helps. But not just normal singing. I'll put a playlist of divas on – Whitney, Mariah, Celine, Barbra, Dina Carroll if you're over forty – and sing like I'm on stage with them. Like if I don't do my best, I'll be letting them down. Jonathan Mayor and I can do an excellent 'Tell Him' by Celine and Barbra. We once did it on the way home from Preston six times on the bounce. I wasn't even tired. Just feeling fabulous.

Confidence goes a long way at hard gigs – even if it's faked. I've faked confidence for so long I'm not sure if I have it or not. What I suspect is that I fake it until I get my first couple of laughs under my belt. Then it's there of its own accord. But sometimes I'll think, You're nailing this! And then immediately forget what I was saying and stop nailing it. Confidence comes with time, experience and consistency. No idea about off-stage confidence; that's still very much a work in progress for me.

A new joke that works can lift the rest of your set. Some people say it's better than sex. It's not. But both at the same time would be awesome and awkward. I have been known to jot a joke down straight after sex that has popped in my head during. But I'm married to a comic so he does the same.

Train journeys can be used for napping, writing, plucking rogue hairs (the lighting is great) and crying if tired. I no longer use the quiet carriage as I get too anxious. If people are annoying or chatty in the normal carriage, I just have to harrumph a bit and live with it. If they are annoying and chatty in the quiet carriage, I get so mad I can't concentrate on what I'm doing or I 'have a word'. I once pulled a woman's friend aside as she went past me to go to the toilet, suggesting she remind her friend that phone calls are not allowed in the quiet coach. I spoke quietly so the woman had to lean in. I used to have a teacher who did that and he was much more terrifying than the one who shouted across the school hall. I went to get off at the next stop and a nearby man, who was clearly on the train for a lot longer, thanked me. (On an unrelated note, I once got off the Tyne and Wear Metro having dropped a terrible fart. I stood on the platform and watched four young lads jump straight into the seats I had just vacated. I got to see the moment my fart hit their faces. It was glorious.)

Learning to drive means you get to go home more and you can do last-minute gigs. Train-ticket prices make the latter almost impossible otherwise. I learnt to drive at thirty-one; it took me two years and three driving instructors. The first one decided he didn't want to work evenings and weekends, which is when I was getting my lessons. And the second and third were just because I moved. When one of my instructors was on holiday he got a pal of his to cover his lessons. I can't remember what he said, but as soon as I got in the car with him I felt so uncomfortable that I got back out. Something wasn't right, so I made an excuse and left. Never stick around somewhere that you instinctively feel is odd or potentially unsafe. 'No' is a great word. Look after yourself with it. I don't know what may or may not have happened if I'd stayed in that car, but it wasn't worth taking the risk to find out.

You'll get lifts off comics and give lifts to comics. It's worth knowing that if people give you a lift back to London, you'll get dropped off at Trafalgar Square. If people give you a lift back to Manchester, you'll get dropped off at your door and some will even wait to see you go inside. Manchester is smaller, I know, but still. Having said that, I might not be good friends with Juliet Meyers if I hadn't been dumped in the middle of nowhere.

Keep parking money in your car. It's useful and a really easy way to impress people. I love impressing people without doing anything that requires much effort, and having parking money in the car is like having an apple in your bag or wearing a bra on a Sunday. Small effort, mighty impressed pals and neighbours.

Keep emergency biscuits and water in your car. I've never been very good at this. I'm good at putting the biscuits in the car, but I'll often eat them, citing the emergency as 'I'm hungry' or simply 'there are biscuits here, look'. Then I had the brilliant idea to put them in the boot so I couldn't just reach them from my seat. But I'd just pull over into a lay-by and get them out. And now I know what people are doing when I see them in lay-bys getting stuff out of their boot. Unless there are two cars, then it's dogging, obviously. Even if one of them is AA Roadside Assistance. Dirty beggars. When I passed my driving test, my dad told me to always have a flask of tea, a blanket and a shovel in the boot of my car. And he was right, because whenever I've just killed a man I'm always parched.

A smart man told me to write every day and gig every night. It's good advice.

Audience-banter skills can be learnt. I was terrified in the beginning. I never talked to the audience; I thought they'd all talk back at the same time, which would be horrific and impractical. Then I realised I could talk to one person at a time, as I do that loads in shops, parks and even at home. I was still very worried about the compère's trick of asking someone their name and what they do for a living. I had no funny lines about someone being a bricklayer. Then, at some random gig in Yorkshire with lovely comic Dan Atkinson, he suggested a route to talking to the audience that I hadn't considered. Ask them a question that I already had a funny answer to. A funny safety net, if you like. Then if they say something funny or I can make something funny out of what they've said, that's great. But if not, I can just say, 'That's lovely. The best answer

I've had is . . .' And that was when I started asking people what I should do with my old wedding dress. 'Burn it' was a popular suggestion, but I also loved the madness of 'put it on and follow him around in it'.

Write your own put-downs. If a heckler gets the better of you, go home and write a suitable put-down so if it happens again, you're bloody ready. You can also do this in an argument if you're not a comedian. Go home, write some good comebacks and hope exactly the same set of circumstances happens again. I usually just react to hecklers. You have to remember, you are always in a better position than they are because you are sober, amplified and probably smarter and funnier.

There's no rush to do the Edinburgh Fringe. Do it when you're ready and do as many previews as you can get your hands on. There's no such thing as too ready for Edinburgh. I always did twenty-eight previews. I did so the first year, it went well, so it felt like a lucky number. I used to have a lucky bracelet for gigs, just a £1 job from the Topshop sale. Oh yes, I can get in their (elasticated) bracelets. My wrists aren't too fat for Topshop. LUCKY ME. It was made of bright-blue beads and I wore it a few times and had some good gigs. While I am silly enough to attach meaning to things where there's none, I'm not an idiot. I lost the bracelet in Gary's car when we started going out (his car is always a shit tip; you could lose a person in among the empty bottles of water and packaging for what he calls 'driving meat'). I was very nervous for my first gig without it. It went well. Turns out I'm just funny. Hooray. •whips off lucky knickers and runs around commando•

I once told Gary I was going to an awards do 'commando'. Turns out I meant 'stag'. Idiot. Alone, beknickered idiot.

Never ever use someone else's material. If you're told your joke about X is similar to someone else's joke about X, get in touch with the someone else. Often it's dissimilar enough to keep using. If it's the same, you will probably have to drop it. But that's fine; you can write more jokes. Integrity is important.

Don't drink before going on stage. You need to stay sharp. (This may seem a little harsh but I am a little harsh.) Also, some folk drink before going on stage then have a good gig and put it down to the booze – like me and my lucky pants, bracelet, amount of previews. If you did well, it's because the booze gave you a little confidence. You can grow that confidence from scratch.

When writing, put the funny bit at the end of the sentence. Standard. Classic.

Travelodges are better than B&Bs. I really hate B&Bs. They treat you like you've broken in and demanded a horrible bed for the night. They never think you deserve a lock on your door. Or clean sheets. I once ordered pie and chips off a very 'and chips' menu only to see the owner leave the B&B and come back five minutes later with a blue carrier bag. He'd got my dinner from the chippy next door. I quite admired the chutzpah of that. It's worth noting that some budget hotels have takeaway menus at the front desk. Thank you, Travelodge Leicester.

Always look in a kettle before using it. Once upon a time, I was fine with kettles – used any one that was put in front of me. But then on my first tour I looked inside one, possibly for the first time. There were a lot of white floating bits of I don't know what. I started looking in kettles in every venue and hotel then. You know, like an obsession. My tour manager at the time decided to get us a travel kettle to take around with us. Smart move. Then if there were white floaters, they'd be our white floaters, which isn't as bad at all. I mentioned this on Twitter and got a fair few horror stories. Someone found a wig in a hotel kettle. Many, MANY men said they weed in the kettle if there was no en suite. And one person picked up the kettle in a hotel to feel the heft, deduced that there was enough water in and set it to boil. It was only when the room filled with a putrifying smell that they looked inside to see they had just boiled a kettle of sick. You're all going to start looking in kettles now, aren't you? Not sure if I should apologise or say you're welcome.

Keep small UHT milks (stolen from hotels) in your cupboard at home for cups of tea after long stints away. This is only really necessary if you live alone. If you live with anyone else, who is good at buying milk, then ignore this one. I lived alone for six years and often had to go via the twenty-four-hour Asda for milk on the way home at 2 a.m. I once bought a £10 dress at the same time. Late-night supermarkets are a wonder. I once ran out of knickers as I was away for longer than expected, and popped to late-night Tesco to get a couple of pairs. The security told me that upstairs was closed as they didn't have enough staff to cover it. Something changed his mind after I told him what I needed. I'm not sure if it was the desperation in my eyes or maybe I looked honest. Or he could smell that I was telling the truth. Whatever it was, it's good to know that you're trustworthy enough to buy knickers during the night, unsupervised.

I hate the self-checkouts. My husband thinks they're fun because he can pretend he's working on a till. The thing is, I used to work on a till and I was really good at it. So I get annoyed at doing it again without the pay, discount or uniform complete with pen slot in the skirt. I have to admit though that they are sometimes handy. I once had a basket of things I'd rather not chat to the young fella on the till about. Again, it was during the night. But, of course, there was too much in my bagging area (story of my life), and he had to come over and help me scan my microwave dinner and tash cream. Then ask if I was that comedian. OH GOD.

Turn up the volume on the audience in your head. So if something that normally gets a round of applause only gets a big laugh, turn up the volume. A small laugh becomes a bigger laugh in your head and a bigger laugh becomes a round of applause. Never comment on a quiet audience or low numbers. Don't piss off the people who came. They don't know they're laughing less at that joke than people did last night unless you tell them. Don't bloody tell them. Ignore chat if you can in a rowdy room, but deal with hecklers.

Don't shy away from hard gigs and tough rooms. What you learn doing those gigs stays with you and makes you more bulletproof. Jerry Seinfeld once said, 'You experiment in the easy rooms and edit in the hard ones.'

Watch from the start of the show if you can. You need to get the feel of the room and find out where any problems are.

If you live and mostly work in London, get out and travel the country. An audience in Hull is so happy you're there.

London audiences must surely look at you thinking, You'd better be good – I could be at *Stomp* right now.

Try to see your friends and family. I'm not great at this. I try but I work too much. I like to slot a friend in when I'm on my way to a work thing. It's not exactly a balance but I thrive on time with my friends, so that little bit of fuel before work is a must wherever possible.

If you're a woman, or a man with a tiny penis, get yourself a Shewee. I was once driving to Birmingham for a gig when a lorry jackknifed ahead of me and I was stuck for two-and-a-half hours. After a couple of hours, and with no idea when we'd be moving again, I started to really need a wee and became very jealous of all the men getting out of their cars and weeing with their fleshy Shewees at the side of the road. Gradually, it became painful and, I believed, potentially dangerous. I don't know if it can get so bad that your bladder just goes BANG. I looked around the car for what I could wee into and spotted an empty Coke bottle. Being very aware of my twin jets, I knew I wouldn't be able to hit the top, but I eyed up the wider bit further down. Without any scissors to hand, I hacked into the bottle with my tweezers and sawed my way around. The jagged top made me nervous but, regardless, I pushed back my seat and tried to squat over it. No joy. My bladder was terrifed. So I did something I'd do again if I had to. I moved across to the passenger seat, pulled down my jeans and pants and did the biggest wee, like something a horse would do first thing in the morning after a big night. I pulled up my pants and jeans and moved across to the driver's seat. God knows what the people in the car behind me thought.

The rescue workers cut through the central reservation and we all went back the way we'd come. I'd been replaced at my gig so I just went home. The next day I took the car to the garage and explained that 'my friend's dog' had weed in it and it needed a deep clean. Years later, I told the story on *Would I Lie to You?* and comedian and excellent friend Joe Lycett, to whom I'd given this car, texted me 'That's where I keep my sandwiches!'

And finally, the eleven o'clock rule (Millican's Law) is great for getting over hard gigs. See page 192.

Chapter 39

Why I'm Not a Criminal

I'M NOT GREAT at winding down after work. I don't read as much as I'd like because when I'm tired I want something to wash over me. Hence telly. I'm a huge telly fan. Some shows I watch are exactly like my life: people being funny, people eating cake or people sitting down. But I also like to place myself in shows and think, What would I do in this situation?

I love a crime drama. In the first episode someone generally gets themselves in a sticky situation. I've done that. You know, the usual things: called a teacher 'Mam', got trapped in a toilet at a gig, ran over a deer. But in crime dramas, it's normally something murdery. Where they look at their hands and they're surprised to see them covered in blood. That's a fun thing I like to do when my periods are very heavy and I get a bit on my hand. Something I've learnt from crime dramas is that it's always a bad idea to punch a hole in a wall, as pretty much anything that happens after that, be it a broken mug or a family murder, will be pinned on you and 'your rage'. When my granda died I threw an address book at the wall. It was a spiral-bound one and I damaged it, so I could never open it again without remembering my rage. There's a lesson there: be more careful in WHSmith.

That character then either styles it out, frames someone else or goes on the run. It made me wonder what I'd be like 'on the run'. For starters, there's one word in those three I'm not fond of. You rarely hear of people being 'on the walk'. So that's the first part I'd struggle with. Maybe I could be 'on the run' for one lamppost and then 'on the walk' for another and build it up.

My handbag is prepared for most eventualities, so if, when I was hiding out, I got diarrhoea, I could sort it (Imodium AND spare pants). If I was really hungry, several times, over a few days, I could sort it (chocolate, biscuits, an old apple with pen on). If I thought of something funny, I could write it down (in my notebook with one of about thirty pens). If I did a solid poo, I could pick it up (dog-poo bags). I could probably fashion a makeshift tourniquet from hair bands and dental floss. And I could stave off any bleeding with a night-time towel, performing said emergency medical care with the light of my travel torch. I think this is why men get caught more. No handbags.

In one show I watched, the bloke on the run stole a hoody off someone's washing line and popped it on, ridding himself of his bloody T-shirt. God, how many back yards would I have to raid before I found something that would fit me? It would be like wandering around the Trafford Centre – some crying and then some chocolate. I can hear it on the news, 'Six houses in the area have reported having clothes tried on by the suspect who then angrily discarded them in a tear-stained pile. Mrs Bainbridge of number 42 said the one item not recovered was a very forgiving wraparound dress in a size 18.'

Some fugitives who are 'on the lam' (always sounds like someone's selected their Sunday dinner of choice) have to steal a car. I hate driving other people's cars. I don't like driving hire cars as they're bigger and the buttons are all different. I'd just be running around trying all of the doors of small cars I think I could park, first checking that they're manual and diesel. 'The suspect was finally captured after holding up traffic at the lights on Brinkburn Street and was taken into police custody repeating the words "I couldn't find the bite" and weeping.'

When you realise you could be done for murder and STILL can't be arsed to lose weight. That's conviction.

HOW TO BE CHAMPION

Always carry a giant handbag full of loads of useless shite that is massively useful in really specific circumstances.

Spend your life driving different cars so that you are able to steal a wider variety.

If you're fat, only go on the run where other fat people live.

Chapter 40

Not Good at Being Famous

I **WAS ON** the Metro once and my sister texted me to say there was a big photo of me in the *Shields Gazette*. I was a few years into stand-up and had done bits and bobs of telly. I was travelling from Newcastle city centre to South Shields to see my parents, and as the Metro got closer to my destination I noticed a change. Hebburn, Jarrow, Bede . . . I realised that people were looking at me a little more and for longer. I was a little unnerved by it but then remembered that this was the area covered by the *Shields Gazette*. My sister had said it was a big photo. Eyes were lingering longer than I was used to but no one said anything. Probably figuring out where they knew me from. And the following sentence went through my head: 'How long will it be before I can't do public transport any more?'

I got off the Metro in South Shields and walked to my parents' house. My mam opened the door and said, 'What's that down your front?' I'd been on the train and lost a square of Dairy Milk. Little did I know that it had melted down my top. They must have been thinking, 'Look at the state of her. Chocolate all down her. And now she's smiling at me and kissing her guns. Very odd'.

One of the first times I was actually recognised was when I was in Brighton with Gary and we were wandering around the shops. A lady was standing outside a chocolate shop with a tray of samples, and Gary and I helped ourselves. But it wasn't then that the lady with the samples recognised me and said, 'Are you on the telly?' Nope. It was when we visited her tray the third time.

It's not all chocolate-based, though. The rest of this chapter is pretty brutal. Fame was a hard subject to write about. I can't imagine it'll be an easy read.

I'm not very good at being famous. I think it's because I'm quite shy. I know. You might think that because I stand on stage and talk about my fanny to thousands of people it means I can't be shy. I was always a shy kid. Quiet. Happiest playing on my own. It was only recently that I discovered KerPlunk isn't a one-player game. My husband said, 'If it's a game for one, there's no competitive element. What is the aim of the game?'

And I said, 'It's to play it quietly enough so that you don't wake your dad who's on nightshifts.' Genuinely, that's what I was told. I developed a real skill for quietly lowering marbles. I also had quiet, quiet hippos.

I've never been great in crowds. Again, weird. So why do you perform to large amounts of fans? There's a gap; I'm up high. It's very different. I still remember as a kid how sweaty I got in the queue to shake Darth Vader's hand downstairs in Binns department store. My mam was also sweaty, possibly for different reasons. Mine was panic; hers was probably the big cape and leather gloves.

You won't see me at a film premiere. Why travel for hours to be judged on what I'm wearing to see a film two days before it's everywhere anyway? Also, I bet you aren't allowed ice cream at those things. Mostly because you've hired a fucking ball gown to watch the big telly in. I can just see the tabloid headline: 'Roly-Poly Funny Lass Sarah Millican Turns Up for Film Premiere Covering Her Chunky Thighs in Size 20 Jeans with Limp Brushed Hair and a Carrier Bag of Sweets from the Garage.'

I'm not very good at being recognised in the street; I'm embarrassed at attention being drawn to me. Some people don't come up and say hi – they just gawp or even point. Which brings back lots of old stuff from my school days.

I'm not great at meeting fans because of some odd experiences that made me nervous. Most fans are lovely and want to say thanks or that they've enjoyed the show. Some are drunk, some put their hand on your arse, some grab at you and occasionally someone tries to get you in their car. Twice I've had someone open my car door while I was in it, and once someone banged on the windows as I drove away, like I was The Beatles. A couple once stood in front of my car in the middle of the road as I pulled out, so I had to slam my brakes on to avoid hitting them. I normally feel safe in my car, but I'm pretty sure I've been followed a couple of times. All of these things are utterly terrifying.

This makes me nervous of everyone, which is a shame, as the majority of my fans – the ones who come and see my shows, buy my DVD and who've laughed at me (in a nice way) for twelve years – are wonderful. The volume of positive messages

I got when my last show aired on Channel 4 was overwhelming. But I suppose that is anxiety for you. It doesn't make an awful lot of sense. It's often not what does happen that causes my heart rate to quicken but what *might* happen.

Also, social media can be odd. I remember when I lived in my old flat and someone tweeted me that they'd just watched me put my bin out. That's some creepy shit. I used to sit in my car for sometimes twenty minutes psyching myself up to do the five-minute walk from the car to my front door. And these days I don't answer the door or the phone, and generally someone else opens my post. Sometimes I think I'm paranoid, but then I remember that all the things I worry about have actually happened at some point. When you're famous, people think you're not a real person. Hence the vitriol on Twitter and Facebook. I'm pretty sure they wouldn't say these things to your face. You're on the telly – you must repel insults. They can't imagine that your anxiety goes crackers or that sometimes you have a little cry.

Whenever fans approach me I always try to be polite. To smile and say thanks, which I genuinely mean. The majority of those who approach me are smashers, lovely people, and I'm so grateful for their continued support and fabulous laughing faces. That's my view from the stage night after night: a glorious sea of smiles and laughs. That's why I do my job; I only ever want to make people laugh. They/you are lovely. This is not their/your thing. It is my thing. My shy, anxious, nervous thing. I try to explain that having a photo taken while I'm with my family doesn't feel right. I'm always in a rush or running late, so I often explain that I'm dashing for a train or I have a three-hour drive home. Some understand, some shout abuse, some take to Twitter to call you names. I'm not in the gang of people who feel that fame entitles everyone to a slice of you. If what makes you happy makes me very sad then I have to put me first. Imagine not liking crowds and causing one. Or hating the way you look (I'm working on it) and people asking for photos.

I feel very vulnerable when I'm out on my own. When you're famous, people listen in to your conversation in restaurants, look at what's in your shopping basket, comment on how you look different to when you're on the telly. That's because there's a team of people doing my hair, applying my make-up and ironing my clothes. When it's just me, I'll have wet hair, a basic covering of foundation to cover the rosacea and clean but wrinkly jeans on. There might even be mud on my trainers because of dog walks.

The teacher who told me to 'always hold your head high' would hate what fame has done to me. I wish I had the confidence others do, just to own it, shoulders back, yes it's me, of course I'll sign your tits. I've really tried but it goes against my personality type. Instead I blend in, disappear. I think it's about your personality rather than fame. I've always hated parties, crowds, people feeling my arse without permission. The same bespectacled nine-year-old who tried to blend in at school is now trying to go unnoticed in shops or in a pub. It's just how I am and have always been.

My anxiety flares up when I'm out and about. There are a handful of places where I feel safe and the anxiety subsides. When it's bad I sometimes cancel social things and just stay at home 'til my brain and pulse chill the fuck out. Ask my husband about Bryan Ferry. We never did get there. I love the cinema because we all sit in the dark and look at the screen. I love being abroad on holiday because no one cares who I am. I'm just the woman asking for a bigger spoon or more bread. On holiday I have a little more confidence. I make people laugh at tills and I complain in restaurants, things I'm too scared to do here. I like nothing better than to be treated like a normal person. A lady in our local Pets at Home recognised me and used to blush every time she served me. She once was honest and said, 'I don't know how to talk to you.'

I said, 'Just like I'm a normal person, flower.' And she did and it was lovely. I understand celebrity culture. I waved at Lee Mack in the street before I'd ever met him. I get it. But from this end, it can be weird.

I mentioned that I'm not great at being recognised at an event the other day. That every time I go in a certain supermarket near us the lady on the till asks where I'm from. Every time. When I tell her, she says I sound like that comedian. Then the lady helping to pack my bags asks the first lady if she finds that comedian funny, and they talk about me without realising it is me. I put my head down and can only hear my heartbeat in my ears. I pack my bags and usually, by the time I get to my car outside, I have the flashing lights and searing pain of a migraine.

At the end of this event, I was saying goodbye to the other guests in the street and saw a girl hovering and looking at me. My anxiety kicked in and heart started racing. But then she said, 'I thought you were really funny,' gave a little wave and went to meet her friends. I could have kissed her.

This is my thing, not yours. It's just a bit weird and I'm crap at this side of things. Forgive me. And feel free to wave.

Chapter 41

#Joinin

I STARTED #JOININ in 2011 and have been doing it every Christmas since. So this coming Christmas Day will be my seventh. It started because I'm a big softie and can't bear the thought of people being alone on Christmas Day. And I don't mean those who choose to be alone. Good for them. They like being alone, they want it, they have a smashing time. They can have a pizza and watch back-to-back episodes of *Benidorm* with no pants on and not even a towel down on their sofa. In some ways, they win at Christmas.

This is not for them. This is for those who don't choose to be alone, but who are, for some reason, on their tod/bob/lonesome. Be it because they have no family, are estranged from their family, it's not their turn to have the kids, even just that their partner is at work, whatever. Alone and would rather not be. This is who #joinin is for.

Though social media has its faults (time-suckage, troll playground, never knowing if the pic you're clicking on is of a cock or not), it's bloody good at lessening loneliness. It's helped me when I've been on the road or on a train or up late because I can't sleep, and I know it does the same for others. So it made sense to use Twitter for this.

By using the hashtag joinin you can join a community made up of those alone, those not alone but lonely (I know that's a thing because it was in a Bon Jovi song once – and I used to work in an office), those who wish they were alone (who often tweet about the horrors of being with other people to make the lonely ones feel better – adorable) and me. Just loads of nice people chatting with me and then each other. As soon as I see conversations start without including me (I'm still watching on the hashtag like a SantaGod), my heart fills with warmth (possibly an overflow of the gravy) and I know it's working.

I start when I get up (which more recently is dictated by what time the dog needs a wazz rather than an excited me wondering, Has he been?), and I explain what #joinin is and encourage people to let us know if they're lonely using the hashtag. Then it sort of takes on a life of its own. The other year I tweeted and retweeted so much that Twitter blocked me – for spamming I assume – and I had to start a new account. Thankfully, the powers that be at Twitter now know what it is and are very supportive. As they should be. And hooray.

I post what I'm watching on the telly so that those alone can watch the same and we can have the Queen- or *EastEnders*-based banter. #Joinin goes down very well. Those who are alone and prefer it that way get a bit annoyed at it, but I can handle that. It's not for them. And they can easily avoid it. For those who were dreading not having anyone to chat to, it absolutely solves that problem. Plus, if you're chatting online rather than in person, you don't have to hoover or wear a bra, and you can eat that whole profiterole pyramid you bought or just always have cheese in your hand.

We do it every Christmas Day and the smashers using the hashtag normally means it carries over to Boxing Day. If people ask, we do it on New Year's Eve in a smaller way. Some folk want it for Valentine's Day but I draw the line at Easter. If you're on your own then, you don't have to share your chocolate eggs with anyone. There should be a #getout for Easter.

Here are some example tweets from #joinin 2016:

Met a lovely vicar yesterday at morning service in Wroxhall. Told him all about **#joinin**. He thought it was marvellous

(Even Jesus approves!!)

I'll be honest- **@SarahMillican75** comedy is not for me. But **#joinin** is brilliant thinking. Well done. X

(Even people who hate me get involved!)

My first year on my own in ten years. I struggled, won't lie. I may not have **#joinin** today but found some help in each tweet

(You don't even have to chat, you can just read it. Like how you used to be able to buy a ticket at the baths to be a spectator. I am not saying #joinin bystanders are paedophiles. Not at all. Let's be clear on that. Bad analogy. Sorry everyone.)

It is just another day, but please keep going we are here and you're not alone **#JoinIn**

(This was in reply to someone struggling. Makes me do a little cry.)

So this Christmas, come and find me. Join Twitter for the day if you have to: I'll be @sarahmillican75, where the door is always open.

Chapter 42

Tips for Turning Forty

'LIFE BEGINS AT forty': so say people who are in their forties. And mugs. Just like people in their twenties say, 'Have you heard the new Yazz record? It's exy*,' and people in their seventies say, 'I'm in my seventies.' People under forty and card manufacturers seem to think turning forty is going to be bloody awful and that the only possible way you can handle it is by getting absolutely shitfaced.

This now forty-two-year-old almost teetotaller dealt with it in a different way. I remember really looking forward to it. I hadn't been a new decade in a while and I've always thought that women in their forties are very together, focused, wear pencil skirts and know how to tie a silk scarf. As an unsophisticated thirty-nine-year-old, I ran a silk scarf down my leg, like they do in the adverts for depilatory cream, and it's been there ever since. I now have to tuck it into my socks.

---

* 'Exy' was a word we used as kids, presumably short for 'excellent'.

I think your thirties are for finding your way.

For learning how to eat in restaurants alone. NAILED. Tip: take this book or listen to my podcast on your phone. Another tip: pretend you have a friend joining you later and order two dinners. Eat both dinners.

For learning how to say no. NAILED. Tip: think of how uncomfortable it is to say no and compare it to how fucked off you'll be when the yes appears in your diary. Another tip: you don't always have to give reasons. Just look a bit sad at having to say no – then say no.

For surrounding yourself with excellent people. NAILED. Tip: your friends are a reflection of you. I sometimes arrogantly twirl around the house at how brilliant my friends are. Another tip: be a good friend. It's almost the best thing you can be.

For accepting who you are and not apologising for it. NAILED. Tip: I'm never going to be a size 10. I like eating and I like having big tits. Another tip: I don't wind my windows up at traffic lights any more. It's about time the world heard a little more Go West.

Surely your forties are about living that life you've created. Reading in a café alone, dancing in your nightie to whatever music you love, spending time with quality mates and hopefully never feeling obliged to say yes to a thing. All in pencil skirts and silk scarves tied a multitude of ways.

Forty is also a new start. I want to be healthier. With a tiny wink at my mortality, before the end of my last day of being thirty-nine, I booked appointments for the doctors, dentist and optician. I had a forty MOT because life continues at forty.

Chapter 43

Recipe for My Very Favourite Cake

MY FAVOURITE CAKE is one I make. How cocky is that? I think it's partly because I don't have to go out to get it. Though I sometimes have to pop to the shops for some of the ingredients as my fridge can look like it belongs to a single man (some cheesy milk and half an onion) and the kitchen cupboards are full of all sorts of tat. I used to keep a jar of my icing heads in there, for fuck's sake. I felt bad every time a fan made me a cake and we couldn't eat it (strangers), so if they'd made a fondant version of me for the top, I'd keep the head. I thought it was funny. Turns out it's just crackers. It looked like a baker had it in for me.

I once cleaned out my cupboards (just the once) and found a tin of marrowfat peas in there. (I'm reluctant to throw old tins away in case of a war. Should that happen, you are all welcome round to mine for custard and marrowfat peas.) I'm not even sure I know what they are. I'm quite new to peas. They were one of the things I definitely didn't like as a child without ever having tried them. Turns out they're really nice, though I only dabble in garden peas. I've heard they are a gateway pea. So how did these peas get in my cupboard? They had a number on the top. Apparently, six years before, I'd won them in a raffle. That's the kind of classy do I go to.

I only started making cakes five or six years ago. I always thought there should be a journey between me and cake – a walk or a drive. And a curfew: no cake after 10 p.m. because the shops are shut. But since I started knocking up the odd lemon drizzle, I've kept a baking cupboard, which is usually pretty healthy. Maybe 'healthy' isn't the word. There's always flour and sugar in there. And 'cooking chocolate', which is just slabs of Bourneville (for brownies) and bags of giant buttons (for cakes and when I'm tired or sad . . . or bored . . . or open the cupboard door for something else).

The recipe for my favourite cake is one off the BBC website with a Millican twist. According to the site, it was donated by John Barrowman, who I love and who once dropped to his knees in front of me in the SECC in Glasgow and I thought I might burst, but my husband was near so I just smiled and helped him up. Who thought you could ever improve on John Barrowman? I have. And I'm sure he'd like it.

The recipe is for banana bread. Bananas and my friend Ruth are the reasons I started making cakes. I was staying at her house once in London and she told me she'd made a cake out of old, dead bananas. I'm sorry, what? Old, dead bananas that I'd normally put in the bin? You're making a CAKE out of them? That's like someone telling me you could turn toilet-roll tubes into chocolate Hobnobs. Or that old cotton buds turn into Matchmakers in the bin. Orange or mint flavour, none of your honeycomb bullshit. The colour of that box is too close to the colour of the orange-flavour one and nearly made last Christmas a disaster.

So in an attempt to help bananas live on, make a better life for themselves and leave a lasting legacy, I looked for a banana-cake recipe. Before this, I regularly left bananas to die in old bags and sometimes my husband's car. I left bananas there so often he called me a forgetful monkey. Now I save bananas. I rescue them. Not so much a forever home as a temporary one in a cake tin. And if I haven't used shite gluten-free flour, an even shorter stay in my tummy.

So, here is my step-by-step guide to making my favourite cake. Don't throw the 'I can't bake' rubbish at me. It's just following instructions. When I started, I was nervous but then thought, I can build a flatpack table; I'm sure I can make a cake.

1. Put the oven on. It's the cupboard that gets hot. Whack it up to 180 degrees.
2. Get a bar of butter out of the fridge. You'll thank me for this later.
3. Get your ingredients out. I like to pretend I'm making a cooking show. So if I'm in on my own, I will chat through the process to the 'viewers', which is usually one or two mewing cats and a snoring dog. I mostly bake at night when the telly turns to shite but I'm too awake for bed. I like having all the ingredients on the bench and putting them away after I've used them. That should avoid what happened when my

friend Lou made a cake for when I came back from Australia. She forgot three of the ingredients and only remembered when the cake was in the oven. She opened the oven door and stirred them in. It was not a success. I mean, I still ate it – I didn't want to appear rude. And cake is cake. The ingredients you need are plain flour, bicarbonate of soda, salt, butter, caster sugar, eggs, bananas, buttermilk (WTF – I'll come to this later) and vanilla extract. As a rule I avoid any recipe that includes something I haven't heard of or can't picture in my mind's eye. Bergamot – no idea. Rosewater – I think that's what I used to make in the backyard with an old washing-up bowl and the heads of the nearby church's rose garden. I haven't got time to make that now, Nigella. Sometimes recipes contain something that might be cheese. We don't like cheese in our house. I don't mind it when it's flavourless on a pizza, acting as a glue for the other, more important ingredients. I found a recipe recently that needed 'fregola'. I thought it might be cheese but I googled it and it's a 1948 musical film from Austria. How I'm supposed to get seven ounces of that I have no idea.

4. Now that you've filled the kitchen bench with your ingredients, you'll need to make some space to work in. For me, I shove the toaster and Nutribullet against the wall and put the slow cooker on the table, taking care not to disturb the dust on the top. The slow cooker is my husband's and he only uses it when I'm away. Like an affair but with really tasty meat. So like an affair. I'm barely off the drive before he's chopping and creating something that I will only hear about in anecdotes and the odd poem. I used to have to

move the soup maker too but that went into the cupboard six months ago. Because Gary hasn't noticed that the soup maker is no longer on the bench it's going to get moved to the loft. If, in another six months, he still hasn't noticed, I'm giving it away. When I moan about the lack of soup in our house, he points to the tiny food processor I bought just for making raspberry coulis and pulsing frozen banana coins and we both laugh and realise we are made for each other.

5. Once you've made space to work, clean the bench. Cat paws have probably been on there. Maybe a cat bum. Also, because we're near the microwave there is bound to be a blob of something inexplicable that is harder than the best of cocks and needs a chisel to budge it. Before you clean the bench, smell the dishcloth. I usually find they smell of the past. Pop it in the washing machine and get a new one out.

6. By now, the oven has been on bloody ages so make a note to remember to apologise to whoever pays the bills in your house. If it's you, remember this is all for cake.

7. Measure out 285g/10oz of plain flour and pop it in a bowl with one teaspoon of bicarb and half a teaspoon of salt. The recipe says to sift it but who can honestly be arsed? I mean, make sure it isn't one big lump, but I've never once had someone eat a slice of my cake and spit it out because 'it's not been bloody sifted'. Is it 'sifted'? or 'sieveded'?

8. In a separate bowl (they always assume you've got two, don't they?) plop some butter (110g/4oz) and some caster sugar (225g/8oz). Don't think about the amount of both of those things any more. It's cake we're making. It's supposed to have butter and sugar in, otherwise why are

we bothering? If you like making cakes with grated cour-
gettes and beetroot, might I suggest you're reading the
wrong book. I love butter and sugar like they're my kids.
I've accepted that you can't have cake and good skin and
I'm willing to make the sacrifice. The butter should be
soft but not melted. If you forgot to get it out of the fridge
before then just cut it into lots of small bits. That'll help.

9. I normally use a tablespoon for this bit. Cream the butter
   and sugar together until they are combined and it looks
   like sugary butter. But not buttery sugar.

10. Add two eggs and mix thoroughly. Wooden-spoon time,
    so get it out of your sex drawer and give it a rinse first.
    I always buy medium eggs and use them for all recipes,
    including the ones that say large ones. Again, no one has
    ever put a slice of my cake down declaring it inedible as the
    eggs were slightly smaller than required. I usually find if
    you make a cake for people, they clap when you tell them,
    look for a kettle and tea bags and eat it willingly, smiling
    all the way. I also make sure I'm in the room to hear any
    compliments. I occasionally ask people to repeat them if
    they're talking too quietly.

11. Mash four ripe bananas with a fork. These are the rescue
    bananas. Look at their little faces. They'd be put down if
    it weren't for you. Make a note to remind yourself you're
    a hero later.

12. Add the mashed rescue bananas to the mix and stir
    thoroughly.

13. Now, buttermilk. What the fuck is that? I hear you ask.
    The recipe (God bless Barrowman) tells you what to do

if you don't live near a buttermilk shop. Pop one-and-a-half teaspoons of vinegar (yes, chip vinegar, not any of the other ones) into 85ml/3fl oz of normal milk and mix it. You can use lemon juice instead of vinegar, but I find lemon juice separates a bit where vinegar doesn't. Also, I've always got vinegar in, whereas unless you catch me around pancake time, lemon juice is unlikely. Add the 'buttermilk', or as I call it 'chip milk', and mix.

14. Add one teaspoon of vanilla extract.

15. Now, this is where Barrowman gets Millicanised. (He wishes. Actually, I wish.) I like his recipe but for me it needed two family bags of giant chocolate buttons. Name me a recipe that can't be improved by giant chocolate buttons. Name me a meal. Name me a sex position. You can't. Cos it doesn't exist. And when I say 'family' bags, I mean the only bags anyone ever buys. The ones with the joke on the bag. You know, 'resealable'. Empty the two bags onto a chopping board. Try five or six of them from each bag to make sure they aren't off. Cut all of the buttons in half and then put them in with the rest of the cake mix and stir thoroughly.

16. Fold in the flour mixture. You're nearly ready.

17. Now, you CAN grease a cake tin if you like, but I just whack in a sheet of greaseproof paper or 'baking parchment' if you've got enough left after writing those letters with your quill. Yes, the edges will be rough, but you can call your cake RUSTIC and you won't have to wash your cake tin. You're welcome. Pour in the mix, pushing it to the edges, and bung it in the oven, which by now must

have been on for an hour. Sheesh. If your kitchen heats up like mine, open a window or just strip down to your bra and pants.

18. The recipe says use a loaf tin but I found it got a bit burnt on the top and uncooked in the middle, and I'd have to make a foil hat for it. Fuck that shit. Instead, put it in a flat, square tin that people make flapjacks in. (Not me. With my IBS, flapjacks are just asking for the shits.)

19. Now, leave it in the oven for about forty minutes. Put a timer on. You don't want to go to all this trouble only to get engrossed in *Quiz Call* and burn the thing. Check on it every five minutes from 40 minutes onwards. When you pull your skewer out, remember that might be banana on the end so don't get carried away and overcook it.

20. When it's done, take it out of the oven and take a photo of it. Put it on your Facebook. If anyone is in the house, shout them down to look at it. If there's only one person in the house, ask them several times if they think it looks amazing.

21. When it's cooled a bit, pop it on a cooling rack. And while it's still warm, cut a slab (no slices in our house) and have it with a cup of tea. That one doesn't count as that's the 'well done' for making a cake. It is the best cake I've ever eaten and I have done some extensive research over the years. It doesn't need filling or icing or silver balls or icing sugar. Or a fork. Or a plate. Just a gob.

22. Now, tell your partner they can do the dishes as you've done all the hard work, remembering to put the wooden spoon back upstairs. Or, if you fancy a change, the fish slice.

BEING CHAMPION

BEING CHAMPION IS about being on an even keel. No one is kissing their guns EVERY DAY. I'm never sure if high-fiving yourself is the saddest thing in the world, or the fucking best. I like to think this might be the book version of a card my best friend gave me when I went to Australia for the first time for a month. Inside she'd written:

You're crying. Are you:
(a) Tired?
(b) Hungry?
(c) Need a wank?

Life is not perfect or easy. But it can be amazing. Like when you see a double rainbow above McDonald's golden arches. Or when you recognise a bird. Or that person or dog you've got your eye on first makes contact (email, text, a look, a lick). Or you make a little headway on a big plan. Or cook something and it's better than edible. Or you find both gloves. Or someone gets you a present you actually want but didn't know existed. Or when you make your friend laugh HARD and then they make you laugh HARDER and your leggings smell even more of wee but you sort of don't mind.

Thank you so much for reading this book. For buying it too, but mostly for reading it. So many books sit on my shelves unread so I know what a time commitment this has been for you. And I'm grateful. I hope I made you laugh. I hope I stopped that man on the train talking to you. I hope I accompanied you for poos and baths. I hope I made you feel normal. God knows, when you lot laugh at me when I'm being funny about being overweight or being bullied or hating how I look or having PCOS or heavy periods or being a cake pigeon or a hamster squeezer or Beyoncé during cunnilingus, you make me feel normal. And for that, I'll always be grateful.

Hope to see you on tour. Stay champion you bunch of smashers.

I never know how to end these things.

So they all went home and had their tea.

ACKNOWLEDGEMENTS

A massive thank you to the following excellent people and things:

To Gary for listening to every word of this as I read it aloud paragraph by paragraph with my 'is it okay?' face on. And for replying, 'Yes, it is.'

To Hannah for waiting 'till I was ready to write a book.

To Tuvok for looking up at me from his bed near my desk with his 'you're great' face on.

To Patrick Doyle whose music calmed the 'what if I can't do this?' noise in my head while I typed.

To three of my fingers and one of my thumbs for doing all of the work on the keyboard.

To Anna for being a constant support and with me all the way.

To Katy for that email three years ago that made me think I could do this.

To Andy, Kat, Boden and Marksies for the cover photo, hair and make-up, top and yellow cardigan.

To my prof-rooders, Emma and Mickey, for correcting the typos caused by my tits grazing the keys.

To my mittens, friends and family for their love, support, and for letting me stroke them.

To my heroes who read this book and gave me quotes and wonderful supportive emails and texts.

To caffeine and sugar for helping a comedian work mornings.

To Trapeze, Orion and all of the other constellations (e.g. all of the ploughs).

To Mr Thomas, thanks to whom I will always try to hold my head high.